STAFFORDSHIRE
and the Black Country
Michael Raven

The upper Dove Valley north-west of Longnor.

Credits

ISBN 0 906114 12 8

Copyright: Text and
photographs,
Michael Raven
1988

Published by: Michael Raven
26, Church Lane
Derrington
Stafford TF9 4HJ
Tel: 0785 55555.

Photosetting
and Print by: Cooper Combine
Telegraph Street
Stafford

Cover illustrations:
Front: Canal scene
between Milford
and Tixall.

Back: 'Old Thatch',
King's Bromley.

Lake Rudyard at evening from the A523.

The author in the garden at Shugborough Hall.

Preface

This book is a gazetteer of the historic county of Stafford and ignores the boundary changes made in 1974. The author freely acknowledges the debt he owes to earlier writers on whose work he has drawn so heavily. However, times change and to bring our information up to date we have visited almost every place mentioned in this survey, often several times. The composition of this book, and a similar volume on Shropshire, has occupied us full time — 12 hours a day 7 days a week — for over a year. The author's cheerful companion in all these travels was his dog, Lady, and to her he dedicates this book. All the photographs were taken between May 1987 and May 1988. With the exception of one or two aerial pictures they were all taken by the author, who used a hand held Nikon FE 35mm camera with a Vivitar 28 - 200mm zoom lens. A few photographs were taken on a Pentacon Six (2·25" square format) and an old but very good Ross Ensign Autorange 820 (6 x 8cm format). Filters and effects were hardly ever employed. Kodachrome 64 ASA transparency film was used in the Nikon and 64 ASA Ektachrome in the other cameras. All the photographs were taken in colour even though it was known the majority would be printed in black and white. Today the author still uses 35mm but takes all important pictures on a Mamiya RZ (6 x 7cm format) with fixed focal length lenses, 50 ASA Fujichrome and a Benbo tripod.

Seighford, the ford and the village beyond.

Contents

ABBOTS BROMLEY *6m. NE of Rugeley.*
A small town on the western edge of
Needwood Forest, famous for its ancient
Horn Dance held annually on the Monday
after the first Sunday after the 4th of
September. Six men wearing reindeer horns
dance at several venues throughout the day
accompanied by a hobby horse, a boy with a
crossbow, a jester and a musician. The horns
are stored in the church on public display. In
origin the dance is probably a relic of a pagan
fertility rite, though there are other theories.

Bagot's Bromley, Goat Lodge.

leaved forest of beech, ash, oak and chestnut.
Now it is gone. Lord Bagot sold the timber to
pay his taxes and the land was bought by the
Forestry Commission who arrayed it with
seemingly never-ending lines of coniferous
trees. However, they have relented in recent
times and are introducing hardwoods with
the intention of creating a genuine mixed
forest. There are deer, rabbits and badgers in
the woods. On the south-eastern boundary of

*Abbots Bromley, Church House and the
church.*

It is unique within Britain. The unspoilt
village has a 17th Century, hexagonal, timber
market cross, pleasantly mellowed brick
houses, a stone church with 14th Century
arcades and a smattering of black and white
buildings. The school of St. Mary and St.
Anne is one of the oldest girls' public schools
in the country. A mile and a half north-west
of the village lie the forests and farms of
Bagot's Bromley. On the west side of the road
to Uttoxeter, at the junction with the lane to
Dapple Heath, is a field (Monument Field)
with a clump of trees and the remains
of a moat (now filled with cow dung) in
which stands a brick monument marking the
site of the manor house of the Saxon Lord
Bagot. His descendant, Ralph, was to desert
this place in 1360 on his marriage to the
heiress of Blithfield, to whose Hall a mere 2
miles away he moved. Amongst his
descendants were the Earls of Stafford and
the Dukes of Buckingham. Bagots Park, even
in this century, had a magnificent broad-

Bagot's Bromley, the Walking Stick Oak

Bagot's Wood the amateur naturalist, Phil Drabble, has his home in Goat Lodge, situated at the entrance to the Bagot Estate Farm, which is located on the north-eastern side of the Abbots Bromley — Uttoxeter road (B5015), signposted Dunstal. Within yards of

A Bagot goat, at Shugborough.

the concrete estate road stands the sole, solitary survivor of the ancient forest: the Walking Stick Oak, now dead and stark and white, standing forlorn. The unique Bagot Goats no longer graze the pastures here, but at least these friendly black and white bearded creatures have been saved, and are now at the Shugborough Hall Farm, near Stafford. Blithfield Hall has been converted into flats. It stands in its park overlooking the 790 watery acres of Blithfield reservoir, opened in 1953 by the Queen Mother. The River Blithe, whose waters were dammed to create the lake, is the 'Withy' of W. M. Canaway's 'A Creel of Willow'. The road crosses the reservoir on a spectacular causeway. The Police Underwater Search

Blithfield reservoir and causeway.

Unit is no stranger here, it being a handy place to deposit the tools and unwanted proceeds of criminal activities.

ACTON TRUSSELL *3·5m. S of Stafford.*
In Domesday Book the village is referred to simply as Actone. At that time it belonged to the Bishop of Chester. The local lord was Robert and there were 10 villagers and 8 smallholders. Between them they had a mill, 8 acres of meadow and a small wood. Acton means 'the settlement by the oak trees' and Trussell was the name of a later Norman lord of the manor (from at least 1342). The old Saxon village stands on a rise above the flood plain of the River Penk. The Staffordshire and Worcestershire canal (constructed by James Brindley in 1772) follows the course of the river; so does the M6 Motorway, with a roar that makes double glazing a necessity

Acton Trussell, the church of St. James.

hereabouts. What little is left of the old village has been swamped by modern middle-class houses, though from a distance the overall impression is of a pleasant little town — almost Italian looking. The church is found in splendid isolation 0·25m. south of the village. It has long been suspected that the reason for this is that the original village stood by the church and moved away either because of the Black Death or possibly because of flooding. Recent excavations have exposed the sandstone foundations and post holes of several buildings to the south and east of the church. Vitreous slag can also be found in the adjacent field to the south.

5

This could indicate either glass or ironworking in the area. To the east of the church the ground is disturbed and there is what appears to be a small quarry. All this confirms that the original village probably stood around the church. As to the church of St. James itself, the nave and chancel are Decorated; the tower is of 1566 in the upper parts and 13th Century in the lower. There was restoration by Street in 1869. Inside is a monument to Richard Neville, d. 1728, and some Clayton and Bell stained glass. North of the church, on the fringe of the village, is the Moat House, part timber-framed and part 18th Century brick. Here also is the Old School House of similar construction. On the other side of the road from the church, to the west, is a fragmentary circular segment of a moat 615 ft. by 110 ft. In the late 1850's fire bricks were manufactured at Acton Trussell. The name Acton Trussell is the original of Stackton Tressel, coined by the comedy duo, Hinge and Brackett. Dame Hilda Brackett, alias Patrick Fyffe, used to live in the village. One mile NE of Acton Trussell, on the lane to the A34, is the splendidly situated haunted house of Acton Hill Farm (SJ 946.195). In March 1835 the shepherd Richard Burton lost 5 children aged between 2 and 17 in a period of 11 days. Another son died in 1838 and 2 more in 1840. All 8 are commemorated on a stone in Baswich churchyard. The cries of ghostly children have been heard by the later occupants of the house.

ADBASTON *6.5m. NNE of Newport.*
Lost in the lanes north of Newport. This is flat farming country which, with the increasingly large fields of today, can be somewhat bleak. The old village consists of little more than the Hall, the Rectory and the Church. One tries to forget the concrete modern houses and the row of brick bungalows. The Hall is now a colour-washed farm and older than it looks. In front of the house is a pool much frequented by ducks. The Rectory is 19th century brick, and the Church of St. Michael is essentially Norman

Adbaston Hall.

— see the chancel windows — with later Perpendicular (1350 - 1550) rebuilding. The silver chalice and plate are Elizabethan and there is an incised monument to Reginald de Adbaston d. 1441. One and, a quarter miles NE is a delightful little lake. Knighton reservoir is almost hidden from the road and looks as though it is a stream temporarily in flood, with grassy meadows reaching to the water's edge. Near the dam end is a derelict farmhouse in a wooded clearing. One mile south of Adbaston is the Shropshire Union Canal. At the junction with the road there is an inn. A quarter of a mile further south is Batchacre Hall. It sits in isolation amongst windswept fields. The Georgian red brick

Batchacre Hall near Adbaston.

facade hides a much older building which shows itself in the strange chimneys and mullioned windows in the basement. Above the porch is a tripartite window with a pointed window above. The house and grounds have known better days. There used to be a lake with an ornamental fort on an

6

ornamental island. Still there, standing forlorn amongst undergrowth by a rectangular remnant of the lake to the south of the Hall is the porch of the long-ago demolished Gerard's Bromley Hall (1584) which was described by Dr. Plot as the finest house in the county. (Gerards Bromley lies some 5m. to the north, near Ashley).

Adbaston, Gerard's Bromley Hall Porch.

One mile SW of Adbaston is the hamlet of **Knighton.** It bestrides the Shropshire Union canal and is dominated by the Premier Brands factory which until 1986 belonged to Cadburys. Dairy based confectionary is manufactured here and has been since 1911. There are a few farms, the old Hall, a roadside development of 20th Century houses with hipped roofs arranged in blocks of 2 or 4, and a social club with a bowling green, tennis courts and a football pitch. It is about as ordinary as could be yet it is unique in the whole of Britain. All but three of the houses here lie on land which was formerly part of the estate of Knighton Manor and by an act of Parliament of 1660 were granted immunity from the payment of local rates and taxes of any kind. The exact wording was very sweeping. The manor was "freed, discharged and acquitted of and from payment of all, every or any manner of Taxes, Assessments or charges Civil or Military". Why should King Charles II have granted such an unusual boon? No one knows. In fact the gift was not actually meant to favour Knighton itself. The purpose of the Act was to authorize the setting up of a free school and almshouses in Newport (Shropshire) by William Adams, a citizen and haberdasher of London. To make his new establishment financially independent he endowed it with the manor and Grange of Knighton. The exemption from taxation already detailed made the income from the manor more valuable. But why was this special concession made? Was the king repaying a favour or a debt and if so was it to Adams, the Haberdashers Company or the town of Newport? Did it have any connection with his flight after his defeat at the Battle of Worcester when at Boscobel and Moseley Old Hall he received succour and protection? Did someone connected with his escape have a connection with Adams and ask the favour? At the time of writing there is talk of abolishing the privilege. The introduction of the new Poll Tax, which is to replace the old local rates system is seen as an opportune moment to

Knighton, Premier Brands factory.

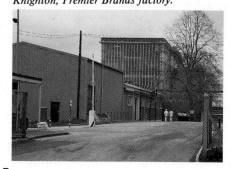

Knighton, Palin's Farm.

Knighton, the Shropshire Union Canal.

remove what some consider to be an archaic anomaly. We hope that it is preserved. It would be churlish and petty, not to say dishonourable, to terminate this ancient right. Note: There is another Knighton to the north of the county, near Woore, which is west of Newcastle-under-Lyme. It is sometimes confused with the Newport Knighton.

ALDRIDGE *2·5m. NE of Walsall.*

The town lies on highish ground NE of Walsall, just beyond the clutches of the Black Country. In Saxon times it was a Royal Manor. After 1066 it passed to William, son

Aldridge, church of St. Mary.

of Ansculf, and under the Normans the area fell just within the southern boundary of Cannock Forest. In the 19th Century the most important industries here were coal mining, brick making and tile manufacture. Limestone was quarried from Roman times until the late 19th century. Today there is a variety of light engineering and manufacturing works, many of which are on the new Industrial Estate. There is very little that is old here. The town centre is full of flat-roofed shops that have the appearance of temporary buildings, the schools are modern square boxes with much glass and there is acre upon acre of post-war housing. That Aldridge was once a great deal more attractive than it is today can be seen by what remains of the old village. It stands around the northern edge of the extremely large and lush village green. Here are three buildings of note: the church, the Moot House and the

Manor House. The church of St. Mary has a 19th century tower, an aisle of 1841 and most of the rest was rebuilt by Salvin in 1853. Inside there is a Jacobean pulpit, a stained glass window by Powell and a cross-legged knight of the early 14th century. South-west of the church is The Moot House. This is a handsome stuccoed house of 3 bays, and 2.5 storeys with a curved porch supported by columns. Each of the slightly projecting end bays has a Venetian window surmounted by a tripartite window, and at the top a lunette (moon-shaped) window. The Manor House lies to the other side of the church. It is a large brick-built building of 5 bays and 2.5 storeys with a hipped roof. The porch does not look as though it belongs. It is of stone, supported by stone Ionic columns, and above it is a pedimented window with stone surrounds. The house is currently used as a Youth Centre.

ALREWAS *5m. NE of Lichfield.*

Alrewas is a communications centre of some importance. Here the A38 (Ryknild Street) crosses the A513 King's Bromley to Tamworth road and the Trent and Mersey Canal crosses the River Trent. The country around is flat and sand and gravel are quarried nearby. The village is most attractive with many timber-framed and black and white thatched cottages. There is a Victorian cotton mill just north of the church. The name Alrewas means alder-wash or alder marsh and was first mentioned in a land grant by King Edmund in 941. The *Alrewas, cottage in the High Street.*

9

village lies on the edge of Needwood forest which was then heavily wooded. The boundaries of Needwood Forest were, generally speaking, the Rivers Trent, Dove and Blithe. A mile and a half west is Alrewas Haye an isolated farm. This is quite possibly the site of a Saxon 'haye' a small, often unenclosed, hunting park. The church is Norman, with two original doorways, but was largely rebuilt in Early English and Perpendicular. In the chancel is a 15th Century wall painting. There are 18th

Alstonefield, harvesting at Harecops.

Alrewas, the old cotton mill on the R. Trent.

Century memorials to the Turton family who lived at Orgreave Hall, which lies 1.5m. NW of Alrewas and is approached by a wide, double avenue of lime trees. It is a small 'L' shaped house built about 1668 with additions over the following 60 years and some Victorian embellishment. The south and north fronts are in different styles. It has a fine door case with fluted Corinthian pilasters and a swan's-neck pediment. There is an early 18th Century stable block. Chetwynd Bridge (1824) lies 1m. SE. This is in cast-iron and was made at Coalbrookdale. It has three arches and was designed by the Country Surveyor, Joseph Potter. It is sometimes called Salter's Bridge and carries the A513 over the River Tame. Half a mile downstream the Tame joins the Trent.

ALSTONEFIELD *14m. NNW of Ashbourne.* The parish of Alstonefield is very large, 23,000 acres, compared to, say, Barlaston at 2,000 acres. The reason is that this is moorland hill country, with a widely scattered population living in isolated farms and small hamlets. It has been this way since medieval times. The underlying rocks are limestone and the stones cleared to make the pastures were used to build the characteristic white stone walls and cottages of the area. The village of Alstonefield is at least Saxon in origin, if not earlier. It is a pleasant stone-built place with a perfect village green shaded by large trees and overlooked by the village pub. It is famous for the fact that Charles Cotton, the fishing friend of Isaac Walton, lived nearby at Beresford Hall. The Hall was pulled down about 1860 and now lies in ruins, but Cotton's delightful Fishing

Alstonefield, detail on Cotton's pew.

Lodge of 1674 still stands in its charming setting by the River Dove at the northern entrance to Beresford Dale (nearer to Hartington than Alstonefield). The Church of St. Peter at Alstonefield has fragments of Saxon interlace sculpture in: the west side of the porch; inside the tower; in the west of the

cup, animal bones and three Roman coins, one of the Emperor Tetricus (AD. 768-773), one of the Emperor Constantine (AD. 307-337), and one which could not be deciphered.

ALTON *3·5m. ESE of Cheadle.*

We were in the grounds of Wootton Lodge, the most handsome house in the county. Across the lovely deer park and the lakes came the raucous sounds of a rock group. Perhaps the Hall had been bought by a pop millionaire, we thought. But no; the music came from the fun fair of Alton Towers nearly 2m. away. The owner of Wootton Lodge is Mr. Bamford of the earth-moving equipment manufacturers, JCB. He must be furious at this untoward intrusion. The quiet little village of Alton lies high on the southern bank of the delightful Churnet valley. There has probably been a settlement here since prehistoric times. It commands the north-south river crossing

Alton village, the High Street.

Alstonefield, on the fringe of the village.

north aisle; and in the north of the north aisle. The chancel is Norman but most of the rest of the church is Decorated (1290 - 1350) and Perpendicular (1350 - 1550). Inside there are 17th Century box pews, a fine two-decker pulpit of 1637, and the Charles Cotton pew with its pale green livery at the eastern end of the north aisle. Alstonefield Hall is a small manor house of 1587 which lies to the north of the church. It is of irregular shape and has mullioned windows. One mile SW is the 17th Century Stanshope Hall. It has gabled wings and a side facing five-bay brick front with a projecting surround to the doorway. In the hills around Alstonefield are several prehistoric burial mounds, or tumulii. These include sites at Narrowdale Hill, Gratton Hill, Stanhope pasture at Hall Dale, Steep Low and Pea Low. The barrow at Steep Low (or Steepe Lowe), 0.5m. NW of Alstonefield, was opened in 1845. Amongst the finds were a skeleton, some smelted iron-ore, a drinking

Alton, the castle.

Alton, the bridgehead settlement.

Alstonefield, the church and the vicarage.

and the east-west road from Cheadle to Rocester. There is good reason to believe that the village lay on an old salt road from Nantwich to Derby because east of Alton is Saltersford Lane which may have formed part of the route. Bertram de Verdun built a large castle here about 1175. (He also built Croxden Abbey). All that remains of the castle is part of one tower. This is in the forecourt of the new castle built by Pugin in 1847. Seen from the valley below this is everyone's idea of a fairy castle, a Rhineland fantasy. It has four storeys and three towers, and sits on a precipice with a ravine between it and the adjacent Hospital of St. John. The castle is 'L' shaped with a chapel wing which

Alton, the Hospital of St. John.

converts the 'L' to a 'T' shape. The chapel has a roof of coloured tiles, the window tracery is geometric and the apse is polygonal. There is an ante-chapel and a chapel proper which is, unusually, rib vaulted in stone. The whole provides an atmospheric place of worship. Today the castle is used as a Roman Catholic boys' school. Across the moat-ravine, traversed by a bridge, is the Hospital of St. John, built between 1842 and 1846 for the 16th Earl of Shrewsbury by Pugin. The castle and the hospital are of one integrated design. It is built in a 'U' shape, the open end facing the castle. The right wing was built last and differs in design from the others. The Hospital, in Pugin's words, was to 'consist of a chapel, school, lodging for the warden, common hall, kitchen, chambers and library, ... lodgings for the poor brethren and a

residence for the schoolmaster'. The schoolmaster's house was actually a conversion of two existing cottages and stands detached. The chapel has a good chancel roof and an ornate plaster reredos. There are brass memorials to the last Roman Catholic Earls of Shrewsbury; the 16th died in 1852 and the 17th died in 1856. Pugin himself died in 1852. The sizeable village is a quiet place. There is a small, pretty hamlet down in the valley at the bridge head, and from here a delightful lane runs parallel with the river to Oakamoor, some 2m. to the north-west. The village church of St. Peter at Alton has a Norman north arcade and a 14th Century tower but was mostly rebuilt in 1830. Probably the best house in the village is the painted Old Coffee Tavern with a pedimented doorway in the centre of three bays. Nearby is the old stone-domed Lock-up of 1819. Alton station lies on the north bank of the river. It was built in the 1840's by H.A. Hunt and has the appearance of an Italian house. The railway is now dismantled and is used as a footpath. Both sides of the valley are wooded. The Churnet Valley has had a long industrial history and, strange as it seems today, there were many mills here making iron and copper. At Alton there are today two buildings which were formerly working mills. The Old Mill Cafe (SK.072.426), formerly Alton Mill, is probably 18th century. It is built of stone with a tiled roof and brick chimney stacks, and a gabled wing at each end. The actual mill has been pulled down. From about 1734 it drew brass for wire pin manufacture, but later became a paper mill. In 1830 it had three water wheels. One mile NW of Alton in the Churnet Valley is a water mill (SK.060.432), built in 1741 as a lead smelting mill and converted to grind corn by 1784. It has a single high-breast water wheel and 3 pairs of grinding stones. North of the river is **Alton Towers** which is today best known as a pleasure park. The old house and gardens are very much of secondary importance to the gaudy amusements first introduced by John

Broome, a businessman and property developer, in the second half of this century. There are 78 listed attractions which include rides that are major works of engineering, such as the gigantic corkscrew roller coaster. It is, to all intents and purposes, a small town in its own right. In the summer months hundreds of coaches pour down the

Alton Towers seen from Farley.

surrounding country lanes. On arrival they stand in endless lines in the enormous vehicle park. There can be no doubt that the greatest achievement of the organisers of the pleasure park was the obtaining of planning permission for this development. So what were the origins of Britain's biggest and most brash fun fair? The hill on which Alton Towers stands is called Bunbury, or sometimes Bonebury. There was an Iron Age (B.C. 600-650) settlement here which was taken over by Anglo-Saxons. It consisted of a double or treble ditch to the north, north-east and north-west sides, with the hill forming sufficient defences to the south. It

Alton Towers, the great house.

was very large, covering about 100 acres. In A.D. 716 Ceolred, King of Mercia, was in occupation of the fortress. King Ina (or Ine) of the West Saxons was advancing to attack him. He camped in a valley, where the Alton Towers' gardens are now, and King Ina himself slept in the shelter of a huge rock now called King Ina's Rock, which can be seen on Rock Walk. The next day King Ceolred left his fortress and descended on the West Saxon army. The battle took place in what is now called Slain Hollow. However, the battle was indecisive and both armies withdrew. The lands of Alton passed on to Bertram de Verdun, a reward for his services in the Holy Land and gifted to him by Richard I, and then to the Talbots in 1412. The Talbots, who were Earls of Shrewsbury, lived at Wingfield in Derbyshire, Worksop in Nottinghamshire and Heythrop in Oxfordshire. All they had at Alton was a small lodge built for their agent. Then, in the

Alton Towers, the Ingestre Stables

early 19th Century, the 15th Earl and his wife visited their Alton estate and were very taken by the grandeur of the scenery. In 1814 the Earl started to lay out the gardens and made Gothic additions to the existing lodge. In 1827, with the work still incomplete, he died but the 16th Earl continued where he had left off, and when the Heythrop mansion burned down in 1831 the Earl moved to Alton. Many architects were employed at Alton, including James Wyatt and Pugin, but who did what is not known. The house measures 460 ft. by 250 ft. It is most ornate and irregular, a fantasy of towers, pinnacles, battlements and turrets. It was originally called Alton Abbey. Today much of the hall is empty and even ruinous. The Banqueting Hall has a fine timber ceiling and stained glass windows. The Flag Tower is rock-faced with 4 turrets and stands in good order. The Chapel was remodelled by Pugin. It is high with two west galleries and has a low polygonal apse between two turrets. The Conservatory and the Stables are restored and very good. The gardens are Alton's glory. More than one observer has declared them the finest in the country. They are heavily planted in a rocky valley that leads down to the River Churnet. There are pools, fountains, terraces, walls, paths and staircases. The two principal gardeners were Thomas Allason (1790-1852) and Robert Abrahams (1774-1850). There are many garden buildings: The Pagoda Fountain (a copy of the To Ho Pagoda in Canton); the Swiss Cottage, now a restaurant but once home to a Welsh harper; a construction called Stonehenge, which is not a copy of the original; and the Choragic Monument, a copy of Lysicrates' work erected in Athens in 344 B.C. The gardens include the great Rock Garden, the Star Garden, the Terraced Garden and the Dutch Garden. The 16th Earl gave orders that any Roman Catholic who applied for a job should be employed without question, hence the vast network of paths through the woods; work that could be tackled by the unskilled. In 1856 the last of the Catholic Earls of Shrewsbury died. There was an unpleasant squabble over the inheritance which finally passed to a remote cousin, the Anglican Earl Talbot of Ingestre, near Stafford. The court case had been expensive and to pay for it the contents of Alton Towers were sold by auction. The sale lasted for 29 days, so much was there to sell. There was a collection of paintings originally owned by the mother of the Emperor Napoleon — which included works by Velasquez, Van Dyck and Bellin — furniture, arms and armour and, all in all, a countless treasure that attracted buyers from

all over Europe. Ingestre Hall became the main residence of the Earls, and in 1860 the gardens at Alton were opened to the public. The family became involved firstly with a hansome cab company and then with the Talbot car company. In 1896 the Earl and his

Alton Towers, the valley gardens.

Countess separated. She had Alton and he lived at Ingestre. The Earl, however, held the purse strings and at Alton both the house and the gardens were allowed to decay. In 1918 most of the Alton estate was sold. In 1921 the Earl died, in 1923 the Countess left Alton and in 1924 the house, gardens, woods and parks were sold. They had been in the hands of the Earls of Shrewsbury for 700 years. The property was bought by a group of local businessmen who formed Alton Towers Ltd. The gardens were restored and the public once again admitted. There were boats on the lake and bands on the bandstand, and the gardens were a commercial success. During the Second World War the house was used as an Officer Cadet Training Unit. By the end of the war the Army had done its worst and Alton Towers was in a delapidated condition. The Army kept it locked up and unused until 1951 when it was finally handed over to its rightful owners. Leaking roofs and dry rot and wet rot made much of the building unsafe so the interior was largely demolished. In 1952 the gardens were once again restored and opened to the public. Then came the modern developments that were to make Alton an international name. One wonders if the 15th and 16th Earls would have quite approved.

Note: Despite common useage the title 'Earl of Shrewsbury' is incorrect; it is officially 'Earl of the County of Salop'.

AMBLECOTE *1m. N of Stourbridge.*

The name means 'the cottage by the river' (or sandbank), but today it is an industrial suburb of Stourbridge. It developed rapidly in the 19th Century. Glass making and fire-clay mining were its most important industries. The church is of yellow brick, built in 1841-4 by Samuel Heming. The centre of the Corbett Hospital is a Georgian house of nine bays with a Venetian window at the back and a handsome staircase. This actually lies in Worcestershire.

ARMITAGE *2·25m. SE of Rugeley.*

It lies on a rise 0·25m. south of the River Trent and alongside the Trent and Mersey Canal (1766-1777), which runs parallel with the road from Rugeley for some 2 miles. This stretch of the canal has recently been improved. The main line railway passes to the east of the village on its way from Rugeley to Lichfield. Armitage is not an attractive place but it does have several black and white cottages, two of which are on the main road. One of these is the well-known restaurant called 'The Farmhouse'. The rest of the buildings are mostly red brick. The village is famous for the sanitary products made here, called Armitage ware. The church stands alone, to the west, close by the river. The old Church of St. John was Norman with a later tower of 1632. All but

Armitage, the Farmhouse restaurant.

the tower was rebuilt in 1844, in Norman style, and was very well done. The font is original Norman and is also very good.

Armitage, a cottage on the main road.

About 1m. W, along the A513 to Rugeley but on the other side of the canal, is Hawkesyard Priory now called the Spode Conference Centre. This started as Armitage Park, a stuccoed Gothic house built in 1760 by Nathaniel Lister. In 1839 it was bought by the

Armitage, Spode House.

widow of Josiah Spode III and the alteration in stone, to the left part of the house, dates from that year. The house has battlements and pinnacles but the chimneys were removed in 1963. The rear of the building backs onto the canal. It has three storeys and looks like a warehouse. There was a short tunnel connecting it to the canal. Mrs. Spode and her son, Josiah IV, lived in the house, the pottery business having passed to the Copeland family. Josiah IV renamed the house 'Hawkesyard' after the original medieval house that occupied the site. He became a convert to the Roman Catholic

Ashley, the Heath in mist from Hookgate. *Ashley, moon rise over Loggerheads.*
Ashley, sunset over Wales from Loggerheads.

detached villas, again in a wooded setting. This occupies the site of the old tuberculosis hospital, the Cheshire Joint Sanatorium. It was situated here because Loggerheads is on a hill, above the damp air of the lowlands and the soot and smoke that used to drift over from the Potteries. It is noticeable today that the weather on the hill is often quite different from that on the plains around it. The Sanatorium lay in woodland that is part of the Burnt Wood. Today this large forest is coniferous, courtesy of the Forestry Commission, but it used to be an oak wood, part of the ancient Blore Forest. The stumps of the great oaks can still be seen. They were mercilessly cut down to make way for the quick-growing crop of softwoods. The whole

Ashley, Clod Hall

area around Ashley is quite heavily wooded, with the Maer Hills Forest to the north, Bishop's Wood to the south and numerous small copses in between. About one mile south-east of Ashley is **Gerard's Bromley.** This is now a single dairy farm. The medieval

Gerard's Bromley. Podmore Pool.

Gerard's Bromley, medieval plaster freize.

settlement is long gone, as indeed is the Hall which was described by Dr. Plot, in 1686, as being 'the most magnificent structure of all this county'. It was built about 1575 by Sir Gilbert Gerard, a handsome stone mansion with ogee capped turrets, shaped gables and high windows. The 7th and last Lord Gerard became a Jesuit priest. The hall passed to the Meynell family and it was they who pulled it down. All that remains on the site today are the later 17th Century gate piers and a 17th Century barn. Inside the barn is an elaborate plaster frieze depicting a hunting scene. The sole remnant of the Hall itself is the Porch which was dismantled and re-

Gerard's Bromley, barn left, old hall rear.

erected at nearby Batchacre Hall. Here it languishes in a patch of scrub where it serves as a piece of garden furniture. The present farmhouse at Gerard's Bromley stands at the back of the large enclosed yard. It is, in fact, quite probably the original Hall, the home of the Gerard's before they built their 'ephemeral palace'. The illustration in

24

Dr. Plot's History of Staffordshire (1686) shows the Old Hall standing beside and behind the New. Below the farm the land falls away to the substantial mill pool and the now disused stone and brick mill. The road runs along the dam. The pastures on the northern bank of the pond have medieval ridge and furrow with distances of between 12 ft. and 15 ft. between the ridge crests. On the other side of this hill is Podmore Pool another man made lake and the probable site of the medieval iron works at Bromley.

ASTON (near Stone) 6m. N of Stafford.

A little catholic enclave hidden amongst the trees and seemingly surrounded by streams, near the junction of the A34 and the A51, just south of Stone. The moated Hall has been a Catholic house since Elizabethan times and today is a home for retired priests. The timber-framed house is now clad in Victorian brick. Alongside the entrance drive is a small chapel of 1844 with a low tower and

Aston, near Stone, from the A51.

Aston, near Stone, from the A34.

spire. The Hall used to belong to the Simeon family who were baronets of Britwell Salome, Oxfordshire. The River Trent touches the northern edge of the village and on it was a mill, now a house. In the outbuildings opposite was a small craft pottery. The Trent and Mersey Canal runs within a few yards of the river and parallel to it for many miles hereabouts. The church of St. Saviour was built by James Trubshaw in 1846, the spire was added by J.R. Botham in 1820 and the stained glass windows,

designed by Gibbs, in 1863. One mile south of Aston, on the A34, is Yarlet Hall School. This is all that remains of the village of **Yarlet.** In 1086 it had 8 households, a large population for its day, but in the 12th Century the monks of Combermere (Cheshire) evicted the tenants, destroyed the village and made a farm — a grange — in its place. Today there is a pub and a garage on the main road nearby, but these are comparatively recent main-road developments, as are the houses to the south. The old deserted village probably lay around the Hall. The present Hall is a Victorian building in Jacobean style, though it almost certainly stands on the site of the old medieval manor house. It is currently used as a Preparatory School. At the top of Yarlet Bank, above the school, is a cone shaped hill which possibly has prehistoric associations. One mile to the south-west of Aston is Pire Hill. This hill gave its name to the Hundred of Pirehill, one of the five Hundreds of Staffordshire. (The others were Totmonslow, Cuttlestone, Offlow and Seisdon). Today the name Pirehill is better known as the new H.Q. of the Stafford County Fire Service, the entrance to which is on the A34 just to the south of Aston.

AUDLEY *4.5m. NW of Newcastle under Lyme.* Audley, called Aldidelege in Domesday Book, is a pleasant small town built on a ridge. There is much suburban housing and a surprise, a small theatre. To the NW of the church is a good group of 3 shops, an archway and a house, all in Gothic brick with arches. They were built by William White and were illustrated in The Builder magazine in 1855. Audley has a 'forgotten castle' which is rarely mentioned in references books even today. It seems that historians had assumed that references to Audley Castle were errors and that the ancient writers were actually referring to Heighley Castle, 2.5m. SW, both of which were owned by the Audley family. It was almost certainly the Normans who built the castle on what is now called Castle Hill. It

Audley, the church of St. James.

lies adjacent to the A52 Newcastle to Nantwich road and consists of a circular mound with a flat top which covers about a third of an acre. A moat protects the northern edge were the mound is at its lowest. There would have been a wooden palisade and a wooden fortress tower for only minimal stonework was found when the site was excavated. The church lies S of the castle

on the other side of the road. This is a typical Norman alignmemt. There was probably a natural gully between them but this was deepened when the road was improved in modern times. The Audley family (who took their name from the Anglo-Saxon settlement) came into possession of the manor some time after 1086 and it was possibly they who built the castle. In 1226 the fortress was mentioned in a document and again in 1272 at the inquest into the death of James de Audley. By this time the family had built Heighley Castle *(see Madeley)* and this had become their main dwelling. The Audley Castle fell into disuse, references to it ceased and it became forgotten. It was rediscovered by local amateur historians at the beginning of this century. It had been long used as an orchard but has now been cleared and fenced around. The most famous squire of Audley was Sir James Audley (ancestor of James de Audley) who led the forces of the Black Prince at the Battle of Poitiers (1356). The battle was won but Audley was badly wounded. The Black Prince is reputed to have embraced him and said: "Sir James, I and all the rest of us deem you the bravest knight in this battle, and to increase your renown I retain you forever as my Knight." In the church at Audley is the tomb of one of Sir James's squires, Richard Delves, who had helped carry his injured lord from the field of battle. On the chancel floor is a tombstone to Edward Vernon, vicar of Audley, who founded the Grammar School in 1612. The church of St. James has a 14th Century tower, a 16th Century aisle and a Jacobean font. It is an impressive building in sandstone with a large east window by Wailes and was restored by Gilbert Scott in 1846. One mile to the NNE are the remains of a tall obelisk to John Wedgwood, erected in 1839. One mile to the E, adjacent to the M6, is Shraley Brook. Most of the male population of this scattered hamlet worked at the Minnie Pit, Halmer End and many were killed in the dreadful explosion of 12th January 1918. *(See Halmer End.)*

BAGNALL *1.75m. S of Endon (which is 5m. NW of Hanley).*

A hill top village to the east of the suburban sprawl of the Potteries. The church of St. Chad is of 1834 with a chancel by J. Beardmore of 1879-81. The Stafford Arms stands opposite, an irregular 17th Century stone house, long and low as though trying to cheat the wind. Half a mile to the north-east is Stanley Pool.

BALTERLEY *5m. SE of Crewe (Cheshire).*

A scatter of houses along the A52; a charming red brick church of 1901 by Austin and Paley; a Victorian blacksmith's shop with green sliding doors and the old hearth still in place; and the beautiful Hall o' th' Wood. The latter is a later 16th Century black and white house which is one of the best in the county, though it has recently been a little over-restored. It stands at the end of a long drive with a backdrop of trees. The Hall is highly decorated with a motif of five overlapping circles. To the front are two large gables in between which are two

porchlike projections with overhanging gables, and in between them is a recessed centre bay with entrance door. The approach drive leads to the back of the house where are to be found some new houses by the pool. Half a mile to the west of Balterley is the county border of Cheshire.

BARLASTON *3m. NNW of Stone (which is 7.5m. N of Stafford).*

In Domesday Book the village is called Bernulvestone which means Beornwulf's estate. At that time seven families lived there. During the whole of the Middle ages the village operated the classic Midland open field system. There was a single settlement and the boundaries of the small parish of 2,000 acres coincided with those of the manor. At one end of the village lay the manor house and the church, and at the other the village green. The farmers lived together in the village and the 3 open arable fields lay around the settlement. Each farmer had a number of strips in each field. These were deliberately scattered so that any

Balterley, the Hall o' the' Woods.

27

variation in soil quality was equally shared. This arrangement lasted until the 16th Century. Within the whole parish there were only two exceptions to this scheme. Great Hartwell farm lay 2m. east of the village and was self-contained with its own fields — and it also had its own chapel and watch tower — and in the 1480's another isolated farm appeared 0·75m. to the NE, called Woodseaves, probably in a new forest clearing. The present Barlaston Hall was built about 1756. The architect is not known but was probably Sir Robert Taylor. It is tall, of brick and of a strong design. It has 5 bays of 2·5 storeys. The doorway has Tuscan columns and a pediment, and at the rear is a large, full length central bow with steps leading to the patio. To the sides are canted bays. The interior had good plasterwork and a fine staircase. A few years ago the house stood in great disrepair. It had been bought by the Wedgwood company who wanted to demolish it and redevelop the site. The building was suffering from settlement cracks, caused by coal mining, and they

Barlaston, the Wedgwood factory.

hoped that it would become too bad to repair. They were thwarted by the Secretary of State for the Environment who rejected Wedgwood's application to demolish the Hall. The company chairman reacted by saying it was a pity that the government hadn't got better things to do than 'save decrepit buildings'. There was a public outcry and Wedgwoods were taken to task in the Times, which spoke of their 'astonishing blindness to the virtue of what they possessed. The outcome was that Wedgwoods sold the property to a trust for

Barlaston Hall.

£1. The trust renovated the Hall and converted it into flats, and it now stands restored to its former glory. The Wedgwood company has in fact had connections with Barlaston since the 1840's when the family lived here at The Lea, and commuted daily to the works in Etruria near Hanley. Then, in 1938-40, the company built a new factory at Barlaston, 0·5m. north of the village, and deserted the old Etruria complex. The new factory is mundane in the extreme and of no architectural interest whatsoever. Apparently, the architect, Keith Murray, was chosen on the strength of some vase designs he had made! A 'model' village for the workers was also built. The factory is still there and now has a small museum for which Wedgwoods, rather surprisingly, charge a substantial entrance fee. There is also a factory shop and a snack bar. Photography is not allowed. Between Barlaston Hall and the Wedgwood Factory is the Park and the Lake. By the works is a railway level crossing. The present church of St. John has a medieval tower but the rest is the work of C. Lynham, 1886-8, with a new vestry of 1969 by A.G. Capey. There are some monuments to the Wedgwood family. The church stands next to the Hall. A little to the south is the large village green. To the west is a considerable surburban sprawl, along the Trent and Mersey Canal and the railway, but this is nicely kept apart from the old village which lies above it on a well-wooded ridge.

Barlaston, canoeists by the canal.

BARTON-UNDER-NEEDWOOD 7·5m. NE *of Lichfield.*

It lies between Lichfield and Burton on Trent just off the dead straight Ryknild Street, the Roman road now called the A34. The name 'Barton' means 'fort-settlement' and 'Needwood' means 'forest-refuge'. Barton under Needwood was originally a dependent settlement of Tatenhill. Both villages lie in the Trent valley on the fringe of the Needwood Forest plateau. The Forest originally filled the area between the Rivers

Barton-under-Needwood, the Old Hall.

Trent, Dove and Blithe, and was well-wooded until the 17th Century. Today there is very little of the Forest left, although a few miles north of Barton there are many copses and small woods which can give the impression of a forest. The village of Barton is quite attractive and is blessed by being a good 0·5m. from the roar of the A34. On the road to Dunstall is the charming 18th Century brick-built Old Hall. In the grounds a deer-shelter is preserved dated 1724. On the opposite side of the road is disturbed ground, possibly the site of old cottages. The Dower House is early 19th Century, rendered with two trellis verandas and a porch of Doric columns of wood. However, the main attraction at Barton is the church and the man who built it. The church of St. James is rare in that it was built all at one time by one man and therefore has architectural unity. It is the work of Dr. John Taylor and was completed in 1517. The tower is short with 8 pinnacles; there is a nave, aisles, clerestory and polygonal apse. In the north wall of the chancel is a blank arch, presumed to have been intended as the founder's tomb. The only alteration made to the structure was the widening of the church to north and south in 1862. The walls were rebuilt to match the originals. The overall

Barton-under-Needwood, St. James' Church.

style is Gothic Perpendicular. Dr. Taylor was born one of a set of triplets. This was an unusual event in those days and they were shown, as a curiosity, to King Henry VII. The King made the remarkable gesture of paying for their education. John the eldest of the triplets, went on to become one of the King's Chaplains, Archdeacon of Derby and Buckingham, Master of the Rolls (1527) and an international diplomat. He attended Henry on the Field of the Cloth of Gold. The church was built on the site of the cottage in which he was born. He died in 1534. Close to the church is the Old Vicarage, a striking stuccoed house with two large, almost semi-circular, gables to the front.

BASFORD *See Newcastle-under-Lyme.*

BASFORD GREEN *1m. SE of Cheddleton.* From the road the lakes in the valley and the mock castle can be seen. These are part of the estate of Basford Hall, an ashlar house of 1858 which is superbly positioned with long views over the beautiful countryside to the SE. It was the home of a junior branch of the Sneyd family which descended from William Sneyd of Keele, M.P. for Newcastle-under-Lyme in 1685. A little further along the road

is Cheddleton Station, now a Railway Museum with a special emphasis on the 'Knotty', the North Staffordshire Railway. The River Churnet and the Caldon Canal flow by here within yards of each other.

BETLEY *6m. NW of Newcastle-under-Lyme.* Betley is a most attractive village. It stands along the A531 in the north-west of the county close to the Cheshire border. The buildings are a pleasant mixture of red brick and black and white. The Old Hall of 1621 has a fine panelled Court Room and amongst the farm buildings are some excellent 2-tier vaulted cow shippons built by George Tollet IV. South of the Hall, at the other end of the village, is Betley Court. This is a large handsome 18th Century chequered brick house with a 20th Century porch which was

Betley Court, from the road.

for long a home of the Fletcher-Twemlow family. In recent years it has been renovated by the present owner, Godfrey Brown, Emeritus Professor of Education at Keele University. He has written a book called 'This Old House' which is an account of the trials and tribulations of restoring an old building. He also commissioned a hand-crafted reproduction of the internationally famous Betley Window which was at the original Betley Hall (now demolished) and is now at the Victoria and Albert Museum in London. This small medieval stained glass window has diamond shaped panes on which are depicted 6 Morris Dancers together with a Fool, a Fife and Tabour Player, the Queen of the May and a Hobby Horse 'ridden' by a King. Its exact age is unknown but it is probably the earliest pictorial representation of traditional Morris Dancers in Britain and is of considerable historical interest. The reproduction is installed in the wing of Betley court that is currently used as a commercial gallery of art, ceramics and antique furniture. The gallery is open to the public and has an excellent selection of beautiful objects. The Court has some excellent iron gates which are at present being renovated with the assistance of English Heritage. The stable block has been converted into dwellings. The village is larger than it may at first appear and there are some small estates of modern houses though these are tastefully tucked away out of sight. The village cricket ground is nicely sited on a hill adjacent to the church but is spoiled by the advertising boards that surround the playing area. The church of St. Margaret is unusual in that it is basically a timber structure with a stone tower and stone aisle walls. Wooden piers carry a wooden clerestory and a heavy wooden roof which is highly ornamented in the chancel. The chancel was rebuilt in 1610. There are monuments to the Fletcher and the Fletcher-Twemlow families and a 17th Century monument to Ralph Egerton, died 1610. The exterior was restored in 1842. To the south-west of the village, approached through a farm, is Betley Mere, a beautiful lake with tall rushes and grasses and wild birds. Adjacent to the Mere is Cracow Moss. In Domesday Book Betley was called Betelege. It was held from the king by Wulfin. Prior to the conquest it was owned by Godic and Wulfgeat. There was once a market at Betley. At **Buddileigh,** 1m. NW on the main road, is the 'Beehive', an engaging half-timbered house of cruck construction with a date of 1662 on the porch but which is probably much older. Here also, is Doddlespool Hall the original Hall was

Betley, cottage in the main street.

31

Betley Mere.
Betley Court, the garden side.

The Betley Window, a reproduction.

Betley, the Mere.

built in 1605 but what we see today is Victorian mock Tudor. The name Doddlespool is thought to be derived from Toad's Pool. The Hall is now an old persons

Betley, Beehive Cottage.

home. South of Betley is **Wrinehill** and here is the Summer House, an old home of the Egerton family which has also been a barracks and a shop. It is built of brick on a stone base and inside is a handsome oak staircase.

BIDDULPH *7m. NNE of Hanley on the A527.* A large sprawling, somewhat characterless, place on the edge of the Moorlands. At the time of the Norman Conquest it was held by a man called Grufydd (Grifin), presumably descended from either an original Celtic pre-Roman settler or a later immigrant Welshman. The Old Hall was built by Francis Biddulph in 1588 and extended in the late 17th Century. It is situated 0·5m. NNE of Biddulph Grange Orthopaedic

Hospital at Ordnance Survey ref.SK.894.003. It was destroyed during the Civil War by the Parliamentarians and today stands in ruins hidden from sight by a large farm. Parts of the front facade remain and a porch leads to the central courtyard. One ogee-capped turret also survives. An area at the back of the house is still lived in. Not far from the Old Hall is the new hall called Biddulph Grange, built by James Bateman (1811-97), but it is for the gardens that it is famous. James was the son of John Bateman of nearby Knypersley, who had made a fortune manufacturing steam engines in Manchester. He was a keen gardener, even in his student days at Magdelene College, Oxford, and was later, in 1864, to lay out the University parks. In 1842 James bought an old farmhouse at Biddulph. It was surrounded by marshy ground on a desolate hillside. Over the next 25 years he laid out the gardens which were to achieve national fame. In 1869 the Batemans moved to Worthing for health reasons and the house was bought by Robert Heath. After a fire in 1896 much of the Hall was rebuilt but the porte-cochere, the outer hall and the low parts of the garden side are original. The main garden facade is of the rebuilding. In recent years the Hall has been used as an orthopaedic hospital and there are some quite awful extensions. The gardens are not very large and have been kept up by the hospital. However, they are something of a disappointment. The main garden only has

Biddulph Grange, entrance hall window.

BILSTON *2·5m. SE of Wolverhampton.*

A flourishing Black Country market town which has survived the closure of its major employer, the huge Bilston Steelworks. It has as many dour streets of cheap Victorian houses as any other town in the conurbation, but the centre of the town is cheerful and busy, whereas so many other town centres have boarded up shops windows and an air of desolation. The large Thursday market attracts customers from far and wide, and at times has the air of a country place; but that it has not been for several centuries. In Domesday Book we are told that the settlement still belonged to the King, that there were 8 villagers and 3 smallholders with 3 ploughs and that there was an acre of meadow and a wood 0·75m. long by 0·75m. wide. The name Bilston is derived from the name of a tribe of Angles who came up the Trent valley and settled here in the late 6th Century — the Bilsaeton or Bilsonii. Coal was probably being mined in Bilston during the late Middle Ages but it was not until the middle of the 18th Century, when John

Bilston, the Greyhound Inn.

Wilkinson (1728-1808) set up his ironworks at Bradeley in 1757-8, that the town began to expand. Wilkinson used the new process developed by Darby in Coalbrookdale which allowed coal, as coke, to be used for smelting iron ore. Previously charcoal had been used because coal would not burn with sufficient heat. Bilston was on the rich '30ft.' coal seams and so had an ample supply of fuel. By 1836 Wilkinson's ironworks had passed into other hands and had been somewhat comically crenellated to give them the appearance of a castle. The Wilkinson works were only the beginning of a large-scale iron making, steel making and heavy engineering industry which 'caused the ground to shake and the night sky to burn like the fires of hell'. Bilston was also famous internationally for its more delicate decorated products, such as enamelled ware, which flourished between 1730 and 1830, and Japan ware (goods made of either papier maché or tin-plate and varnished to give a high gloss finish). Japanning was a dead art by 1900 but a firm called Bilston Enamels has recently revived

the enamelling crafts and is doing very well, especially in the limited edition collectors' market. Note: Papier Mache is a misnomer although the term was used by the trade at the time. The articles were actually made from sheets of a special paper pasted together and then stamped into shape. They were originally called 'paper ware' but the public preferred the French name. Examples of both japanning and enamelling can be seen

Bilston, path off Greencroft.

and even had small back gardens. However, many of these gardens were later built on. Small workshops and sometimes more houses were crammed in by the owners and landlords. Bilston has been fortunate in having good communications. The Holyhead road used to pass through the town until the 1820's when Telford built a bypass. Between 1772 and 1786 Brindley constructed the Birmingham canal which linked Bilston with other major Black Country towns and Birmingham, as well as the rest of Staffordshire and Worcestershire. The parish church is something of a surprise — a great white piece of stucco that commands the attention. It lies in the centre of the town and was built in 1825 by Francis Goodwin. It replaced the old medieval church but is of a classical design. It was rendered in 1882-3. The windows of the sides are long and arched and the front has five bays and a chamfered turret. The interior is quite elegant with galleries and Ionic columns, and a sense of space. It is nice to see monuments to other than landed gentry. Here they are to Mrs. Williams, died 1834, Mrs. Riley, died 1835, and Mrs. Pearce 'descended from three children of Edward I'. There are two Commissioners' churches in the town — St. Luke in Market St., of 1851, and St. Mary in Oxford St., by Francis Goodwin, of 1857. Commissioners' churches were built with financial assistance from the government under the Act of Parliament of 1818 which established a fund of one million pounds to provide churches in districts of

Bilston, St. Leonard's over the railway

at Bilston Museum (which is above the town library), and in Bantock Park House, Wolverhampton. The early industrial towns were squalid places and in 1832 there was a severe outbreak of cholera in Bilston. The local vicar demanded the rebuilding of 'brick graves called courts, alleys and back squares where the poor are buried alive, amid gloom, damp and corruption . . . . .' The old courts were pulled down and replaced by streets of terraced houses which, though not by any means oppulent, were at least more sanitary

View from the A5 to the Morridge.
Blithfield reservoir at Sunset.

Brewood, field near Chillington.

the enamelling crafts and is doing very well, especially in the limited edition collectors' market. Note: Papier Mache is a misnomer although the term was used by the trade at the time. The articles were actually made from sheets of a special paper pasted together and then stamped into shape. They were originally called 'paper ware' but the public preferred the French name. Examples of both japanning and enamelling can be seen

Bilston, path off Greencroft.

and even had small back gardens. However, many of these gardens were later built on. Small workshops and sometimes more houses were crammed in by the owners and landlords. Bilston has been fortunate in having good communications. The Holyhead road used to pass through the town until the 1820's when Telford built a bypass. Between 1772 and 1786 Brindley constructed the Birmingham canal which linked Bilston with other major Black Country towns and Birmingham, as well as the rest of Staffordshire and Worcestershire. The parish church is something of a surprise — a great white piece of stucco that commands the attention. It lies in the centre of the town and was built in 1825 by Francis Goodwin. It replaced the old medieval church but is of a classical design. It was rendered in 1882-3. The windows of the sides are long and arched and the front has five bays and a chamfered turret. The interior is quite elegant with galleries and Ionic columns, and a sense of space. It is nice to see monuments to other than landed gentry. Here they are to Mrs. Williams, died 1834, Mrs. Riley, died 1835, and Mrs. Pearce 'descended from three children of Edward I'. There are two Commissioners' churches in the town — St. Luke in Market St., of 1851, and St. Mary in Oxford St., by Francis Goodwin, of 1857. Commissioners' churches were built with financial assistance from the government under the Act of Parliament of 1818 which established a fund of one million pounds to provide churches in districts of

Bilston, St. Leonard's over the railway

at Bilston Museum (which is above the town library), and in Bantock Park House, Wolverhampton. The early industrial towns were squalid places and in 1832 there was a severe outbreak of cholera in Bilston. The local vicar demanded the rebuilding of 'brick graves called courts, alleys and back squares where the poor are buried alive, amid gloom, damp and corruption . . . . .' The old courts were pulled down and replaced by streets of terraced houses which, though not by any means oppulent, were at least more sanitary

View from the A5 to the Morridge.
Blithfield reservoir at Sunset.

Brewood, field near Chillington.

greatest need. The Roman Catholic church of Holy Trinity is also on Oxford St. It is of 1883 with a chancel by Pugin. The Town Hall of 1872 has a tower and Gothic capitals but has a style that leaves all the experts baffled. The most notable secular building is the Greyhound Inn in the High St. It is of about 1450. The handsome black and white timber framing has closely-set uprights and two gables. Inside is a good Jacobean plaster ceiling with leaf scrolls. In recent years a large Asian community has developed in Bilston.

BISHOP'S OFFLEY *See Offley*

BISHOP'S WOOD *6·5m. E of Oakengates (Telford).*
The village lies 0·75m. south of the A5 in pleasant rolling country and has a church spire that is a well-known landmark. The church of St. John lies just outside the village to the south-east. It was built in 1851 by G.T. Robinson, much in the style that had developed in the second quarter of the century by the constructors of Commissioners' churches, i.e. those wholly or partly financed by the government under the Act of 1818, which alloted one million pounds to provide places of worship in districts of greatest need. They were often very utilitarian and there are many examples in the Black Country. The Bishop of Bishop's Wood would have been the Bishop of Chester whose diocese used to include all

Bishop's Wood, view NE over the A5.

the land between Chester and Lichfield, including the cathedral town itself. Two miles to the west of Bishop's Wood is Weston Park, home of the Earl of Bradford, and two miles south-west is Chillington Hall, home of the Giffard family. The famous Boscobel House and the Royal Oak Tree lie 0·75m. south. *(See Chillington.)*

BLAKE MERE *5m. NE of Leek.*
Blake Mere, or Blackmere (SK.030.613) is a small pool in the moorlands between Leek and Buxton. It lies alongside the spectacular road that follows the Morridge — literally 'the moorland ridge' — an ancient track that must have been well used by pre-historic man. It is most easily approached off the A53 at Stake Gutter which is 2m, NE of Upper Hulme but can also be reached via Thorncliffe. All manner of tales and superstitions are connected with this 40 ft. heart-shaped pool. Animals will not drink

Blake Mere, the Mermaid Inn sign.

39

there, birds will not fly over it; the pool is bottomless; it can never be drained; there is a mermaid who protects it from harm, etc. It is said that in recent years there was a moorland fire and the fire brigade pumped water out of the pool non-stop for many hours without the level lowering. It is very likely that Blake Mere had religious significance for early man and that these legends are a folk memory of ancient beliefs. Some say the mermaid story originated in medieval times when Joshua Linnet had a young girl branded as a witch and drowned

Blake Mere, the mere.

her in the pool. As she floundered in the water she cursed her accuser and said he would suffer the same fate. Three days later Joshua Linnet was found drowned in the lake with his face torn to pieces. The mermaid has been known to walk alongside travellers and try to entice them with her deep green eyes to follow her to her watery home. In 1679 there was a murder here. Andrew Simpson, who worked at the Red Lion in Leek, overheard a young woman speaking of how well she had done selling her lace wool and thread. He followed her home across the moors and murdered her for her money. He threw the body into Blake Mere but the corpse was found and he was hanged on Gun Hill. Just south of Blake Mere is a prehistoric burial mound called Merryton Low and south of that is the stone-built and gabled Mermaid Inn. This is all that remains of the village of Blake Mere. In the 16th and 17th Centuries there were several houses, a

Blake Mere, the Mermaid Inn.

chapel and a pub, the original Mermaid Inn. At that time the present pub was a house, called Blake Mere House. The remains of the old hostelry are at the end of the car park. The field opposite the inn is used by a Gliding Club. All around are wild moors parts of which are used by the army for exercises.

BLITHFIELD *8m. E of Stafford and 3m. N of Rugeley.*

In 1066 Edmund held Blithfield. By 1086 it had passed to Roger de Montgomery, the right hand man of William the Conquerer. It was held from him by another Roger who had 4 slaves. There were also 7 villagers, a

Blithfield Hall.

priest and a smallholder. For its time this was quite a substantial settlement. In 1367 the manor passed by marriage to the Bagot family, of nearby Bagot's Bromley. It remained in their hands until this century. The present hall has an Elizabethan core but was remodelled in 1820-4. It is approached

40

from the entrance lodges in Adbaston (on the Rugeley-Uttoxeter road), over a long drive through agricultural parkland. The country is very pleasant, with the great 20th Century reservoir-lake a new and impressive landscape feature. The house is very irregular, with courtyards and stables attached. The oldest part retains its timber framing inside. The facade is rendered and has turretts, pinnacles and castellations. The south side of the north range contains the sumptuosly redecorated great hall with traceried windows and a screen passage. The panelled library lies in the postion of the old solar. North of the north range is the eleven-bay Orangery, and to the north-east is the octagonal game larder of 1895. It is altogether a most interesting and unusual house, though it must be confessed that one's first impression is of a rather drab jumble of tired looking building going slightly to seed. The church of St. Leonard is approached by way of the rose garden behind the house. The nave and chancel are 13th to 14th Century. The nave has Early English *Blithfield Hall.*

Blithfield reservoir from near the Hall.

arcades with later clerestories (upper nave walls pierced by windows). The furniture is good, especially the Perpendicular screen and the bench ends. The pillar piscina (wash basin) is Norman. In the west window, c.1526, is depicted Sir Lewis Bagot, died 1534, and his wives, one of many monuments to the Bagot family. Sir Richard Bagot's grandson was created a baronet in 1627 and it was the baronet's son who became the Royalist commander in the Civil war. In 1780 the 6th baronet was created a peer. It was his

The Robin Hood, Brierley Hill.

enterprise which Brierley Hill was well known for was the Marsh and Baxter sausage and pie factory, reputed to have been the largest in the country. This is gone and the site is now partly occupied by the Moor Centre. Re-development is no stranger to Brierley Hill. Stretching SW of the town, between the Delph and Stourbridge, there were numerous coal mines and clay pits. These have now been cleared and in their place is a mammoth housing estate. The Delph is synonymous with the Nine Locks that carry the Dudley Canal No.1 up hill of the ridge on which the town stands. There are actually only 8 locks now, one being lost during re-building in 1857. They are in very good repair and the area is most attractive. The canal lies to the SW of the church, below the looming tower blocks. At Withy Moor village, near the Delph, is the Vine pub which is famous for its home-brewed ale. Locals know it as the Bull and Bladder. To conclude mention should be made of another inn, the Robin Hood on Pedmore

Road, Merry Hill. This is home to the Citizens Theatre where, amongst other attractions, there are regular performances by the popular 'Black Country Night Out' group of local singers and comedians which was first devised and organised by Jon Raven of Wolverhampton.

BROCTON *3·5m. SE of Stafford.*

The village lies between the A34 Stafford to Cannock road and the A513 to Rugeley on the eastern fringe of Cannock Chase. The village is of Saxon origin and the name means either 'the settlement by the brook' or 'the settlement by the badger's den'. There are several black and white half-timbered houses, probably the finest being 'The Cottage' in Pool Lane. However, in this century the area has become an up-market dormitory for the county town of Stafford. There are many attractive modern houses in the leafy lanes but this is not a real village — there is no church, no pub and no feeling of

Brocton, Oldacre Valley, adder country.

a remnant of medieval oak forest called Brocton Coppice. Most of the trees are no more than 200 years old but we know from the insect life and other vegetation in the area that this has been a deciduous forest for many, many centuries. Robin Hood would have been at home here. It is approached along a lane leading off the village green. Near the top of the hill, just past the quarry, is an unmade track on the left that leads to a parking area from which a well-trodden footpath leads to the wood. In the early 19th Century flax was grown at Brocton.

Broughton Hall, from the front.

BROUGHTON *5m. W of Market Drayton and 0·5m. E of Wetwood on the Eccleshall to Loggerheads road.*

Broughton lies in what is often called the 'wooded quarter' of the county, that is, the north-west corner which has few villages or towns of any size, virtually no industry and which has a most pleasant rural aspect, almost medieval in places. The gently rolling country provides views not obtained in flat areas where hedges, important as they are as wild life habitats, often obscure the land they lie in. Broughton is in the parish of Eccleshall which, at around 20,000 acres, is the second largest parish (after Worfield) in the county. To the south of Broughton was marsh — the name of nearby Wetwood perpetuates the memory — and around and beyond the marsh was, and still is, the forest of Bishop's Wood. Today this is largely stocked with coniferous trees by the Forestry Commission but amongst their endless ranks can be found the stumps of the oak trees that once flourished here when Bishop's Wood was a part of the larger Blore

Broughton Hall, from the rear.

Forest. It is likely that the villagers of Broughton depended quite heavily on the forest because at the time of the Domesday survey the arable land was described as waste. The name means 'the settlement by the fort' and the settlement was almost certainly of Saxon origin. It was never more than a hamlet but today only the Hall and chapel to the Hall remain. However, they are both splendid buildings. The Hall lies north of the road from which it can be glimpsed through the woods of its park. it was the home of the Delves-Broughtons from the 13th Century though the present house is dated at 1637. It is without any doubt the finest black and white house in the county.

Broughton Hall, from the gardenside.

The Delves-Broughtons moved to Cheshire in the 18th Century and only used Broughton as a second home. They sold the house in 1914 and between 1926 and 1939 it was renovated and greatly extended. Most of the stone work is of this date, including the great hall, now a chapel. Inside there is a

good staircase of the 1630's and in the long gallery is a freize depicting monsters and other beasts. The house has three storeys and gables over the right and left wings. When the new owner died the house was given to the Fransiscan Order (in 1952) and is now a home for retired lady missionaries. Attached to the Hall is a park with meadows, a lake and a large walled garden. The house is not open to the public but once a year the nuns hold a summer fair. They also sell fresh eggs. Broughton Hall is not only a splendid house it also has a splendid ghost, a Royalist cavalier of the Civil War who wears period dress and Red Stockings. He was fatally shot by Roundhead soldiers whilst taunting them from a window in the Long Gallery and died in a room adjoining it. A bloodstain was found there in 1926 during restorative work and the ghost of Red Stockings has been seen on several occasions. On the opposite side of the road from the Hall is the delightful

Broughton church, a Pre-Raphaelite window.

Broughton, the Langut valley near Fairoak.

church. This was built in 1630-4 as a private chapel to the Hall, though it is now a public church of St. Peter's. It is of a Gothic design and has an east window over the chancel arch which contains some sparkling 15th Century glass with figures of the Broughton family. There is also a beautiful pre-Raphaelite style window. The monuments are, as one would expect, mainly of members of the Broughton family. It is very likely that the church occupies the site of the old Saxon fort. The vicarage is in Wetwood, 0·5m. to the west. Iron was probably being worked at Broughton in the 14th Century; one of the tax payers was called Roger Iremongere (Ironmonger). There is believed to have been a supply of iron ore in Bishop's Wood and, of course, the forest provided an ample supply of fuel. What is more certain is that glass was manufactured hereabouts. In 1580 Bishop Overton, Bishop of Lichfield and the owner of Bishop's Wood, brought Lorraine glass makers from Hampshire and established them in the forest here. Glass

Broughton, shed covering the glass furnace.

was a very profitable business at that time because the owners of large houses and stately mansions were building much larger windows and enlarging those that already existed. Glass was also beginning to be used in the homes of the developing middle classes — farmers, craftsmen and merchants. In the Wood the glassmakers had all the necessary raw materials — sand, clay, ferns (which were burnt to make potash) and of course timber for fuel. Two of the glass families were the Tyzacks and the Henzeys (or Hennezels). In 1615 there was great concern nationally about the depletion of the country's timber supplies and a law was passed prohibiting the use of wood as fuel in glass furnaces. Much to the Bishop's regret the glassmakers were forced to leave. Some went to Newcastle on Tyne and some to Brierley Hill, in south Staffordshire, where coal was available to fire their furnaces legally. However, they left a memorial. In the 1930's the remains of one of their furnaces

The glass furnace in Bishop's Wood.

was found and renovated. It is the only surviving 17th Century glass furnace in the whole of the country. It lies just off a track in Bishop's Wood at Ordnance Survey ref. SK.760.312, half a mile NW of White's Farm. The forest here is most attractive. The furnace is covered by a substantial, but somewhat wonky, open-sided timber shed. The furnace is about 7ft. square and 3ft. high. It is constructed of sandstone lined with vitreous shards. There are four crucibles on two platforms which lie either side of a

61

sunken 2ft. wide fire tunnel. The road from Wetwood, south to Fairoak and on to Outlands and Bishop's Offley, follows the lovely valley of the River Sow. The source of the river is at two attractive pools some 250yds. SW of the farm called Broughton Folly, which is on the main Loggerheads — Eccleshall road, 0·5m. NW of the church. The Ordnance Survey map still shows the wood called Broughton Birches, a little further NW from the farm, but this was ripped out several years ago to make pasture. A few token trees were left along the roadside.

BROWN EDGE *3·5m. NE of Hanley and 1m. W of Endon.*
The old stone-built village lies to the north of the considerable suburban development along the main road from Burslem to Endon. It adjoins the southern slopes of Cowall Moor with untamed areas still under gorse and heather. To the north-west by half a mile is Greenbank Country Park, with its attractive lakes and woods. The River Trent

Brown Edge village seen from Ridgeway.

has its source there. *(See Knypersley).* The present church of St. Anne at Brown Edge was built in 1844 by James Trubshaw (junior) in Norman style. The spire was added by Ward and son of Haley in 1854. The west doorway and the arch between the tower and the nave are very ornate and there is a beautiful William Morris-Burne Jones

Brown Edge, the Chatterley-Whitfield Mining Museum.

window of 1874. The parsonage looks to be contemporary with the church. Also of the same date is the unusual stable and coach house placed in front of the church. This was

built for his own use by Mr. Williamson, a wealthy local worthy, who paid for the steeple. Perched high on a ridge, and facing the prevailing winds from the north-west, Brown Edge is a notoriously chilly place. One mile to the south-west is the Chatterley Whitfield Mining museum.

BROWNHILLS 4·5m. SE of Cannock.

The main shopping street of Brownhills is the Chester Road. It runs in a dead straight line NW-SE To the NW the town is approached via Holland Park, an area of grass and newly planted woodland. The shops are

Brownhills, the town centre.

very largely of the 20th Century and have very little character but are nevertheless well patronised. To the SW the shops give way to blocks of skyscraper flats and then to semi-detached suburbia. No-one goes out of their way to visit Brownhills. However, the A5 skirts its northern fringes making the name known to many. In fact, the town is situated on one of the two main routes from London to Chester. The Royal Mail coaches came along the A5 from London and then turned north-west, via Lichfield, Rugeley and Stone, and so on to Chester. A much used alternative route came up from Coventry via Castle Bromwich and joined the A5 at Brownhills. It followed the A5 for 14m. before leaving it at Weston under Lizard to go to Whitchurch and on to Chester. This road was much favoured by cattle drovers, because the country was more open, and by passenger stage coaches which found it was a

faster route. Brownhills lies on the Cannock coalfield and shallow pits had been worked there long before the boom years of the mid-19th Century. Cannock coal lies deep, and it was not until the mines of the Black Country failed to keep pace with demand that deep mines became economically viable. Iron had been smelted and worked at Cannock up to the mid-18th Century using charcoal as fuel. When coal, as coke, began to be used, Cannock could not compete in the iron trade because of the costs of obtaining the deep coal and the lack of transport. By the time the Wyreley and Essington canal arrived in 1797, and the spur to Brownhills built a year or so later, it was too late and the iron trade was dead. The canal and the new financing methods (the formation of Joint Stock Companies) did save the coal trade, though, and today the area is littered with spoil heaps as a memorial to the success of the industry. On the northern fringes is a suburb called Newtown. This consists very largely of a new industrial area centred on an iron foundry called Castings Ltd, established here about 1960. This is surrounded by similar and connected businesses such as steel stockholders, toolmakers and pressing manufacturers. The local council is, at the time of writing, attempting to close down the iron foundry on environmental grounds. Why, is something of a mystery because there is little noise or smell, the area has a long industrial history and the company has some 500 workers, all of whom would become unemployed if the foundry closed.

Brownhills, Castings Ltd., Newtwown.

Mr. Cooke, the owner of the company and the man who built it nearly 30 years ago, is very upset about the affair. Brownhills is still

Brownhills, yachts on Chasewater.

very much an industrial area, but unlike the Potteries or the Black Country has very little character. Just over a mile to the north-west is the vast expanse of Chasewater, a reservoir used for various water sports such as sailing, canoeing, sail-boarding and power boat racing. There is a permanent boat club, and on the opposite shore to this is a pleasure area which in the summer months is akin to a seaside holiday resort. In character with the area in general, however, even Chasewater is somwhat scruffy and the nearby raceway buildings are an absolute disgrace. Half a mile north of the A5 (Watling Street) is Hammerwich. There is a wild Morris dance, performed by the Lichfield Morris, called The Vandals of Hammerwich.

Brownhills, sailboarding on Chasewater.

BURNTWOOD *3m. W of Lichfield.*
A colliery town on the Cannock coalfield

that offers a dismal prospect. Burntwood lies in an area of Cannock Chase that was cleared of woodland as late as the Middle Ages. (Much of the forest of England had been cut down and most of the settlements established by the time of the Norman Conquest). The name 'Green' that occurs in the names of nearby villages such as Goosemoor Green, Cresswell Green and Spade Green refers to a clearing in forest — a green field amongst the dark woods. The name Burntwood itself implies that the land here was cleared by burning. Between Burntwood and Cannock Wood, and Longdon to the north, are a characteristic tangle of little lanes linking small hamlets and isolated farms. On the eastern fringes of

Burntwood, graffitti near the library.

the suburban growth is Burntwood Green and here, on the main road to Lichfield, is Edial House (pronounced Ed-yal). This is where Samuel Johnson opened his school in 1736. His famous advert read: 'Young gentlemen are boarded and taught the Latin and Greek languages by Samuel Johnson.' It was a disaster. The school had only 3 pupils and closed the following year. Johnson left Burntwood and went to London accompanied by one of these 3 pupils, a young man by the name of David Garrick, who was to become the country's leading actor. To the east of Burntwood, and almost in Lichfield, is Maple Hayes, a good late Georgian house where Erasmus Darwin laid out his Botanic Gardens. The house later became the property of the Worthington brewing family. Today it is a boarding house for Lichfield School. In 1840 a horse race meeting was held at Burntwood. It was held anually for 10 years and at one time nearly ousted the long-established Lichfield races.

BURSLEM *3m. NE of Newcastle under Lyme.* Burslem is a hill town, a nice town and is quite rightly called the 'Mother of the Potteries'. There was a flourishing pottery industry here by the mid 17th Century. Local farmers had kilns (about 8ft. high) in which they produced rough ware such as butter-pots for Uttoxeter market. There were some 20 small potteries using clay and coal dug locally from opencast pits. The town developed around the old Anglo-Saxon village – the name Burslem is a corruption of Burgheard's Lyme, meaning either 'Burgheard's woods' or 'Burgheard's clearing in the Forset of Lyme' – and by 1710 there were 43 pot-banks in Burslem out of 52 recorded in the whole area. It is believed that

Burslem, the old Town Hall.

Burslem, the church of St. John.

the quadrangle format of many of the later factories was a perpetuation of their origin as farmyard buildings. By the 1750's the trade was growing rapidly and the quality and variety of wares was increasing greatly, though Burslem was especially known for its white crockery ware. About this date Thomas John Wedgwood had a windmill at the Jenkins constructed by James Brindley (the canal builder), who had recently set up as a millwright in Burslem. The town, and the Potteries in general, were still comparatively isolated, but in the late 18th Century the roads were turnpiked and improved, and in 1777 the Trent and Mersey Canal arrived. In 1829, despite being thoroughly industrialised, Burslem was described by a visiting clergyman as 'spacious, airy and clean'. Today, although it has its share of grim Victorian terraces, the town could still be so described. The overall impression is of a Georgian market town, though the impressive Old Town Hall of 1852-7 by G.T. Robinson, with its giant columns and baroque decoration, speaks of civic pride rather than rural. Today it houses a sports and recreation centre. Covering much of the area between the Old Town Hall and Queen Street (after Queen Charlotte) was the site of the famous and very large Brickhouse works, an ancient pottery which was in the hands of the Adams family until 1762, at which time Josiah Wedgwood became the tenant. It was here that he developed his 'Egyptian Black' and produced the cream crockery called 'Queen's Ware'

Burslem, Wedgwood house, Morland Road.

of the best known buildings in the Potteries is the Wedgwood Memorial Institute in Queen street. It is built of red brick and terracotta in what has been described as Venetian Gothic, with some large and very fine sculptured figures and a statue of Josiah Wedgwood by Rowland Morris above the lavish porch. It was purpose built to house the museum, library and art gallery. The impressive Burslem Sunday School in Westport Road is of 1836 by Samuel Sant. It has 5 bays, 8 columns and a pediment. Adjacent to the Sunday School is the Wade Heath Pottery of 1814, one of the better pottery works with a typical Georgian facade consisting of a canted arched doorway, a Venetian window and a pediment. Close by, in Hall Street, is the Roman Catholic church of St. Joseph by Sydney Brocklesby of 1935-7 — a pleasant enough building but one which would look more at home in the sunshine of Tuscany. The parish church of St. John the

Burslem, the grave of the witch Molly Lee.

(after Queen Charlotte). South of the Old Town Hall is the Leopard Inn with 3 storeys and columns between the parts of the bows. Still in the centre of the town, on the corner of Wedgwood Street and Chapel Bank, is Wedgwood House, the finest house in Burslem. It was formerly a home of the Wedgwoods. Inside are the initials of Thomas (father of Josiah) and John Wedgwood, and it is dated at 1751. It later became the Midland bank and is now owned by a firm of architects who have restored it to its former glory. The house has 5 bays, 2·5 storeys, a one bay pediment and a Tuscan columned porch. Opposite the Wedgwood House (the Big House as it used to be called) is the site of the Ivy Works rented by Josiah Wedgwood in 1759. It is now a lawned area with public toilets and a bandstand. The new Town Hall in Wedgwood Street is in classical style with pairs of columns and was built in 1911 to a design by Russell and Cooper. One

Baptist stands with a quiet dignity in most undignified surroundings. It lies a little way from the present town centre, down the hill towards the canal. The medieval stone tower is of about 1536, the brick chancel is of 1788 and the rest is brick of 1717. Inside are 2 terracotta figures by a teenage Enoch Wood, later to be a potter of some stature in the town. In the large churchyard, close to the church, is the grave of the witch Peggy-Lee. Margaret Leigh, to give her her proper name, was reputed to have caused herds of cattle to die, chimneys not draw and other such evils. When she died in 1748 she was buried in the churchyard just south of the church. However, when the funeral party returned to her old home they found her there knitting by the fire. To lay the spirit her body was dug-up and re-interred in a new grave which had been cut north-south. Close by Peggy Lee's grave is a stone coffin believed to have come from Hulton Abbey. Lanes lead from the church down to the wharves of Longport, Middleport and Newport on the Trent and Mersey Canal. From the town centre the A50 leads southwards along the Waterloo Road. This road was begun in 1815 and named after the famous battle of the previous year. The George Hotel stands at the Burslem end. This was The Dragon of Bennett's novels, a Georgian-style building of the 1920's. Arnold Bennett lived at number 198 and also at number 205, which was once a museum dedicated to him but is now an old persons home. On this road is the America Inn of 1830 with one large bow window.

Burslem, Arnold's house is second right.

BURSTON *4m. NE of Stafford.*

A tiny, pretty village in a quiet cul-de-sac off the busy A51 between Weston and Stone. There is a row of terraced houses, several cottages, a large red brick farmhouse, facing a pool frequented by ducks, and a church built in 1859 on the site of a ruined chapel.

Burston, the old mill pool.

The pool was constructed as a part of a water-mill complex. The mill was at Burston Villa Farm just downstream. It has been demolished but was grinding corn up until about 50 years ago. Within half a mile to the west lie the River Trent, the Trent and Mersey Canal and the main line railway to Stoke on Trent. Despite all this hustle and bustle the village slumbers peacefully and remains quite rural. To the south-east is Sandon Park, the seat of the Earl of Harrowby. The 'ton' ending in the name of the village implies an Anglo-Saxon origin but it does not appear in Domsday Book.

BURTON UPON TRENT *11m. NE of Lichfield.*

In the Early 7th Century the Angles came into the Midlands along the valley of the River Trent. At Burton they built a fort around which developed a small settlement, hence the name 'burh-tun', (fort settlement). Today, of course, the name Burton is synonymous with beer:

'Say for what were hop-yards meant,
Or why was Burton built on Trent?'

A.E. Housman

The trade was first developed by the monks of Burton Abbey. After the Dissolution of

Burton-on-Trent, boathouse by the bridge.
Burton-on-Trent, Ind Coope brewery.

Burton-on-Trent, parish church of
St. Modwen.

the Monastries local inn-keepers manufactured their own beer, and by the beginning of the 17th Century ales brewed in Burton were being sold in London. At the end of the 17th Century the river was improved and became navigable between Burton and Gainsborough in Lincolnshire, thus allowing rapid and cheap transport to the east coast. In the 18th Century the town thrived on trade with the Baltic and Russia, and the foundations of the modern industry were laid. (Catherine the Great is said to have been 'immoderately fond' of the ale brewed in Burton.) In 1777 the Trent and Mersey Canal opened, and facilitated transport both to the east and the west coasts. During the 19th Century the brewers developed the famous East India Pale Ale and enjoyed great success in the huge Indian sub-continent. In 1839 the railway arrived and trade was given its biggest boost yet because Burton brewers could now compete more effectively with local breweries in other parts of England, and they greatly expanded their home business. The secret of Burton's success was, and is, the special qualities of its hard water. This is pumped to the surface from subterranean springs. The rocks here contain gypsum and the water dissolves out and absorbs minerals such as magnesium and calcium sulphates. (In the past brewers from other parts of the country have actually sunk wells at Burton and transported the water, at great expense, to their breweries.) The breweries at Burton totally dominate the town. Beer is a bulky product. It needs large vats to produce it and huge containers to store it, and the maltings require massive areas of floor space for the grain to be spread over and turned, to dry the malt and encourage germination. Until 1967 Burton was criss-crossed by an elaborate system of private railways which connected the maltings on the outskirts of the town with the breweries in the centre. In this century the industry has been rationalized and is now controlled by a handful of big amalgamations and alliances. Despite their 'chemical beer'

they still dominate the market, but in recent years they have been troubled by the growth in the Real Ale movement. The wheel could go full circle for there are now many small breweries, and they are back in the countryside, operating the length and the breadth of the land. Things could be returning to how they were in the Middle Ages when every locality had its own special brew and was proud of it. Still, the brewers of Burton won't be short of beer to cry into. Burton has had a market since the year 1200 when the Abbey created the borough, and the heart of the town is still the Market Place. It is one of the few areas in Burton with any character. Around the square are shops, and facing the main road is the parish church of St. Modwena, named after the Irish lady Saint who, in the 7th Century, is reputed to have built the first church here on the island of Andressey (St. Andrew's Island) in the Trent, which lies at the back of the present

Burton-on-Trent, Marston's brewery.

local government, estate agents, banks, solicitors etc. The Cannock Chase District council administers many nearby towns such as Rugeley and Hednesford which are described in this book under their own names.

CANNOCK CHASE *It lies between Stafford and Rugeley and south to Cannock Wood.*
Cannock Chase covers 25 square miles of varied country, from wild heathlands to gentle wooded valleys, marshlands and coniferous forests. It is a remnant of the great Royal Forest of Cannock which in medieval times extended from Stafford in the north to Wolverhampton in the south, and from the River Penk on the west to the River Tame on the east. There were wolves here as late as 1280 and there are still substantial herds of deer — red deer, roe deer, barking deer and fallow deer. One of the old deer leaps has recently been restored by the Forestry Commission. *(See Rugeley).* The Forest had been a Royal hunting ground in both Saxon and Norman times. The term 'Forest' was a legal one. It meant that the land belonged to the King and that forest law applied. It was well-wooded but there were also large areas of moor and meadow. Some of these open areas would almost certainly have been cleared by prehistoric man. The

Upstream from the Stepping Stones.

Cannock Chase, the Stepping Stones.

extensive Neolithic flint working 'factory' discovered at Court Bank Covert, and the 8-acre Iron Age hill fort of Castle Ring, both near Cannock Wood, speak of a considerable pre-Roman population. In 1189 Richard I, desperately seeking funds to finance a Crusade to the Holy Land, sold the Forest to the Bishop of Coventry and Lichfield and from this date we must refer to Cannock Chase, not Forest. The Bishops built a palace at Beaudesert near Upper Longdon. In 1546 Henry VIII bought back the Chase and gave it to one of his 'new men', Sir William Paget, reputedly the son of a Wednesbury nailor. Beaudesert was held by the Paget family from 1546 to 1918, except for one short period between 1584 and 1597 when the third baron was in exile for treason. (He was a Roman Catholic and was suspected of being involved in the Throckmorton Plot). In 1815 Henry Paget was made Marquis of Anglesey as a reward for the services he rendered at the Battle of Waterloo. In 1935 the magnificent Beaudesert Hall, the Paget home for many generations, was pulled down and the stone sold by auction. All that remains today is the early 19th Century lodge and a fragment of the Tudor great hall. The lands of the estate are now home to a golf course and a camp site for scouts and guides. It was the Pagets, and in particular their lessee, Sir Fulke

valley that has had an interesting and intriguing history. This valley is served by two small streams which join at a small wood called Courtsbank Covert. (This is not named on the 1·25 inch Ordnance Survey map but is the wood just to the east of Red Moor - SK.042.116). There are six sites of interest — see the plan below. 1. The neolithic flint working site was quite extensive, a veritable factory, but this was totally destroyed during the early years of the Second World War when the eastern banks of the stream were subject to open cast coal mining. Three train loads a day were stripped by a huge American drag bucket machine, the farmer told us. Flints from the site are at Birmingham University. 2. The Nun's Well was an ancient well lined with sandstone and capped with a brick arch. The waters were thought to have healing properties for complaints of the eye. Just after the end of the Second World War the woods around the well were cut down by a local timber merchant, a Mr. Barratt. He

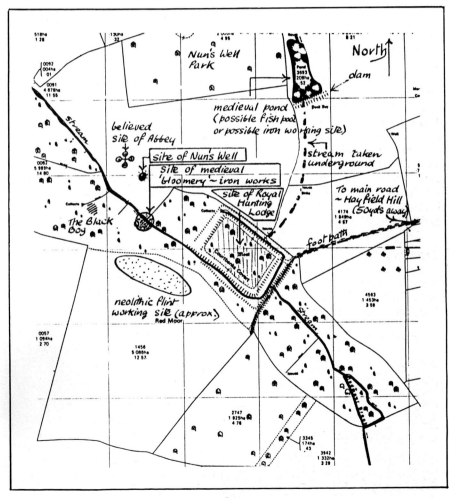

81

used teams of eight horses to drag the trees away. A few old oaks were left and stand there today, but most of the area was bull-dozed level. The well was capped with corrugated iron sheets and now lies below about 4ft. of earth. Some years after the well was capped a man working a dredger said he saw the ghost of a nun. 3. Just north of the well is the reputed site of the Radmore (Redmore) Abbey. That this existed is beyond dispute. It was originally a Hermitage endowed by King Stephen. About 1145 it became a Cistercian Monastery but later Henry II gave the monks land at Stoneleigh in Warwickshire in exchange for Radmore Abbey. The site was investigated after the Second World War but nothing was found. It has been suggested that the Abbey was only made of timber. Since that investigation the land has been bull-dozed, as already mentioned, so any post holes or differences in earth colouring are now long gone. 4. The King had acquired Radmore Abbey because he wished to build a Royal Hunting Lodge there. No trace of this has ever been found but we know that Henry II stayed there in 1155. It has been suggested that the lodge could have been built a little further down-stream in the woods where there is a rectangular 'moat' (SK.043.117). However, it is now suspected that this 'moat' was actually a pond reservoir for a medieval water driven wheel which worked the hammers of an iron working factory, that is, a 'bloomery'. Slag has been found over quite a wide area and the farmer has found irregular coarse bricks up to a foot square by 3ins. deep, both in the stream and in the field, in the area marked on the map. 5. Up the hill to the east is a pond (SK.044.118), quite clearly created by a man-made dam. This is thought to have originally been a fish-pond for the Abbey and then later used as a mill-pond in connection with medieval iron working. 6. The westerly stream runs red. This is because it cuts through ironstone rocks and earths. The road to the north is called Ironstone Road. (By the pub at New Hayes it becomes Cumberledge Hill). The westerly stream has

Cannock Wood, the Black Bog of Court's Covert.

been chanelled along underground pipes from the hillside pond to the Courtsbank Covert. All in all, this is a fascinating site and ought to be properly investigated. Visitors should beware of the nasty little Black Bog. There is a considerable depth of soft peat here. The ground is thoroughly putrid and

Cannock Wood, Court's Covert pool.

nothing, not even mosses and lichens, live there - an evil place if ever there was one. The entrance to the valley and all the sites listed above is off Hayfield Hill. A five-bar gate gives access to a track between a row of houses at SK.046.117. In 1342 some Lichfield merchants sent two of their servants to Stafford. They were carrying goods to be sold at the market there, but as they passed through Cannock Wood they were set upon by Sir Robert de Ridware and his men who robbed them of their silks and spices. Sir Robert repaired to the priory at Lapley where he shared out the goods with other robber Knights, amongst whom was Sir John de Addyngesles. Sir Robert then rode to

Gentleshaw, the Windmill Inn.

Blithbury but the abbess there refused him hospitality, whereupon the knight broke into the barns and took fodder for his horse. Meanwhile, one of the servants who had been robbed escaped and reported to the Sheriff of Lichfield. The Sheriff and his men intercepted Sir Robert and his band and a battle ensued. The Sheriff won the encounter, recaptured the stolen goods and beheaded four of Sir Robert's men on the spot. The robber knight, however, escaped and rode to Hamstall Ridware to seek the assistance of his relative, Sir Walter Ridware. Together they led a band of men, attacked the Sheriff and retrieved Sir Robert's booty. The Lichfield merchants went to Stafford to seek justice but found the town gates locked and manned by men from Ridware. The plaintiffs were forced to flee for their lives. This is a true story. Medieval lords and knights lived very much by the sword, and

Cannock Wood, Court's Covert wood.

the sword they wielded was not always that of Justice.

CANWELL *6m. SSE of Lichfield.*

Canwell lies 1m. NE of the intersection of the A453 and the A38. There is no village, only a park and a church. The Hall is long gone. It was the home of the Lawley family, Lords of Wenlock, who are buried at Hints church. The attractive church at Canwell was built by Temple Moor in 1911. It has a vaulted roof and Decorated style windows. The large park lies to the east of the busy A38 which at this point follows the route of one of the country's most famous coaching roads - the road from London to Chester and Holyhead - described in John Ogilby's road book of 1675 as 'one of the most frequented in the Kingdom'. It entered Staffordshire at Bassett's Pole, 1m. SW of Canwell Gate in Canwell, and proceeded to Lichfield, Rugeley, Wolseley Bridges, Stone and Darlaston (near Stone) to Woore (Shropshire) and Nantwich (Cheshire). In the 13th and 14th Centuries the route was slightly different. From Stone the road went to Newcastle-under-Lyme and then to Nantwich.

CAULDON (or Caldon) *7m. SE of Leek.*

A tiny village on the northern Weaver Hills. Godiva owned it in 1066. It then passed to the Norman, Robert of Stafford, the younger son of Roger of Tosny (or Toeni). In 1086 it was described as 'waste' and could well be so described today, for the village lies below the

Cauldon Low, Tarmac limestone quarry.

hill of Cauldon Lowe which is being rapidly diminished by quarrying. To the south-west are several disused quarries and there is a certain grimness to the country hereabouts. The village consists of the Yew Tree Inn, a few stone cottages and a little 18th Century church with a tall 17th Century house close by. A stretch of road from Cauldon to the

Cauldon, Blue Circle cement works.

Crown Inn at Waterhouses is called 'Yarlsway'. This is a corruption of Earlsway, the name of the romantic medieval road used by the Earls of Chester when they visited their estates in Staffordshire, Derby and Nottingham. It was a well used route from the 11th to the 13th Century and is almost certainly that taken by Sir Gawain in his quest for the Green Knight whose castle was probably sited at Swythamley Hall. Today it is a series of minor roads running parallel with the main road to Leek. The 'low' in the name Cauldon Lowe refers to the ancient burial mounds found there, in particular the Big Low. There can be little doubt that more

Cauldon, the church of St. Mary and St. Lawrence.

prehistoric remains were here but they have been destroyed by the limestone quarry workings. Near the top of the hill Tarmac produce road metal, and lower down Blue Circle have a cement works. To some people quarries are a blemish on nature's handiwork but to others they have a gaunt attraction. What is beyond doubt is that the materials produced are essential and have to be obtained from somewhere. Quarrying on a large scale began here in the late 18th Century when the Trent and Mersey Canal Company bought the mineral rights and in 1777 brought a spur of the Caldon Canal to Froghall Wharf. The canal was connected to the quarries by a plateway. The stone, as lime, was used in ironworks as a flux, by builders for lime mortar, and by farmers as a fertiliser. The stone itself was used locally for house building. In the 1890's the firm of Brunner Mond, later to become ICI, bought large quantities of limestone from here for their alkali works in Cheshire. Today the canal in only used by pleasure craft and the stone and cement are transported by lorries.

The Blue Circle Cement works can be seen quite clearly from the A52 between Leek and Ashbourne near Waterhouse. In ancient times copper and lead were also mined in the Cauldon area. The Staffordshire Peak Arts Centre is located in the Old School, Cauldon Lowe, on the A52. All manner of local arts and crafts are exhibited and most of the goods displayed are for sale. There is also a restaurant specializing in whole foods and a snack bar.

CAVERSWALL 2·5m. E of Longton.
Caverswall lies just beyond the suburban growth of the Potteries and is still very much a place with its own character. It has a superb castle, two churches and north of these a little village square. There was a castle here in medieval times, (Licence to Crenellate was given in 1275), but in 1614 Matthew Craddock had the present fortified house built within the old castle. (Matthew Craddock came from a wealthy wool merchant family based in Stafford). A dry moat surrounds the balustraded inner

Caverswall Castle.

gardens in which the house stands tall, elegant and most handsome. At the corners of the moat wall are polygonal towers. The house is approached via a bridge that leads to a small gatehouse. As late as the last century the moat held water, and old pictures show the castle apparently sitting amidst a lake.

Caverswall Castle, guard dog.

Ownership of the castle passed through several hands until it was purchased by a long established local Roman Catholic family, the Coyneys, and in 1811 they established it as a convent for Benedictine nuns from Ghent, who fled in fear of the excesses of the French Revolution. In this century it was still in the hands of the nuns who ran it as a kind of guest house. When they left it became somewhat run-down. About 12 years ago it was bought by a businessman and restored as a private house. At the time of writing it is being offered for sale. There are two churches, one on either side of the entrance drive to the Castle. The parish church of St. Peter has a long nave with an arcade rebuilt in the 17th Century, a long chancel and a perpendicular tower. There are monuments to the Cradocks and the Parkers of Park hall, Longton. Outstanding of these is the monument of 1818, by Chantrey, to Countess St. Vincent who was the wife of Admiral Parker and daughter of Lord Chief Baron Parker. However the treasure of St. Peter's is the remnant of a tympanum discovered during restoration work in 1962. The sill of the east window in the north aisle was removed and the underside was found to

be carved. It was determined that the stone had formed a part of a 12th Century tympanum (the area between the lintel and the arch above a doorway). This had been removed in the 13th Century and left outside for some considerable time. (The marks of grass roots were found). The back of the stone was then cut into shape to form a window sill, the carved side being embedded into the mortar. The carving consists of a human figure between two griffins with wings and feathered bodies and four-clawed-feet. The top half of the picture is missing. Scholars have concluded that the carving represents the celestic journey of Alexander the Great. Alexander wished to ascend to heaven. He sat in a basket attached to two eagles. To encourage them to fly upwards he attached meat to the ends of long rods and held these above their heads. In art this story became modified. The basket became a quadriga and was then confused with the bottom half Alexander's dress. The rods became sceptres. The philosophical meaning of the story here was 'man in communion with animals', not 'pride before a fall' as it was in some representations. The carving is on display inside the church. On the other side of the entrance to the castle is the Roman catholic church of St. Filomena, of 1864, designed by Gilbert Blount.

CHAPEL CHORLTON *7m. NE of Stone.*
Chapel Chorlton is most easily approached by turning off the A51 at the Cock Inn, Stableford. The lane heads SW, uphill. Near the top of the hill, on the left-hand side, is a rusty five-bar gate near a little wood. This leads to one of the old sandstone quarries for which the village was once famous. The rock-face has been earthed over and grass now grows on the steep slope, but the stone can be seen at surface outcrops only feet away from the gate. This stone is fine, white and stain-free, and was used for prestige buildings. At the top of the hill is the large, triangular village green with an oak tree near the centre. The ground is slightly marshy in

places. On the north edge of the green is a large, reed edged pool. The whole area is pleasantly open with only a handful of red brick farms and a white stuccoed cottage to take advantage of the views over the forest of Swynnerton Old Park to the north-east. The small church of St. Laurence lies slightly downhill on the lane to Lower Hatton. It stands on a high mound with two ancient yew trees, one of which is hollow. The stone tower is medieval but was remodelled by James Trubshaw (junior) in 1826 who also rebuilt the nave and chancel in ashlar. The nave has five windows and the east window has a lunette. The pulpit is Jacobean. Opposite the church is Schoolhouse Farm, a large, red brick complex that, although lived in, looks derelict and is very tumble-down indeed. All in all, Chapel Chorlton is a charming place. Along the lane to Maer from Chapel Chorlton are some new houses, perched on the edge of the high ground. Just past these is a right-hand turn leads down a delightful, deep and wooded hill to the main road. This is the eastern fringe of **Hill**

Chapel Chorlton, pond by the village green.

Chorlton. The lane opposite will take the traveller to a farm called Springfields and near here is an unusual old stone mill, rebuilt by the Duke of Sutherland and until recently

Chapel Chorlton, Springfield Mill at Hill Chorlton.

almost forgotten; it was only Listed in 1987. It is now being renovated and converted into a dwelling house. Most of the village lies further west along the main road. The undulating wooded country between Stableford and Woore is really most attractive.

CHARTLEY (HOLME) *7m. NE of Stafford.*
The Saxon Earl Algar held it before the
Norman Conquest when it past to the king.
Today the hamlet is small and scattered
around the Stafford to Uttoxeter road east of
Weston. There are a few cottages, two blocks
of modern semi-detached houses, a medieval
castle and the Old Hall. Hidden behind a hill
is another attraction, far less well known - the
large 'quaking bog' of Chartley Moss. The
settlement is placed on the edge of the Trent
Valley, on the hills of the attractive rolling
country that stretches from Chartley to
Uttoxeter. The view from the mound of the
castle keep is well worth the short climb.
There are three ancient sites; the castle itself,
possibly built within the earthworks of a
previous pre-historic fort; the moated Hall to
the west; and a rectangular earthwork on the
hill to the north. The original castle was
probably of timber, built by Ranulph de
Gernon, the Earl of Chester, and was in
exsistence by at least 1153. In 1232, on the
death of his grandson, Ranulphe de Blundeville, also Earl of Chester, the castle passed to

Chartley Castle, from the A518.

William de Ferrers, fourth Earl of Derby,
who had married Ranulph's sister, Agnes de
Blundeville. In the early 13th Century the
castle was rebuilt in stone. It has a motte
(keep mound), and two baileys (enclosures)
protected by walls and towers. The walls are
12ft. thick and the towers have arrow slits.
The inner bailey is 83 yds. long by 43 yds.
wide, and the outer bailey is 66 yds. long by
60 yds. wide. There is an engraved cross, a
mark that the builder had been on a crusade
to the Holy Land. In 1461 the castle passed

Chartley Hall from the castle.

by marriage to Walter Deveraux, who was created Baron Ferrers in the same year. By that time the castle had already been abandoned and a moated timber manor house, Chartley Hall, had been built at the foot of the hill, just to the west. By 1540 the castle was in ruins. The altitude of the castle is 313ft. above sea level. Just to the north is a stream. In 1575 Queen Elizabeth I visited the Hall and stayed for 10 days. The queen was entertained at Chartley by her cousin, Lettice, who had married the 1st Earl of Essex, the grandson of Walter Deveraux. Robert, the son of the 1st Earl, would almost certainly have been at Chartley then and would have met the Queen. The following year his farther died and Robert became the 2nd Earl of Essex, was introduced to Court and became the Queen's favourite. He so arranged things in Staffordshire that he was able to nominate six of the county's 10 Members of Parliament in 1592. He lost his

Chartley Castle from the Hall.

earldom and was executed in 1601 after an attempted rebellion. On the accession of James I in 1603 the 2nd Earl's son, also Robert, was restored as the 3rd Earl. During the Civil War he was the parliamentary commander-in-chief. In 1646 he died

Chartley Manor.

childless and the Chartley estate passed eventually to Sir Robert Shirley, the grandson of the 3rd Earl's sister. In 1677 he was created Baron Ferrers and in 1711 his son became the 4th Earl Ferrers. In 1760 the 4th Earl killed his steward. His punishment was death. Somewhat bizarely he dressed himself as a bridegroom and was driven in his state landau to Tyburn Hill in London where he was hanged before a crowd of 200,000 people. From December 1585 to September 1586, Mary Queen of Scots was held captive at Chartley Hall before being taken to Fotheringay Castle, in North-ampton, where she was duly tried and executed. It was whilst she was staying at Chartley Hall that Gilbert Giffard of Chillington smuggled letters to and from her in beer barrels and laid the trap that was the Babington Plot. In 1781 Chartley Hall was accidentally burned to the ground. The present house was built in 1847 but an older wing survives at the back. It is approached along a wooded avenue and lies within the old moat. To the front of the house is the lake, which forms part of the moat, and beyond that are the ruins of the castle and the park. There are woods all about and the setting is delightful. The Hall remained in

Chartley, the old moated site.

the hands of the Shirley family until 1905 when it was sold. There have been several owners since. On the hillside north of the castle is an earthwork. It is a perfect rectangle, measuring 57yds. by 31yds, with a bank and ditch on the longer sides and a ditch only along the shorter sides. It is marked on the Ordnance Survey map as a moat but has yet to be properly investigated. From time immemorial the Chartley estate was the home of the famous wild Chartley cattle. These were a pale tan in colour, with black ears and long curved horns. They are believed to have been descended from the prehistoric British Aurochs that roamed wild in nearby Needwood Forest. In the early part of this century they were struck down by disease and the survivors cross-bred with Longhorn cattle. Their progeny are now at the Duke of Bedford's Estate at Woburn. Half a mile along the main road towards Uttoxeter is Chartley Manor Farm House a good early 17th Century, black and white timber-framed building with gables. It stands on higher ground than the castle and the road that climbs the hill has some misleading bends which have been the cause of several fatal car accidents. Across the fields, less than 0·5m. S of Chartley Manor Farm, is Chartley Moss (formerly called the Anglesey Coppice). It lies on the western edge of the wood and adjoins the overgrown track of the disused railway. (The Moss is centered on SK.021.279). This is a very special place. It has been virtually untouched by man since

its formation in a glacial hollow 20,000 years ago. It looks today much as it did then. In a basin 70ft. deep is a pool of muddy water. On the water floats a thick layer of peat and sphagnum moss. As one walks across the surface of the Moss it moves, or trembles, and for this reason is called a 'Quaking Bog' or Schwing-moor. Trees grow in the peat layer but as they grow taller and heavier they slowly begin to sink and small black pools appear around their boles. When they exceed about 24ft. in height they become unstable and collapse. Because of the special conditions here there are many rare plants. The site is not only the best example of its kind in Britain but is probably the best of its kind in the whole of Europe. The Moss is a Nature Reserve of the Nature Conservancy Council and entry is by permit only. Surrounding the Moss is an Area of Special Scientific Interest. The whole site covers 104 acres. Anyone venturing onto Chartley Moss

Chartley Moss, a 'quaking bog'.

should remember that it can be very dangerous. In particular beware of areas where trees do not grow; it probably means that the peat cannot take their weight. Snakes, especially adders, are here in great numbers and in the summer there are some very nasty biting insects. This is a wild and interesting, but potentially dangerous place. To the south and west are drainage ditches. A mile NE of the Manor Farm, along the road to Uttoxeter, is the hamlet of Grindley. The houses lie along the lane to the SE and there is no sign of a village on the main road. Between the main road and the disused railway line is the site of Grindley Forge (SK.043.296). It lies on the land of Grindley Forge Farm. Here are the remains of an early 17th Century forge. There is a large mound of black earth and forge cinder, and the leat and forge stream still survive. The leat drew water from the River Blythe. This forge worked 'rough iron' and produced 'merchant bar'. The supplies of iron came mainly from Meir Heath and Vale Royal (in Cheshire).

CHASETOWN *4m. E of Cannock on the A5190.*
The village did not exist before about 1850

Chartley Moss, a primeval place.

91

and was built to house the colliers who worked in the nearby pits. The Cannock Chase coalfield was heavily exploited in the second half of the 19th Century. By 1900 there were some 40 mines in the area. It is a dull, drab place of endless rows of modern houses and straight roads, and is noticeably lacking in trees for somewhere so close to Cannock Chase. All around are slag-heaps and waste land, a dismal place like Brownhills which adjoins it to the north. The church of St. Anne at Chasetown is most unusual. It was built in 1865 to the design of Edward Adams who worked for the South Staffordshire Railway Company and the South Staffordshire Waterworks. It is neo-Norman of red, purple and black brick. It does not have a tower and the nave and chancel are as one with a low apse and high windows. Inside are brick columns with Romanesque capitals inlaid with black and jagged arches and an open timber roof. There is a marble bust of John Robinson McLean, a local coalowner, who founded the church.

CHEADLE *8m. NW Uttoxeter.*
An unassuming little market town that stands on a hill in the Moorlands of North Staffordshire. There are several good houses in the High Street: the Police House with ashlar front, fluted capitals around the doorway and Venetian windows; the Wheatsheaf Inn with a Tuscan porch; and No. 77 with it's timber-framing and decorative motifs. The Market Cross is probably of the 17th Century. The Market Place is an open area off the High Street formed by the setting back of a terrace of late Georgian 3-storied houses. In Tape Street the large textile mill of J. & N. Philips once stood, but this was mostly dismantled in 1973. Only the warehouse remains, with its central pediment. In Watt's Place is the former workhouse of 1775. The dominant building in Cheadle is the lavish, red-stone Roman Catholic church of St. Giles built in 1841-6 by Pugin. The Earl of Shrewsbury, of

nearby Alton Towers, commissioned and paid for the church. Pugin was told to spare no expense and decoration here runs rife; indeed, the overall style is Decorated. The steeple is a very good piece of Gothic revival with a sharp spire and two sets of pinnacles. Inside the church is painted throughout and stenciled with crowns, crosses, flowers and trellises - a colourful place. The church has a matching school, the Convent of St. Joseph,

Cheadle, the spire at St. Giles, R.C.

and a Priest's House (in Chapel St.). The Anglican Parish Church is also called St. Giles and was built in 1837-9 to a Perpendicular design by J. P. Pritchett. It stands on higher ground on the other side of the High Street and replaced the medieval church. One mile to the NE is Hales Hall, a very good house of 1712 with five bays and two storeys with even stone quoins (cornerstones). It was built by the grand-daughter of Chief Justice Sir Matthew Hale. In the recent past it was used as an educational establishment by the County

Cheadle, view on the road to Oakamoor.

Council at the time of writing is up for sale. There is a Toll-house (Sk.002.430) of 1833 by George E. Hamilton, 0·5m. SW of the town centre, on the Cheadle to Blythe Marsh and Calton Moor Road. At Woodhead (SK.010.442), 0·25m. N of the town centre on the Froghall road, was a coal mine. In the wall fronting the road can be seen stone sleeper blocks with iron spikes that were taken from the now dismantled tramway that carried the coal to the Uttoxeter canal between Oakamoor and Froghall (SK.035.453). A double-track inclined plane, 900ft. long, ran through Gibridding Wood. The Woodfield mine hit badly faulted seams and was closed by 1900. There were several long flame coal mines in the Cheadle area; the last was Foxfield. In the 12th Century iron was mined at 'le Brodedelph'. In the 18th Century copper from the Ecton mine was smelted near the town. In medieval times Cheadle lay on the Salt Road, used by pack horse trains travelling between Nantwich and Derby, taking salt out and bringing back malt. In 1686 Dr. Plot, on his journey through Staffordshire says he saw conical houses made entirely of turf in the Cheadle area. We tend to forget that up to about the beginning of the 18th Century the houses of poor country people were often little more than mud huts. They were made of 'cob', earth and cow manure, white-washed to make them waterproof and roofed with thatch and turf. Such buildings can, if properly maintained, be quite durable as evidenced by those that exist in Cornwall today. However, they soon disintegrate if left unattended and almost literally melt away, leaving little sign that they ever existed. We recollect a farmer in Churchtown near Mainstone in Shropshire, telling us that he could remember just such primitive dwellings in a state of collapse on the hillside above the church there.

CHEBSEY *5m. NW of Stafford.*
Chebsey lies just north of the A5013 Stafford to Eccleshall road. The country from here westwards to the border with Shropshire is

Cheadle, the market.

most attractive. The village lies close to the River Sow which is joined by the Meece Brook less than a mile to the SW. It is a quiet place of old cottages, Victorian houses and some modern villas, not especially pretty but quite pleasant. The Norman church lies on an ancient site, high-mounded with a watery

Chebsey, the church of All Saints.

ditch forming an enclosure to the SW. In the churchyard are the remains of an Anglo-Saxon cross, a thick round shaft becoming square and decorated mainly with interlace. There was almost certainly a Saxon church here and before that quite probably a timber stockade-fort. The present church has a Norman window in the north chancel, a Norman window in the north nave, a late Norman north doorway, several shallow Norman buttresses and Norman masonary. The 4-bay south arcade, the south doorways and the chancel arch are Early English and the tower, with its eight pinnacles, is Perpendicular. There are several William Kempe, and Kempe and Tower windows. Wriothesley Noel, who died at sea in 1941 whilst serving with the Royal Navy is commemorated by a tablet. He was descended from Robert and Celestia Noel who founded nearby Ranton Abbey in 1147. *(See Ranton).* In the Domesday Book Chebsey, called Cebbisio, is recorded as having 20 villagers, 9 smallholders and a priest with land for 12 ploughs. The village was owned by Henry Ferrers and within the manor was the land on which Stafford Castle was built. This would have been the castle at

Chebsey, Saxon cross shaft

Broadeye, near the present windmill. It had been built on the orders of the King but was destroyed prior to 1086, also on the orders of the King, because some of the Saxon lords in the area had been rebellious. A quarter of a mile SW of Chebsey is Walton Hall, a substantial Victorian house in Classical style dated at 1848. It has good ashlar masonry and at the back a very large coach-porch with

Chebsey, Worston Mill.

94

Jones and William Morris. There is a pub, The Star, and several large brick houses with an ominous development of new villas in progress at the entrance to the church. Park Hall lies 0·5m north of Church Leigh. It has a good wrought iron entrance gates and close

Church Leigh, the church of All Saints.

to the house is an old moat, presumably the site of the medieval farmstead. At the back of the Hall is a wood called Hell Clough. At Upper Leigh is the modest but attractive Manor House of 3 bays, 2·5 storeys and a hipped roof, set at the end of a long drive that commences at Lower Leigh and traverses the park in which three donkeys were grazing at the time of our visit. There is a village green at Lower Leigh. To the east of Church Leigh is the curiously-named Nobut Hall and the hamlets of Upper Nobut and Lower Nobut.

CLAYTON *See Newcastle-under-Lyme.*

CLIFTON CAMPVILLE *9m. S of Burton upon Trent.*
The village lies in flat country watered by the River Mease. In 1086 the manor was owned by the King himself and it was a sizeable village with 33 villagers, 7 smallholders, 2 slaves and a priest, plus all those who did not owe service to the lord and who were therefore not recorded in Domesday Book. Today the village is dominated by the church of St. Andrew with its tall, elegant steeple (a term meaning the tower and spire together). It is a spacious building, largely of the 14th Century, and has some good interior

decoration of the same period – the south chapel screens, the seven misericords and the painting in the south aisle. There is a brass plate of a lady of about 1360, with a fragment of a knight on the back, and a fine alabaster monument to Sir John Vernon, died in 1545, and his wife, with some excellent sculptures around the tomb chest. In the chancel are non-figurative monuments by Rysbrack to Sir Charles Pye, died 1721, and Sir Robert Pye, the 4th and last baronet, died 1734. There is a curiosity in the small north transept. Above the vaulted chapel, partially hidden by a modern oak screen, is a priest's chamber with a fireplace, a garderobe (lavatory) and a gilded crucifix in the medieval altar recess. As to the rest of the village: the Vicarage stands to the NE of the church. Manor Farm has a large brick dovecote and a square gazebo, and there has been the usual invasion of modern villas in the main street. Less than 0·25m. to the east is Clifton Campville's second curiosity - Clifton Hall. At the end of a rough track are two stately 18th Century brick pavilions, each of seven bays and each with two imposing doorways. These are in fact the two wings of the house of which the centre part was never built. The architect was probably Francis Smith but his design was not completed because the owner, Sir Charles Pye, ran out of funds. However, he and his family and their descendants have lived there quite happily for some 200 years. Today these noble structures are derelict and used as farm store rooms. One mile west of Clifton Campville is the hamlet of Maunton. Here is the Convent of John Bordeaux, now a school, with a chapel of 1840 by Manson.

CODSALL *3·5m. NW of Wolverhampton.*
Codsall is basically a dormitory town for Wolverhampton, but amongst the acres of suburban housing is a pleasant shopping centre and a little railway station. The church of St. Nicholas has a Norman south doorway, a restored Perpendicular tower and the rest is of 1846-8, in Decorated style, by E. Banks of

101

Colwich, riders at Wolseley Bridges.

Colwich, the gates to Wolseley Park. *Colwich, sunset over the Black Hills.*

The Dorothy Clive Gardens, Willoughbridge on the A51 north of Market Drayton.

Codsall, the railway station.

Wolverhampton. There is stained glass by O'Connor of about 1870 and by Bryans of about 1900. Walter Wrottesley, died 1630, lies here in effigy. One and three quarter miles SSE of Codsall, in Wergs Hall Road (off Wergs Road), is Wergs Hall, a good Italiante country house set in grounds with lovely specimen trees. It is now owned by Sir Alfred McAlpine and is used as a regional office by his construction company. At

Codsall, Wergs Hall.

Wood Hall Farm, 1·25m. WNW of Codsall, is a moated site, and at Kingswood Common, 1·5m. ESE, is a small church of 1861 and areas of rough heathland that gives a good idea of what the country around would look like if left uncultivated. Adjoining Codsall to the east is **Oaken**, a charming tree-lined place of mature detached houses overlooking fields and woods. Of particular note is Oaken House, 18th Century with three bays and three storeys, a pedimented doorway and parapets to the gables. Today Oaken is a suburb of Codsall, but in 1086 it

was the larger of the two villages. A nature trail starts at Oaken Lane, opposite the foot of the railway drive. A leaflet is available from nearby shops. South-east of Oaken, and on the other side of the A41 Wolverhampton to Shifnal road, is the entrance to **Wrottesley** Hall and Park. Here lived the Wrottesley family who, like many Norman settlers, took the name of the Saxon manor they occupied after the Conquest. They had been here in unbroken succession for 23 generations, from 1164 to 1963. Amongst their forebears were Sir Hugh Wrottesley who became Governor of Calais, and Major General Wrottesley, the 19th Century historian. The family was awarded a baronetcy in 1642 and a barony in 1838. During the Civil War they were Royalist. In 1963 the 4th Lord Wrottesley died and the whole of the estate was sold. Wrottesley Hall stands on rising ground with good views over the attractive though undramatic Staffordshire countryside. The original mansion was built in 1696 and had a central block of three storeys with a pediment and projecting wings. However the house was virtually destroyed by fire in 1897 — only the walls were left standing — and was not rebuilt until the 1920's. The central block was lowered to two storeys and the wings to one storey. The original pediment has been re-used but is not of the correct proportion for the smaller house. Nevertheless, it is a handsome place and so much better than the alternative of total demolition and rebuilding. The Wrottesley coat of arms in

Codsall, Wrottesley Hall.

103

the pediment maintains a tenuous link with the old family. The Hall has been several things since 1963, including a Country Club, and in the grounds is a small golf course. Most of the extensive Park has been dispersed. Close to the house is a long Georgian stable range surmounted by a cupola. Although there is some commercial activity in the grounds the house itself is now, once again, a private residence. In 1066 the Saxon Hunta owned the manor of Wrottesley, but after the Norman Conquest it was taken from him and given to Robert of Stafford. In 1086 there was a small village here but by the 17th Century this had disappeared, almost certainly destroyed by the Wrottesley family when they extended their Park. This was an unkind but not uncommon practice amongst the landed gentry. Wrottesley has an intrigueing archeological mystery, namely a **Lost City**. In 1686 the reputable and learned Dr. Robert Plot published his Natural History of Staffordshire. In it he tells of having seen the remains of a large stone-built city, or fort, between Wrottesley and Patshull. Since Dr. Plot wrote his account squared stones, have been found in the area at various times, but little else of interest has come to light. All trace of the settlement seems to have disappeared. Within the locality is Low Hill Field where many human bones have been found. However, it appears that there has never been a thorough, modern investigation of the site which is quite remarkable when one considers the potential importance. This is Dr. Plot's account. "It being thus made at least probable that the original inhabitants of this county might also be Iceni, as well as those of Norfolk, &c. who though they at first carried themselves fair to the Romans, yet seeing them use their neighbours in that manner as they did, thus stoutly interposed: let us next take a view of what markes there yet remain, of their places of habitation, defence, &c. to one or both of which I think I cannot refer that noble antiquity near Wrottesley in this county, where there yet remains, either the foundation of some ancient British city, or other fortification, of great extent; it including above a moyety of Wrottesley, and part of Pateshull, Pepperhill, and Bonningal parks; also some parcell of the two Commons of Kingswood and West-bach, the whole containing in circuit about 3 or 4 miles, lyeing part of Staffordshire and part in Shropshire, as mark't out by the shaded line in the map. Within the limits whereof there are several partitions yet visible, running divers ways like the sides of streets, tho' hard to be fully traced, because interrupted both by the mattock and plow, the foundations being dayly dugg up by the former, to mend high-ways, make inclosures, and pavements; and then all levell'd by the latter: which together with the large hinges for doores, an antique dagger, that have been found here, and some of the stones squared; make me rather think it some ruinated city, than a fortification only: otherwise I could have been content to have thought it some such British vallum, or encampment, as Tacitus acquaints us Caractacus made upon a hill in Shropshire, upon the banks of the River Clun, with great stones rudely heap't upon one another, to defend him from the impressions of the Roman army, the remains whereof, faith Camden, are to be seen this day. Such a Rampire as this, I say, I could have easily believed it, there having been just such great stones found hereabout, as we read Caractacus, and other British princes, were used to fortify withal: whereof I was told of one, that contained 100 loads: another so great, that after 10 loads of stone were hewed off it, required 36 yoaks of Oxen to draw it, and made the great Cistern in the Mault-house at Wrottesley, which though left very thick both at bottom and sides, is yet so capacious, that I will wet 37 strike of barley at a time. Or at least I could have thought it some camp of the Danes, who as Simeon Dunelmensis, John Brompton and Florentius Wigorniensis all testify, were overthrown at Totenhale, Teotenhale, or

Tbeotfanbele, now Tettenhall not farr off; the whole, or greatful part of it, being I think in that parish at this very day: but that the parallel partitions within the outer wall, whose foundations are still visible, and represent streets running different ways, put it I think out of doubt, that it must have been a city, and that of the Britains, for that I could hear of no name it ever had, nor have the inhabitants hereabouts any tradition concerning it, of any sort whatsoever, somewhat whereof would have certainly been preserved, had it either been Roman; or so late as either Saxon, or Danish conquests of this nation".

COLTON *2m. NE of Rugeley.*

It lies between Rugeley and Blithfield Reservoir. Though not large it was a borough by 1364, one of only 23 towns in the county. It was small and agricultural but the people who lived within the boundaries had rights and privileges above those of their neighbours. The church of St. Mary has an Early English tower with twin lancet bel'

Colton, the High House.

Colton, the church and the village green.

105

Colton, the house opposite Bellamour Lodge

openings and a late 13th Century south chapel with lancet windows. The rest was rebuilt by G. E. Street in 1850-52. He also supplied most of the furnishings. There are three misericords, brought here from Tenby, and some stained glass windows by Wailes. Colton House is a brick mansion with nine bays of about 1730. Like so many large houses close to towns and villages the grounds have been sold off and filled with modern villas, a practice to be deplored. Bellamour Hall is long gone — demolished

between the Wars — and all that remains is the wall that enclosed the Park and a 2-storey fragment in ashlar about 10 feet square with mullioned and transomed windows. The village green is quite remarkable. It is a roughly circular raised platform some 3 to 4ft. high and about 55yds in diameter. About it stand the church, the school and a couple of large houses. A stream runs close to the green and is crossed by a brick built bridge. It is altogether a most attractive ensemble. Up the hill the Victorian developments have been greatly extended in recent years and the village is now quite substantial. Littlehay Manor is of 16th Century origin but only the 2 chimney stacks survive from the original house. North of Colton and almost adjoining it is Stockwell Heath, a charming hamlet set around a small pool.

COLWICH *2m. NW of Rugeley.*
The village has achieved national notoriety as the scene of two terrible railway crashes, both of which involved substantial loss of life. The main lines from Stafford and Stoke

Colton, the pool at Stockbrook.

meet here before going onto Lichfield. The gabled Tudor station was built in 1834. Colwich is little more than a dormitory town for Stafford and has never developed as it might have considering its excellent communications. Besides the railway lines there are two main roads, the River Trent and the Trent and Mersey Canal. Between Colwich and the adjacent village of Little Haywood is the Abbey of St. Mary, in which resides a Benedictine order of contemplative nuns. The order was founded in Paris in 1651 and settled here in 1834. The abbey was originally a private house known as Mount Pavilion. It had been built in about 1825 for Viscount Tamworth, the son of the 7th Earl Ferrers, but he died before it was completed. The house is of stone and constructed in a neo-Tudor-Gothic design with battlements to the long main front. There are good views over the water meadows of the River Trent to the hills of Cannock Chase. Not far from the Abbey is the gabled Tudor station, built in 1847 to a design by Livock. The School is of 1860 by Ewan Christian. The church of St. Michael has a Gothic tower dated at 1640 but most of the rest was rebuilt by H. J. Stevens of Derby in 1856, though inside there are Early English arcades. The chancel is highly decorated and the stalls are canopied. Overall, the church is large and spacious. There is an alabaster monument to Sir Robert Wolseley, died 1646, a tablet to Charles Trubshaw, the architect and builder, died 1772; and monuments to the Anson family of Shugborough Hall. The Wolseley

Colwich, the lake in Wolseley Park.

family lived one mile SE of Colwich at Wolseley. They took their name from the manor. The family crest includes a wolf's head, a reference to their legendary role as slayers of wolves in medieval times. (Wolves lingered long in the local forests). The main entrance to Wolseley Park is on the A51 at Wolseley Bridges, just opposite the big barn with red doors used as a craft shop. The iron gates are locked now because the old Hall was demolished some time ago. The Wolseley's were established here by the 10th Century and a Wolseley still lives here, in a new bungalow with an entrance a little further up the road towards Rugeley. The Park and the old stables are still in their control and they recently applied for planning permission to make a leisure centre here. The Irish branch of the family produced Field Marshall Wolseley, a leading soldier of his day who saw service in the Crimean War, the Indian Mutiny, the Chinese War of 1860 and Canada. It was he who led the force sent to relieve General Gordon at Khartoum, but which arrived too late. The elegant Wolseley Bridge, which carries the A51 over the River Trent, was built by Sir John Rennie in 1800. This replaced the previous bridge which had carried the famous stage coach road from London and Lichfield to Stone and on to Chester and Holyhead - 'one of the most frequented roads in the kingdom', said Sir John Ogilby in 1675. Less than 0·25m. NE of the bridge is Bishton Hall, an attractive

Colwich, barn craftshop at Wolseley Bridges.

Coven, Grange Farm. 221

Toeni of Stafford, who let it to Burgred. Robert was a major landowner in the county. In 1086 there were two villagers, two small-holders and the lord of the manor had four slaves, or serfs. At Coven Lawn, 1m. SSE of Coven (SJ.903.053), are the remains of

Coven, American gun site at Coven Lawn.

concrete foundations upon which were fixed American Guns and the service buildings associated with them. The site covers some 5 acres and has been used in post-war years by the Territorial Army. At the time of writing it

Coven, American gun site at Coven Lawn.

is up for sale. The guns protected the Boulton and Paul aircraft factory 2m. SSW and Pendeford Aerodrome 2m. due S. The aerodrome is now disused and the old buildings house a gypsy-like industrial estate. However, model aeroplane enthusiasts congregate here on many weekends. *(See Brewood for mention of an old iron working site near Coven Sewerage Works).*

CRADELEY HEATH *Between Brierley Hill and Blackheath.*

There used to be two settlements, Cradeley and Cradeley Heath, but now the distinction is largely academic. Here they are treated as one. Cradeley is a Black Country town that was famous for hand-made chains, especially the large anchor chains used by ocean-going ships. In the old forges men stripped to the waist in open-fronted workshops, even in the depths of winter, so hot were the fires and so strenuous their task. The last of these chain shops was that of Noah Bloomer which only recently closed. For many years small chains have been made by machines in modern factories, and now even large chains can be made mechanically. Cradeley is also reputed to be the home of the Staffordshire Bull-Terrier, a cross-breed developed specifically for the baiting of bulls. Blood sports were practiced in the Black Country and illegal cock-fights and dog-fights are still held, one regrets to have to say. One of the most famous breeders of Staffordshire Bull-Terriers was 'Champion Gentleman Jim' a local character who died in 1947. In 1935 the breed was acknowledged by the Kennel Club. The village of Cradeley Heath, as its name would suggest, developed as a squatter community on wild heathland north of the River Stour in the 18th Century. (There had ben a water-mill operating a forge from the early 17th Century). One of these unplanned, higgledy-piggledy settlements has survived later redevelopment and is now protected. This is Mushroom Green, off Quarry Road, about 0·5m. NW of Cradeley Heath town centre. It is a delightful hamlet of old brick cottages, gardens, hedges and an overgrown piece of heath by a stream, surrounded by the uniformity of more recent housing estates. Here also is a small craft chain shop run by the local council. The squatters engaged in a variety of trades but around Cradeley they specialized in chains and nails. Nailmaking was the cottage industry par excellence. At the back of his house the nailer had a little workshop which housed a hearth and the few simple tools needed. Iron bar was supplied by a local nailmaster who took away the finished nails and paid the nailer a pittance. Whole families slogged away day and night to scrape a living. A nail was not just a nail; there were dozens of varieties of all shapes and sizes. Indeed, it was this variety that delayed their production by machine. Despite the huge urban growth of this century there are still patches of scrubby heathland to be seen all over the area and, increasingly, these are being adopted by councils as places of recreation. The church is of 1843, a Commissioners church, with a chancel added in 1874.

Opposite is Barclay's bank, housed in the striking Victorian Gothic structure erected for the old United Counties Bank. Congreave Hall and Congreaves Road perpetuate the name of the vast Congreaves Iron Company whose works and collieries dominated Cradeley between 1810 and 1894, when they closed. The site became derelict and not until the 1970's did new, smaller industry move in. Congreaves Hall is a late 18th Century house with a 19th Century castellated Gothic facade. It was the home of the Attwood family, local ironmasters, but has fallen into disrepair. Adjacent to the Hall is a golf course. At Two Gates, Cradeley, is a Ragged School of 1867. There were many of these schools in the Black Country but only a few have survived. William Caslon, the type-founder who gave his name to a printer's type still used today, was born in Cradeley in 1693. (He died in 1766). Halesowen's Caslon Hall is also named after him. Attempts are being made to revitalize Cradeley. There is a main line station, a shopping precinct with branches of most of the chain stores and new

Cradeley Heath, Mushroom Green.

115

Cradeley Heath, Noah Bloomers chain shop.

housing estates. Perhaps Cradeley's greatest claim to fame, at the moment anyway, is its motor-cycle speedway team 'The Heathens' whose supporters slogan is 'Ommer 'Em Cradeley!'

CRESWELL *5m. SE of Longton.*
Not a place to linger over long. Here are suburban houses, a large factory, the main line railway, the River Blythe (or Blithe) and some old houses in Creswell Old Lane. Attached to one of the latter is the simple Roman Catholic church of St. Mary, built of brick in 1816 with lancet windows and stained glass window of the Annunciaiton by Pugin.

CRESWELL *2m. NW of Stafford.*
Creswell is no longer a separate community but is now a suburb of Stafford on the road to Eccleshall. Junction 14 of the M6 Motorway has divided the old settlement into two parts. To the SE is Creswell Manor, hidden from sight in its well-wooded grounds. A new,

largely Georgian style housing estate has been built on land once belonging to the manor. At the back of this estate is the River Darling and the Doxey Marshes, an important wild life site. North-west of the motorway is an area of inter-war style houses and the site of The Mount, an old mansion now demolished. The entrance gate and some of the outbuildings remain and in the grounds are the remains of Creswell church (SJ.896.261), which lies opposite another set of iron gates a little further along the road

Cresswell, the ruined church.

Croxton sunrise (no filters).

Croxall Hall.

117

towards Eccleshall. This was once a substantial church but it has been a ruin for many years, and all that remains is a part of the chancel with lancet windows. Around it is some disturbed ground, probably shallow sand and gravel workings, but it is believed that there was a small village around the church. Domesday Book also mentions that there was a mill at Cresswell. The manor was then owned by Earl Roger de Montgomery, King William the First's right hand-man and most trusted friend. (The King left his Queen in Normandy under the protection of Roger de Montgomery whilst he made his Conquest of England in 1066).

CROXALL 5·5m. NE of Lichfield.

Croxall is most easily approached off the A38 at Alrewas. The name means 'Croc's secluded place' and is thought to be of Danish origin. Croxden was in Derbyshire until 1894 and much of that county was in the Danelaw, where a high proportion of invading Danes settled and where in Anglo-Saxon times a modified form of Danish law prevailed. The little hamlet is best known for an incident recorded on the wall monument in the church to Sir Robert Wilmot-Horton and his wife, Anne. It was Anne who inspired Byron to write his famous poem which begins:

> 'She walks in beauty, like the night
> Of cloudless climes and starry skies:
> And all that's best of dark and bright
> Meet in her aspect and her eyes.'

Croxall, church of John the Baptist

Byron first saw Lady Anne at a ball. She was wearing a black gown with starry spangles, and the poet was so taken with her that he wrote his immortal lines that same evening. The wide church, which has no aisles, lies on high ground amongst trees to the east of the hamlet and is approached across a field. It is mostly of the 12th and 13th Centuries and contains a great number of monuments and tablets, mostly to members of the Curzon family of Croxall and the Horton family of Catton. First amongst the tablets is that to Eusebius Horton, died 1814, by Sir Francis Chantrey. Croxall Hall is a large, handsome late 16th Century 'L' shaped house built of brick with additions and alterations after a fire in 1868. It has wide courtyards and stands amongst meadows close to the River Meese. The windows are mullioned and transomed and the chimneys are tall. Near the road there is a Dovecote with a cupola roof. The Curzons lived at Croxall Hall, and after them the Earls of Dorset lived here. Half of the villages in the area around Croxall have been deserted, mostly in the period 1330 - 1530, probably due to de-population through plague and famine but also, it is believed, because of flooding. The remains of the deserted ancient village of Croxall are in fields opposite The Grange, which is on the SE fringe of the hamlet. South-east of the churchyard, against the River Tame, is a burial mound with a diameter of 117ft. and a height of between 18ft. and 29ft. There is also a moated site. Catton Hall lies 1·25m. NE of Croxall. It is a modern house set in a small park. In the grounds is a rockery in which are the fragments of windows and a font believed to be Saxon, the last remains of a chapel now long gone. Oakley Farm lies 0·5m. SW of Croxall. It once belonged to John Stanley, ancestor of the first Earl of Derby, died 1474. Edward IV was often a visitor here.

CROXDEN 4·5m. NW of Uttoxeter.

Croxden is most easily approached from the minor road between Rocester and Tean. A

Croxden, the Abbey ruins.

the Abbey during the 14th Century, and this valuable document is now in the British Museum. The heart of King John lies either here or in Croxton in Leicestershire. (His body lies in Worcester Cathedral). The Abbey was built between about 1179 and 1280 and the church was consecrated first in 1181 and again in 1253. The two largest fragments still standing are of the south wall of the south transept, and the west wall of the nave. Both have tall, elegant lancet windows and the west wall has a superb doorway with clustered pillars. The east wall of the cloister court still stands with three arches of clustered pillars, the middle one being the entrance to the chapter house. There are many other smaller remains of parts of the kitchen, the common room, the abbot's house, the sacristy and the 14th Century guest house. The choir plan is marked out in the grass; it is to the French 'chevet' plan of five radiating apsidal chapels and ambulatory − most unusual in this country. The present road, almost unbelievably, cuts through the site of the abbey church. The Abbey Chronicle tells of the Great Famine of 1316, of the Murrain of Cattle in 1319 and of the Black Death of 1349. Little wonder the 14th Century saw a general decline in the population of the country as a whole. The monks cleared woodland in the valley and sold it for charcoal, probably for use in the Churnet Valley iron works. Today there is a small hamlet at Croxden − a few cottages, the 5-bay Georgian-fronted Abbey Farm and the little village church of St. Giles (1884), which replaced the former chapel. The church is rock-faced, of early 14th Century style and was paid for by the Earl of Macclesfield, who no doubt occupied the south chapel pew which has a fireplace. The valley is still secluded and well-wooded, and the streams are ponded in several places, the haunt of fishermen.

sunken, tree-lined lane leads northwards from this road to the remote, spectacular ruins of Croxden Abbey, the finest Abbey ruins in Staffordshire. Croxden means 'Croc's Valley', a Danish name. The Abbey was founded in 1176 by the Crusader, Bertram de Verdun, who also built the first castle at Alton. It was constructed of sandstone taken from the Hollington quarry, a mile to the SW. (Stone from this site is particularly good, being soft and easy to cut when first quarried and becoming most durable when exposed to the air). The Abbey was a Cistercian house of monks from Aunay in Normandy. Cistercians were sometimes called White Monks because of the light colour of their robes. They seem to have been attracted to the Moorlands for they had several monasteries in North Staffordshire. They sought out remote places and were good farmers. One of their members, William de Shepesheved, kept a chronicle of

CROXTON *9·5m. NW of Stafford.*
It lies on the B5206 in the handsome wooded country between Eccleshall and Logger-

heads. There are houses old and new, and several farms. Today the fields are mainly laid to pasture, but 150 years ago this was arable farming country. Croxton is quite a long village. Most of the main road development is somewhat nondescript, but at either end of the village are two little off-road centres that are most charming. The SE centre has a handful of old Georgian brick houses set above the steep banked lanes, one of which leads to a disused windmill at the top of the hill. Opposite the windmill is a tall, modern Scaffold-tower from which clay pigeons are fired. The NW centre is again high-banked and here is found the small church by Ewan Christian, of 1853, with its polygonal apse and bellcote. The rectory was built about the same time and lies adjacent to the church. Together they occupy a site which may well have been favoured by the earliest settlers — easily defended and with good views of the country around. The road from the top of the edge to the valley below is steep and winding. Here, on the fringe of the village, is the Vernon-Yonge Arms, named

after the family who used to live at Charnes Hall, which is 1·25m. NW of Croxton. The turning to Charnes is opposite the turning to Wetwood. The Hall is 17th Century with an 18th Century facade and has a most attractive park. In fact, all the country around here is quite delightful. There is however a gruesome tale told hereabouts. Some 300 years ago the young wife of one of the Yonge family took ill and died. On the night of the funeral, a coachman broke into her tomb. He tried to remove the valuable jewelled ring that she wore but it stuck fast to her finger. In desperation he took out his knife and cut her finger off. As he did so the finger spurted blood and the corpse sat bolt upright. The coachman still clutching the ring ran off in terror. The young wife staggered back to the hall and lived for many more years. She had, in fact, been buried alive. The tomb was in Chapel Wood, opposite the entrance to the Hall. The ghost of the girl is said to haunt the house looking for the ring so cruelly, yet so fortunately, taken from her. There is not a village at Charnes and it appears that there

Croxton, Charnes Hall.

never has been. The Old Hall and an adjacent moated site lie 0·25m. NE of the 'new' Hall. In 1086 Croxton was a part of the Bishop of Chester's extensive Eccleshall estate. It is likely that this was previously an old Anglo-Saxon estate which continued intact after the Conquest.

DARLASTON 4m. ESE of Wolverhampton.

Darlaston lurks deep in the heart of the Black Country surrounded by Wednesbury, Bilston, Willenhall and Walsall. Today, nowhere is more industrialised or urbanised, and yet it appears in Domesday Book as a small agricultural village owned by the Abbey of Burton-upon-Trent. Darlaston owed its early industrial development to its position on the '30ft. coal', a rich seam which actually outcropped here but which is never more than 400ft. below the surface. The most important metal working industry was gun

Darlaston, derelict land at Forge Street.

making, especially the manufacture of the firing mechanism — the lock. These were sent on to Birmingham where the finished guns were assembled. By the mid 18th Century the trade was booming. One of the most important markets was Africa where guns were traded for slaves. In Darlaston at that time there were more than 300 gunlock filers, and more than 50 gunlock forgers. With the abolition of slavery the trade went into recession but recovered, specializing in quality guns, and has survived into the present century. The other trade especially associated with Darlaston is the manufacture

of nuts and bolts. Indeed, the town has a claim to be the home of the modern industry because the first machine to make nuts was invented by a local man, Thomas Oliver. One

Darlaston, the Staffordshire Knot.

of his machines is in Bilston museum. By 1860 the trade was firmly established in the town with eight large manufacturers and many smaller concerns. The largest single company in Darlaston was Rubery Owen, formed in 1893 by John Turner Rubery and Alfred Ernest Owen. The company manufactured a variety of components for the cycle, motor vehicle and aviation industries. Their Booth Street factory closed in 1980 but the firm continues. There are many other industries in the area and many factories, large and small, making the most diverse products. During the Industrial Revolution the lot of the labourer was hard. Even skilled men were poorly paid and lived in small, dark unhygienic houses. This can, perhaps, partly explain the prevalence of

Darlaston, the police station.

121

blood sports. Cock-fighting, dog-fighting, bull-baiting and bear-baiting were widely practiced in the Black Country, and Darlaston is well known for its Bull Stake. This is both an area of the town (now a shopping precinct) near the Library and the

Darlaston, the new shopping centre.

actual stake, a large iron ring. This is normally on public display at a site close to the original position. Bulls and, on occasion, bears were tethered to the stake and attacked by bull-terriers. The 'sport' was practiced in medieval times but was widespread here through the 17th Century to 1825 when it was made illegal. There is believed to have been a church at Darlaston from 13th Century but the first parish church of St. Lawrence dates from the 17th Century. This was rebuilt in 1721, rebuilt again in 1801 and rebuilt yet again in 1872 by A.P. Brevitt with a new tower and spire in 1907. Inside there are two galleries supported by cast-iron piers and large cast-iron capitals. In the churchyard is an oversized Mother and Child sculpture by Thomas Wright, 1958. (Wright also made the statue of St. George, 1959, which stands at the north end of The Green). In Walsall Street is the modern church of All Saints, of 1952 by Lavender, Twentyman and Percy which replaces, somewhat belatedly, the previous church of 1872 by Street, which was destroyed by a landmine during the Second World War. The church of St. George at The Green is of about 1852 by T. Johnson. In the 1960's Darlaston was in danger of dying but the centre was revitalised with the development of the new shopping area, and the construction of new housing estates. Today the town looks prosperous enough and has an openness and a feeling of the fresh air that belies its location. This is partly due to the landscaping of the old railway cutting which now forms a welcome green area close to the town centre. Darlaston's literary claim to fame is that in the 1890's Mrs. Henry Wood wrote her novel 'King's Lynne' whilst staying with relatives at The Poplars, a house now demolished, which stood in King Street. The town itself was immortalised in a song written by Tom Langley, a retired policeman, and called 'The Darlaston Dog-fight', which was recorded by 'The Black Country Three' in the 1960's.

DENSTONE *5m. N of Uttoxeter.*
The very largely modern village lies in the valley of the River Churnet, some two miles north of its confluence with the River Dove.

Denston, the church of All Saints.

122

There are two houses of note: the Stone House of 1712 and Barrow Hill House (now the Corbellion Restaurant) of 1780. The church of All Saints was paid for by Sir Thomas Percival Heywood of the Manchester banking family, designed by G.E. Street and built in 1860-2. The style is English Gothic of about 1300 (Middle Pointed) and is considered to be an example of Street at his best. The chancel is, unusually, higher than the nave, and outside is a round, turret-like tower capped with a tile-clad spire. The stained glass is by Clayton and Bell and the front carving is by Thomas Earp. Street also designed the lychgate, the School and the Vicarage. The well-known Denstone College lies 0·75m. WSW of the village in a high position, with good views all round but especially northwards to the Weaver Hills. It is a 'Woodward School', one of the colleges established by the Rev. Nathaniel Woodward, who had a mission to achieve 'union of classes by a common system of education'. He built schools at Hurst Pierpoint (1851), Lancing (1854), Bloxham (1860), Ardingly (1870) and Denstone (1873). Denstone College is in Middle Pointed Gothic style to an 'H' layout. The buildings were designed by Slater and Carpenter (junior) and constructed in pink sandstone. The chapel was built later (1879) with a polygonal apse and a tall lancet window. Overall, the school and its chapel are impressive but unfriendly structures.

DERRINGTON 2·5m. W of Stafford.

At the beginning of this century the population of Derrington was probably little more than at the time of the Domesday Book, when the lord of the manor, William, held it from the great Earl Roger de Montgomery. There were 3 villagers and their families and 1 hide of land (about 120 acres). Today it is a place of modern villas, pleasant enough but with little or no real character. There is a pair of black and white cottages and the half-timbered Blue Cross Farm of 1612 (which has many anachronistic

Derrington the church of St. Matthew.

mahogany windows) to remind one that the settlement is ancient. The church of St. Matthew was designed by a local architect, Henry Ward of Stafford, and was built in 1847. It has a nave and a chancel in one with 13th Century details and a bellcote. A practice occurs here which is to be frowned upon, namely the broadcasting through public address loudspeakers of pre-recorded bells to announce the Sunday morning service. The principle is distasteful enough but it is compounded by the choice of bells — great cathedral-like swirls of sound apparently emanating from a humble village church. On occasion the tapes get mixed up and more than once worshippers have been summoned to prayer by Bing Crosby and

Derrington, Stafford Castle from Billington

Frank Sinatra singing songs better suited to a night club. Floodlit at christmas, though, the church looks very pretty. On the approach lane to the village from the Stafford to Newport road, is an untidy factory. This used to produce dog food and the smell was awful.

123

Dilhorne, Foxfield Colliery at sunset.

Derrington, Stafford from Billington Bank.

Mr. Boon, the owner, was forced to desist by a High Court order. There is also a shop, a post-office and a pub in the village.

DILHORNE *1·75m. NE of Blythe Bridge, which is 2m. SE of Longton in the Potteries.*
To the north of the small village are the remains of the old Foxfields colliery. It was one of the last coalmines in the area and is linked to Blythe Bridge by a mineral railway. Some of the locomotives and rolling stock have been preserved and 'steamings' take place on Sundays and Bank holidays during the summer. Gone too is Dilhorne Hall, home of John Holliday who planted many thousands of trees on the moors hereabouts. Here also lived the Bullers and the Manningham-Bullers in the 19th Century, and Lord Dilhorne, a former Lord Chancellor, took his name from the village. All that remains of the Hall are the red brick Gothic, turreted gatehouse and the gabled lodges. The church of All Saints is noteworthy for its octagonal tower, one of very few in England. It is 13th Century in the lower part and 13th - 14th Century in the upper part. The 4-bay arcades are 13th Century and the chancel late medieval, restored by Ewan Christian. The aisles are of 1819 and the doorways rusticated Gothic. The communion rail is Jacobean. The Old Parsonage has 4 storeys, 3 bays, a semi-circular porch and Venetian windows. Houses of note in the country nearby include Heywood Grange, 1·25m. NW of Dilhorne, dated at 1672; and Stansmore Hall, 1m. WNW of Dilhorne, an early 17th Century house of stone with gables and mullioned windows.

DOSTHILL *2·25m. S of Tamworth.*
To all intents and purposes Dosthill is a southern suburb of Tamworth. The River Tame runs close by to the west and the A5 (Watling Street) passes by to the north. Mostly a modern place. The church of St. Paul has a remarkable, if not comical, small broach spire. The old church stands to the NE with Norman doorway and windows, and

is now used as a parish hall. North of the old church is a barn, probably of the early 15th Century, with very good crucks (inverted curved 'V' shaped frames). Sitting by itself beside the river is Dosthill House, of 1830.

DOVEDALE *The southern entrance near Thorpe is 4m. NW of Ashbourne.*
It is a place of unsurpassed natural beauty with scenery that varies from precipitous limestone cliffs to gentle meadows with caves and woods and secret corners. Dove Dale lies between St. Mary's Bridge (SK.146.514), 0·5m. W of the village of Thorpe, and Hartington Bridge (SK.121.508), 0·5m. W of Hartington, a distance of 7·5m. The most dramatic and most walked stretch is the Dovedale Gorge. This stretches for 2·75m. northwards from

Dovedale, near the Thorpe entrance.

the car park near the Isaac Walton Hotel to Viator's Bridge at the picturesque hamlet of Milldale, where there is also a car park. The journey can be made from either direction but we shall start at the south and head upstream. The word 'Dove' is from the Celtic word meaning 'dark'. It is the 'dark river'. For much of its course and for the whole of this journey it forms the boundary between Staffordshire and Derbyshire. The car park is on the W bank of the river, the Staffordshire side. As one walks northwards along the main path the hill to the left is Bunster Hill (1,000 ft.) The conical hill on the right is Thorpe Cloud (942 ft.). After about 0·75m. the river makes a sharp left-hand turn and at

A Weir; below, near Dove Holes.

Dovedale, view from the Izaac Walton Hotel.

Below: Thorpe Cloud and Stepping Stones

Dovedale, fisherman near Milldale.

126

this point are the Stepping Stones which we use to cross to the E bank. The flat area of grass here is called Sow Sitch. On the left, on Bunster Hill, is the rock called Dove Dale Castle (or Dove Dale Church), and on the corner of the next bend are the limestone outcrops called The Twelve Apostles. By now the woods are established and will be our companion for much of the way. this is a natural forest. The trees are predominantly ash and provide a rich sea of green that contributes greatly to the valley landscape. The walls of the gorge stand high now, to about 450ft. above the river. Opposite the Twelve Apostles the path rises to a promontory of rock called Sharplow Point.

Dovedale, Ilam Rock and Pickering Tor.

Spires on the right and beyond them leads to Reynard's Cave. A short, steep side track leads through the impressive entrance arch to the cave itself which is some 30 ft. high and 15 ft wide. To the left of the main cave and a little above it is another smaller cave called Reynard's Kitchen. In July 1761 Dr. Langton, Dean of Clogher in Northern Ireland, had picnicked near Reynard's Cave and was riding up the steep hill towards Tissington, with a young lady in the saddle behind him, when his over-loaded horse lost its footing and threw its riders. The young lady recovered from her fall but the Doctor died from the injuries he sustained. The riverside path continues to the Straits, where the rocks on either side press hard against the river. Beyond lies the large crag called Lion's Head Rock, again on the right-hand side. High above the Lion's head is the Watch Tower. Next come the great rock walls of Pickering Tors and opposite them, on the Staffordshire side of the river, is the bulk of Ilam Rock which is usually in *Dovedale, the Dove Holes.*

Dovedale, Sharplow Point.

This is also known as Lover's Leap because a young girl who had been jilted by her lover leapt from the rock in an attempt to commit suicide. Fortunately, however, her fall was broken by the bushes and she survived. The path descends to the river, passes Tissington

127

shadow. There is a footbridge across the Dove here which leads to Hurts Wood and Hall Dale, the upper northern slopes of which are bare and are called the Greek Temple. The main path continues on the

Dovedale, Raven's Tor.

Derbyshire bank, the right-hand side, and the ground rises again before the descent to the spectacular Dove Holes. These are big shallow caves, the largest one being about 55 ft. wide and 30 ft. high. The valley now opens out. On the left-hand bank are the Shepherd's Abbey Rocks and beyond them the cliffs of Raven's Tor, set back from the river above a steep grassy bank. Dry stone walls appear and sheep are seen grazing. A long, narrow meadow leads to the ancient packhorse bridge called Viator's and the charming stone-built hamlet of Milldale. Here there is a car park and a tea shop. Several tracks converge at this point. There are footpaths to Wetton, Hope and Alstonefield on the Staffordshire bank and tracks through the hills which join the Buxton to Ashbourne road on the Derbyshire side. For half a mile the metalled road now becomes the route along the left-bank of the river as far as Lode Mill. Here the walker crosses the bridge to the Derbyshire side under the shadow of the hill of Shining Tor. The valley is pastoral with occasional rocky outcrops. At Iron Tors the hill is clad in conifers and a half mile further on Biggin Dale joins the Dove valley from the E (the right-hand side). From now on the valley of the Dove is called Wolfscote Dale after

Wolfscote Hill which rises to 1,272 ft. to the E. After a mile of cliffs, pinnacles and screes the hills fall away and a path leads over a meadow and across a footbridge to Beresford Lane, a metalled road which ends at the river in a wood. The traveller is now in Beresford Dale. The river flows through high banked woods, over weirs and through Pike Pool (named after the rock that sticks out from the pool, not the fish) to the Charles Cotton Fishing Lodge of 1674, which still stands in good repair but which is not accessible from the Derbyshire bank. The Fishing Lodge (SK.126.592) is stone built, about 17 ft. square and has a tall pyramid roof. The round headed doorway has Tuscan pilasters to the sides. It is placed on a little promontory in a well-wooded area. The approach to it is somewhat boggy, and is being deliberately left like this as a small nature reserve. Access to the Fishing Lodge is gained from the big gate pillars on the

Dovedale, Cotton's Fishing Lodge.

above: Lode Mill; below Iron Tors.

above and below: Wolfscote Dale.

below: Wolfscote Dale.

below: Beresford Dale.

B5054 which are 300 yds SW of Hartington Bridge (which is about 0·75m. SW of Hartington village). The gate fronts a long, dead-straight drive which leads to the site of the old Beresford Hall. This is now a mere pile of stones behind a stone wall, 40 yds to the left of the gate at which the drive ends. In the woods between the gate and the river are three abandoned statues. Incidentally, near its end the drive curves around an old stone barn with massively thick walls. This is called Og's Barn and is almost certainly very old indeed. The name is Celtic. Strangely, it is not marked on the 2·5 inch Ordnance Survey

Dovedale, farmer repairing Og's Barn.

map. To return to the Fishing Lodge, this can be found on the river bank, on the left of the drive, about half a mile beyond the gates on the main road. It is difficult to see until you are very close to it. The Tower, which lies in the grounds of the old Hall, also still stands, less than 0·25m. S of the Lodge. North of the Fishing Lodge the country is open and the

path leaves the Derbyshire bank of the river to terminate near the Charles Cotton Hotel at the village of Hartington.

DRAYTON BASSETT *3m. S of Tamworth.*
At the time of Domesday book Drayton Bassett was simply Draitone. The manor belonged to the King who had 2 mills, 9 villagers, 3 smallholders and 8 burgesses of Tamworth who worked here. The Bassett suffix was added later when the Norman knight of that name became the lord of the manor. Today the village is best known for having been the home of Sir Robert Peel (1788-1850), who was Prime Minister in 1834-5 and 1841-6. He was a Conservative but also a reformer. He repealed the Corn Laws and produced the Tamworth Manifesto (1834). Drayton Manor had been rebuilt by his father, a wealthy Lancastrian textile manufacturer, who came to Staffordshire in 1791 and rented the Castle Mill in Lady Meadow, Tamworth, for a cotton factory and the Castle banqueting hall for a forge. By 1795 he also had two cotton-spinning factories and a calico printing mill at Bonehill (Fazeley), about 1m. SSW of Tamworth. The Bonehill Mill (SK.199.021), used for calico printing, subsequently returned to grinding corn by water power and did so until 1965. The iron breastshot wheel is 12 ft. in diameter and 14 ft. wide, which is unusually wide. The 4-storey brick-built mill is now used as a builder's workshop. One of the two cotton mills has also survived and stands at the end of Mill Lane, now known as the Old Mill and owned by William Tolson Ltd, smallware manufacturers. The main block is of brick, 3 storeys high, 164 ft. long and 33 ft. wide. Sir Robert Peel was very fond of his home at Drayton Bassett and regularly bought plants and seeds for the gardens there. The Manor was demolished some 60 years ago and today it is the site of the well advertised and well signposted Drayton Manor Park and Zoo. Some of the Gothic estate houses remain, as do parts of the gardens which were laid out

by Gilpin. The village of Drayton Bassett lies 1m. S of the zoo. The church of St. Peter has a Perpendicular tower, a nave of 1793 and a chancel of about 1855. There is a monument to Sir Robert Peel, an inscription in black under a Gothic canopy. North-east of Drayton Bassett and close to the main road (A4091) is a foot bridge over the Birmingham and Fazeley canal with round, Gothic brick towers.

DUDLEY 5m. SSE of Wolverhampton.

Dudley has been styled 'Queen of the Black Country'; yet if there was one town that does not conform to the popular, grim conception of the region it is Dudley. The town sits on a limestone ridge that is a watershed. Rivers and streams flow east from here to the North Sea and west to the Atlantic. Paradoxically, although the castle has always been in Staffordshire, the town has for centuries been a part of Worcestershire — an island in

Dudley, statue of William Earl of Dudley.

an alien sea. In 1974 the whole of the Black Country was removed from Staffordshire and became part of the West Midlands Metropolitan County. In this book we have ignored all such nonsense. To us Dudley is in the Black Country and the Black Country is, with the exception of Stourbridge, in Staffordshire. The history of the settlement starts with the castle which stands on a mound high above the town. The castle site was occupied in Saxon times when it was held by Earl Edwin during the reign of Edward the Confessor. In 1066 it passed to William Fitz Ansculf who also owned 25 manors in Staffordshire, 14 in Worcestershire and 5 in Warwickshire, as well as others elswhere in the country. Little is left of the 11th Century castle. Most of what we see today — the gatehouse, the barbican and keep — is of the 14th Century. The castle passed to the de Somerys and from them to the de Suttons, who became Lords of Dudley. In the 16th Century John Dudley, the Duke of Northumberland, built a Tudor mansion, or Great Hall, within the old castle. In 1575 Queen Elizabeth stayed here. The Sutton family line ended in 1621 and the castle passed to the Wards who later became, and still are, Earls of Dudley. During the Civil War the castle was a Royalist stronghold until captured by Cromwell's soldiers in 1646 when the defences were slighted. The Tudor mansion was left intact, though, and many splendid balls were held in the great state rooms until 1750 when it was destroyed by a fire which raged for 3 days. The shell of the mansion, with its mullioned and transomed windows, still stands and forms the inner court. After the fire the castle was abandoned and the Wards moved to Himley Hall. About 1850 the castle became a place of recreation and an annual 3-day Whitsuntide Fair was held here. In 1916 as many as 20,000 people attended the festivities. In 1937 a zoo was built in the grounds and the earthwork defences of the castle. (There are seals in the moat). The concrete buildings were designed

131

Dudley: the Black Country Museum; above, Lord Dudley's Limekilns; below, left, reconstructed Newcomer Engine House.

Dudley: above, a ship's anchor chain below, Dudley Castle in mist.

Dudley: the Racecourse Colliery at the Black Country Museum.

Dudley: the Dudley Canal Tunnel entrance.

133

by Messrs. Tecton who had also designed London Zoo (1934). Their work was unorthodox for the time but has since been accepted and even applauded. The curved entrance gates are a 'listed' building. The Zoo company (now a charitable Trust of 1978) has invited and encouraged excavation of the castle site and this is now proceeding. However, the castle is not open to the public and this is to be regretted. The town of Dudley grew up around the foot of the castle. There are few old buildings and the town seems to have developed largely in the 18th and 19th Centuries. It is not noted for its involvement in any particular industry though nails, fine glass, anvils and vices, cars (Bean's), beer and GPO post boxes have all been made here. It has a wide market place in the High Street, (though the Old Town Hall stood here until demolished in 1860), and a fine fountain of 1867 which was exhibited at the Paris Exhibition of that year. There are Council Offices of 1935; the Italianate County Court of 1858; the Baroque Central Library of the early 18th Century; a Technical College; a Grammar School; a Girls' High School; and the usual professional services which the presence of such bodies attracts, solicitors, bankers, estate agents and the like. The town has a busy shopping centre and a Freight Liner Terminal on the site of the old station. The ruins of the Priory lie on the NW fringe of the town centre at the foot of the castle hill in a grassed park area. It was founded by Gervase

Dudley, cavern at Wren's Nest.

Pagnell about 1160 for Cluniac Benedictine monks. It was never very large and there were never more than four resident monks, though there would no doubt also have been several guests staying at any one time. In brief, the remains consist of a nave of the early 13th Century, the south transept, the choir, two chancel south chapels, the outline of the cloister, the west wall of the west range and a spiral stair on the east range. After the Dissolution of the Monasteries the buildings were occupied by a tanner, a thread manufacturer, glass grinders, polishers of fire irons and polishers of fire fenders. The neo-Tudor Priory Hall was built in 1825. It is now used as offices. There are six churches worthy of mention: St. Edmund in Castle St., (1722-4) of brick and stone with monuments to Edward Dixon, died 1806, and Thomas Badger, died 1856; St. Augustine (1884) with lancet windows; St. James (1840); St. John (1840); Our Lady and St. Thomas (1842) by

Dudley, the Priory ruins.

Pugin; and St. Thomas (1815-18) by William Brooks, attractive and with some unusual features and iron window tracery. The Priory Housing Estate, built about 1930, stretches from the town almost to the foot of Wren's Nest Hill to the NW. Here are now fenced-off entrances to the old limestone mines. Huge black holes in the rock face lead by way of passages and shafts to a multitude of great caverns. The workings are very extensive and not at all properly mapped. There have been some alarming

Race Course colliery, Black Country Museum.

collapses — craters appearing overnight in playing fields and houses subsiding. The Goverment has authorised the spending of considerable sums of money in order to attempt to fill in these workings, but the job will take many years. Fossils, especially trilobites, were once commonly found in the outcrops but these are now rarely found such has been the extent of depradation by collectors. At one time there were 3 fossil shops in the town. One of the 'Dudley Locusts' appears in the town's coat of arms. The Wren's Nest Hill is now a nature reserve with two organised trails. At 3,172 yds. (nearly 2 miles) the Dudley Canal Tunnel is the longest in Staffordshire. It was built in 1792 and connects the Birmingham Canal to the Stourbridge Canal. An extension of 1,227 yds. leads from the main tunnel at Castle Mill basin (which is open to the sky) to an underground basin at Wren's Nest. This was paid for by the Earl of Dudley because its purpose was to serve his limestone mines

there. British Rail had plans to seal off the canal to make safe an embankment above its Birmingham New Road entrance, but local enthusiasts formed a Preservation Society in the 1960's and through their efforts the tunnel was saved. They wrote a song called 'Push Boys Push' (recorded by 'The Black Country Three') which describes a journey through the tunnel. The title refers to the means of propulsion which is by 'legging'. There is no towpath so in the days before engines the horses were led over the hill and the boatmen lay on planks and propelled the boat by pushing with their feet against the tunnel walls. Regular trips for the public are run through the tunnel to the limestone caverns, and some 100,000 people a year avail themselves of the service. In recent years a new 65 yd. tunnel was cut to the Singer Cavern, the first new tunnel of its kind to be constructed in Britain for over 100 years. The Black Country Museum was established in

Dudley, the Black Country from Wren's Nest.

1975 on waste ground between the Birmingham New Road and the entrance to the Dudley Canal Tunnel. It is a remarkable enterprise. Buildings from all over the Black Country have been dismantled and re-erected here to form a typical street of the region. There is an ironmongers shop from Oldbury, a chemists and a chapel from Netherton, a row of cottages from Old Hill, a pub from Wordsley, a bridge from Wolverhampton, a stable block (now a restaurant) from Wednesbury, the headgear of a colliery, a boat-building dock, a rolling mill, a bakery, a chainshop and many more such-like. All this was initiated by local enthusiasts, ordinary people, not by professionals or local government. This is a reflection of an awakening pride in the region's history and traditions wich occurred in the 1960's with performances of local songs by 'The Black Country Three' on Midlands television in 1964, the publication of several books by M. & J. Raven in 1964-5 and the formation of the Black Country Society in 1966. Dudley has produced two great ironmasters and innovators of iron-making techniques. They are Dud Dudley and Abraham Darby. Dud Dudley was one of the 5th Earl of Dudley's eleven illegitimate children. In 1619, at the age of 20, he took charge of his father's iron works in the town. At that time iron was smelted using charcoal as a fuel. Coal would not burn with sufficient heat. However, timber supplies in this country were being depleted at an alarming rate, and becasue of insufficient fuel the production of iron was curtailed. Imported iron was coming in from Spain and Sweden and a crisis was imminent. Dud Dudley experimented with coal as a fuel and it is likely that he did tests using coke. He had many trials and tribulations — rioters and floods damaged his works and competitors persecuted him with lawsuits — and finally the Civil War curtailed his experiments. He fought for the King as an engineer, casting iron and fortifying towns. At the end of the war he became an ironmaster again, but after

the Restoration was denied the patents he had earlier been granted. He died in 1684, embittered and poverty stricken. With him died his secret coking process. In 1677 Abraham Darby was born at Wren's Nest, the son of a Quaker farmer. He became interested in iron-casting, especially of pots and pans which were being imported from the Continent. He went to Holland and returned with Dutch craftsmen, and established a successful foundry, first at Bristol and then at Coalbrookdale in Shropshire. He initially used charcoal to smelt his iron but after several years of experimenting achieved success with coke as a fuel. The results were dramatic and enabled him and his successors to produce vast quantities of iron cheaply and quickly with a fuel supply that was virtually inexhaustable. He died in 1717 and his sons carried on refining the process which, much to their credit, they did not attempt to patent and which was very soon adopted by all their competitors. Personalities in other fields born at Dudley include Dorothy Round (1909-82) who won the Ladies' Singles Championship at Wimbledon in 1934 and 1937, and was three times mixed doubles champion (twice with the great Fred Perry); and Duncan Edwardes, considered by many to be the greatest and most versatile professional footballer ever. He died in the Munich air crash which virtually wiped out Manchester United F.C. in 1958. He was born on the Priory Estate and there is a stained glass window to his memory in the church of St. Francis. Billy Russell (1893-1971), the comedian, was born in Birmingham but brought up in Dudley; he was the first popular exponent of Black Country humour. 'Devil' Dun of Dudley (died 1851) was a very famous 'wise man' who specialized in charms that enabled stolen property to be recovered. He had a national reputation and clients came from all parts of the country.

DUNSTALL *4·5m. SW of Burton upon Trent.*
A small, pretty village on the edge of

136

Needwood Forest. The Hall is ashlar with a 10-bay centre to which wings were added about 1850. The entrance has a coach-porch and a striking top facade with turret-like pediment. Inside there is an original Roman floor mosaic from Tivoli, and a staircase carved with animals and foliage by Edward Griffiths of about 1900. Griffiths also made the beautiful front door (1898) which features a fantastic landscape with beasts, horsemen and a castle. Outside is a 7-bay orangery and a good stable block. The approach to the church of St. Mary is lined with holly trees. It was built by Henry Clutton in 1852 and paid for by John Hardy of Dunstall Hall. The south-west tower has a round staircase projection and is topped by a tall spire. Inside it is vaulted, as is the porch. The chancel is lined with alabaster. Clutton also designed the School and the Rectory. In the church is a tablet engraved: 'In memory of Charles Arkwright Esq. of Dunstall, founder of this church and the schools connected with it. Fifth son of Sir Richard Arkwright of Willersley, Derbyshire.'

DUNSTON *3·5m. S of Stafford*

It lies on the A449 close to Junction 13 on the M6 motorway. Dunston is a small scattered hamlet which was for long in Royal ownership, being first the possession of the Saxon King Edward and then of William the Conqueror. The present Italianate stuccoed hall was built in the 1870's. Lord Thorneycroft was born in this house. There has been a building on the site since the 13th Century when there was a farm here. The present stable-block pre-dates the present Hall which is today owned by the Staffordshire County Council and leased to the North Staffordshire Polytechnic who use it as a student hostel (80 places). The large, rock-faced church of St. Leonard dates from 1876, was designed by W.D. Griffin of Wolverhampton and paid for by F.C. Perry who lies outside in an enormous marble tomb. It replaced an earlier church. The brick Rectory lies further south and has been divided into several seperate homes. The M6 cuts through the country here on a raised embankment, broadcasting its drumming din mercilessly.

ECCLESHALL *7m. NW of Stafford.*

Eccleshall lies in the midst of well-wooded undulating country. The name means 'the place of the church' and it is likely that the Bishop of Chester's extensive medieval estate, centred on Eccleshall, which was previously a Saxon or even a Romano-British estate which was passed on more or less intact. There was certainly a Saxon church in Eccleshall, probably founded by St. Chad in the 6th Century. There are re-used carved Saxon stones in the south arcade of the tower of the present church, and also a stone in the vestry with carvings of two men, one thought to be a bishop and the other St. Chad mounting a horse. The nave of the church is 12th Century, the chancel and tower 13th Century and the clerestory 15th Century. Internal features include stained glass by Clayton and Bell (1870), the reredos by Champneys (1898) and a finely carved Lady Chapel and organ case by Caroe (1931). In 1866 the church was restored by Street and it was he who rebuilt the east wall with its fine, stepped lancet windows. The tower, the clerestory and the south aisle have *Eccleshall, curbside petrol station.*

137

battlements and pinnacles. It is a large church but well proportioned and held in high regard by students of architecture. Five bishops are buried here. The earliest is Richard Sampson, chaplain to Cardinal Wolseley and friend of Erasmus. He also assisted Henry VIII to obtain his divorce from Catherine of Aragon. The others are Thomas Bentham, William Overton, James Bowestead and John Lonsdale. There is possibly a 6th bishop buried here. This is Robert Wright who garrisoned the church for King Charles during the Civil War, and whose monument may be the worn stone figure that lay for many years in the churchyard but is now inside the church. Eccleshall Castle lies just to the north of the church but is hidden from view by a small wood, which was grown for this purpose, and is approached off the Eccleshall to Newcastle road, the A519. It is quite possible that the Saxon bishops had a house on the site. Certainly, this has been the main residence of the post Norman Bishops of Lichfield and before that of Chester. (William the

Eccleshall Castle.

Conqueror gave the Saxon diocese of Lichfield to the Bishop of Chester but it was later re-instated.) A licence to crenellate a castle here was granted as early as 1200, but the first castle of which we have certain knowledge was built by Bishop Walter de Langton in the late 13th Century. All that remains of this castle is a 9-sided corner tower with small pointed trefoiled windows. The site is surrounded by a moat, crossed by

Eccleshall, the High Street.

a 14th Century bridge, and probably had 4 towers originally. In 1643, during the Civil War, the Castle was besieged and Bishop Wright was killed participating in its defence. The fortress fell and was partially dismantled. In 1695 Bishop Lloyd rebuilt the 'castle' and it is his substantial 13-bay brick house with projecting wings that we see today. The house continued to be used as the Bishop's main residence until after the death of Bishop Lonsdale in 1864. (The new Bishop's palace at Lichfield was built in 1687 but was little used.) The castle was sold and in about 1900 it passed to the Carter family who are the current owners. The house and gardens are open to the public on certain weekday afternoons during the summer months. There is a small mere in the castle grounds, a remnant of the old marshes and pools that formed part of the defences. The mere and the wet meadowland that fringe it are a Nature Reserve which contains many wetland plants. The bishops had an important corn mill that stood on the bar north of the town along which Castle street runs and which was in fact the dam wall that held back the waters of one of the branches of the River Sow to make the large mill pool that lay NW of the Castle. With regard to employment the leather trades such as cordwainers, saddlers and tanners were important in Eccleshall and in the mid 19th Century shoe-makers were only exceeded in numbers by farm workers. Eccleshall is not so much a village as a small town. It is sited at the meeting of many roads. The High Street

138

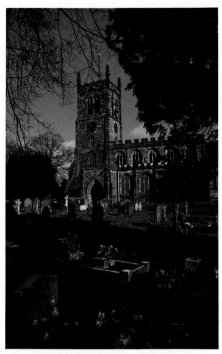

Eccleshall, the castle tower.

Eccleshall, the church of St. Chad.
Dunston Hall in winter.

Eccleshall, sunrise near the church.

is wide with cobbled verges, and there is a good selection of shops and many Georgian houses. The Royal Oak and the Crown have attractive arcades over the pavement, and opposite is one of the very few kerbside petrol pump stations left in the Midlands. The town has a typical village cricket pitch adjacent to the church and a rugby club that is renovating the 'house on stilts' near to the Co-operative store. In medieval times there was another street called Usulwall Street which ran south of and parallel to the High Street but this wasted away through depopulation and is now given over to gardens. On the fringe of the village, on the road to Stone, is a brick-built **Roman**

Eccleshall, the Fire Station.

Eccleshall, Johnson Hall.

Catholic church, and on the road to Newport is the new Fire Station with an old cart-type fire engine very nicely displayed. Half a mile SW of Eccleshall, with access off the Newport Road, is Johnson Hall. This is a large neo-Tudor mansion set in pleasant agricultural grounds. In 1978 it was bought by an arms dealer who runs his mail order business from the Hall. The road from Eccleshall to Swynnerton, 4·5m. NNE, takes one past the Raleigh Hall Industrial Estate, Drake Hall open Prison, the Army Weapons Testing Depot at Coldmeece and then past the Old Army Camp at Swynnerton, now fenced off and guarded. It is here that radio-active dust was scattered over a vast area during an exercise, and here atomic weapons convoys stay overnight on the journey from Scotland to the south. By the time you reach

Swynnerton you might be thinking you are lucky to be alive! To end on a pleasanter note, the folklorist Charlotte Sophia Burne (1850-1923), whose book Shropshire Folk Lore (1881) is internationally known as an important and early work on British traditions, songs, games and customs, lived at Eccleshall towards the end of her life.

ECTON *0·75m. ESE of Warslow, which is 7·5m. ENE of Leek.*
Ecton is a hamlet in the vally of the River Manifold. The track of the old Manifold Light Railway passes by here. This has now been surfaced and is a public footpath. Above the valley towers Ecton Hill, from which have been taken vast quantities of high-grade copper and lead ore. The ores were first worked commercially by German miners for Sir Richard Fleetwood, the Earl of Devonshire, but by the late 1680's the mines had closed and were soon almost forgotten. They were 'rediscovered' in 1720 and worked by a Cornish miner in association with a company of Ashbourne adventurers. They struck a rich mass of copper ore, but in 1764 their lease ran out and the mine was taken over by its owners, the Dukes of Devonshire. They excavated a huge cavern in the side of the hill which became a well-known tourist attraction. There were some 60 or 70 men underground, with many women and children on the surface washing and grading ores. Altogether several hundred people were employed here. About 1830 the mine

showed signs of being worked out and the Devonshires leased the workings to a partnership of miners. by 1838 the seam of ore was virtually exhausted. Several companies were formed in the latter part of the 19th Century. They all hoped to find new deposits, but all failed. The Dukes of Devonshire had got out just at the right time after having made several large fortunes, some of which they spent on developing Buxton as a spa town. Noteworthy sites on Ecton Hill include: the Dutchman Mine now covered by the huge spoil-heap (SK.098.582) that looms over Ecton village; The Ecton Deep Adit driven by Robert Shaw in 1774 which can still be seen (SK.096.581); and the Ecton Engine House (SK.098,583) which consists of a stone and tiled shelter for a Boulton and Watt steam engine of 1788 and the chimney stack now reduced to a height of about 10 ft. Just to the north is the site of a gin-race. Ecton Low is an early burial mound, 0·25m. E of Ecton Bridge, with a diameter of about 80 ft. and a height of 6 ft.

Ecton, the R. Manifold at Swainsley.

Ecton, the Manor House, Back Ecton.

141

Half way up the hill near the hamlet of Ecton is a large house with a copper spire. It was built as a castle-folly in 1931-3. One of the farms on the Hill perpetuates the ancient Longhouse format where a man and his animals sleep under one roof. The central house is flanked by byres. There is a lane that runs around the east side of the hill, opposite to that which faces the valley, called Back Ecton. There are several small farms along this lane and at the very end in a delightful setting is the Manor House (SK.104.567). The road used to continue on down to Wetton Mill but is no longer passable in a vehicle. The Manor House is a small stone-built house with mullioned windows which has had a varied history. It began life as an estate lodge and then, with many thirsty miners in the area, became a public house called 'The Peppercorn'. It was not officially licensed but as the Duke Devonshire had commissioned it the authorities turned a blind eye. Nearby the stream was dammed to provide a head of water to power a water wheel of the copper smelting plant situated here. When the mines ceased to be worked the Manor House became a farmhouse. The farmer's wife had a side-line, namely the manufacture of lead buttons, and a workshop was created by adding a third floor to the house which had a separate access from the rear up outside steps. When the Manifold Light Railway was being built there was an outbreak of cholera amongst the workers and the Manor House was used as an Isolation Hospital.

EDINGALE *7m. ENE of Lichfield.*

A compact village close to the River Mease which meanders across its flood plain hereabouts. The most striking feature of the settlement is the tiny, mounded, green at its centre upon which stand the remains of 3 large and ancient elm trees. Facing the green is the Black Horse pub and several half-timbered cottages. Church Farm House is a black and white building of 1664 and close by is the church of Holy Trinity which was

Edingale, the village green.

rebuilt by C. Lynam in 1881. It is of red brick and has a short tower with a pyramid roof and the vestry E window has a Saxon head. Opposite Rose Cottage is the old, green-painted village water pump, set into the roadside bank. There are some new houses in the village but it remains a pleasant little place.

ELFORD *5·5m. E of Lichfield.*

In 1066 the manor was owned by Earl Algar but after the Conquest it was taken by the king himself. It was a village of considerable size for its day, with 24 villagers and 8 smallholders and their families, plus all those who did not owe service to the lord of the manor and who are not therefore mentioned in Domesday Book. The list of local lords reads like a litany: Ardernes to Stanleys to Smythes to Bowes to Howards to Pagets. There is an early burial mound called Elfordlow alongside the Tamworth road. The country around the village is flat but pleasant, and the settlement itself is very quiet and dignified. It is well-wooded and there are some very attractive houses. The Old Hall, the home of the 4th Earl of Berkshire, was demolished in 1964 and there are now new villas in the grounds. The church of St. Peter is approached along an avenue of lime trees. It has a tower of 1598 and the rest is by Salvin of 1848, except for the south aisle and the south chapel which are by Street of 1869. It is the monuments for which the church is best known. These were very thoroughly restored by E. Richardson in 1848. The most popular of the monuments is without doubt the effigy of the child, John Stanley, who was killed by a blow from a Real (Royal) Tennis ball, which is very hard, in about 1460. In fact, there are anachronistic details, the hairstyle and face being more in the style of the 13th Century. Richardson was also responsible for the unsubstantiated attribution of the name of the great Sir John Spencer (who crowned Henry VII on Bosworth Field) to the splendid alabaster figure of an unknown knight of about 1370. There are also monuments to Sir Thomas Arderne, died 1391; William Staunton, died circa 1450; Sir William Smythe, died 1525; and Craven Howard (who married the Bowes' family heiress) and his son, Henry Bowes-Howard, who became the 4th Earl of Berkshire and the 11th Earl of Suffolk. The church is heavy with painted coats of arms and gilded angels. The stained glass windows are by Wailes and by Ward and Hughes. The south aisle west window is 16th Century Dutch, brought here in 1825 from Herckenrode Abbey near Liege. At the half-timbered house recently re-named Franheim, Stanley Whitehead established (in 1953) a non-profit making organisation which enables young people to participate in adventure holidays both in this country and abroad. They use Land Rovers called 'Frams'. Fram is Norwegian for 'forward'.

ELLASTONE *5·5m. NNE of Uttoxeter.*
There are two parts to the village, Upper and Lower. Lower Ellastone lies close to the River Dove on the road to Norbury (in Derbyshire). It is a pleasant enough place with some old stone houses. In the middle of the village is a lane running north. This formerly went on to the Abbey, but now comes to a dead end just beyond a little stone bridge. Here are two farms and an old stone mill now used as an agricultural merchants. The mill was built in 1822. the water wheel is gone but the mill pool remains. It was still working after the Second World War. The

previous mill on this site belonged to Calwich Abbey. The Abbey (or Priory) lay 0·5m. NW. It was founded in about 1130 as an Augustian house. The monks were driven out in the late 1530's at the Dissolution and the buildings were taken over by John Fleetwood and made into a private house. It was said that he 'made a parlour of the chancel, a hall of the church and a kitchen of the steeple'. In 1630 Richard Fleetwood was living here. He married a girl of 6 years of age and she had born and buried a child before

Ellastone (Lower), stone mill.

she was 13. In 1611 Fleetwood bought a baronetcy (from James Stuart) and as Sir Richard Fleetwood became a Catholic, left the Abbey and 2m. away built himself the most splendid house in the county, namely Wootton Lodge. His son, Thomas, stayed on at Calwich but in the early 18th century the Abbey passed to Bernard Granville. He pulled down the building and built a new house by the stream which he dammed to form a lake. He was an eccentric and a semi-

Ellastone (Upper), the village.

143

Works of 1881 - a handsome factory, much smaller but a little taller than the Boundary Works, with a similar arched doorway and pediment. However, the middle window is not Venetian and the stop chamfered mullions are a Victorian addition. A few yards further down the road is the boundary

Fenton, shops in King Street.

between Fenton and Longton, marked by a council sign. Frank Bough, the popular television presenter of topical and magazine programmes, was born at Fenton, though he was brought up in Oswestry, Shropshire.

FLASH *7m. NNE of Leek and 4m. SSW of Buxton.*

At 1,518ft. above sea level Flash is reputedly the highest village in England, with the highest pub and the highest post office. It is a somewhat nonedescript little place and is best seen from a distance. The country all around is magnificent - wild moors and long views in every direction from the A53 Buxton to Leek road. Romantic country too,

Flash, view of village from A53.

Flash, view W of A53 1m. S of Travellers Rest.

for this is the setting Sir Gawain and the Green Knight, the epic medieval poem. The church of St. Paul is a sombre looking structure by W.R. Bryden of Buxton, with a carved stone pulpit which was given by Lady Harpur-Crewe. There is also a Methodist Chapel of 1821. Three Shire Heads (SK.009.686) lies 1m. NW of Flash on Axe Edge. This is the point where Staffordshire, Cheshire and Derbyshire meet. It is a beautiful and dramatic spot. The River Dane

Flash, bridge near Three Shire Heads.

is joined by a stream and at their confluence there are waterfalls, bridges, rocky cliffs, trees and stony pools. Several tracks meet here and it is a favourite place of walkers and horsemen. It can only be reached on foot though if approached from Knotbury a car can be taken within 0·5m. of this idyllic place. Three quarters of a mile NNE on the Buxton to Leek road, and within a few feet of the county boundary sign between Staffordshire and Derbyshire, is the source of the River Dove. The river itself is the boundary line

Flash, source of the R. Dove, Flash Head. *Flash, Three Shire Heads.*
Flash, sunset, south of village looking west.

between the 2 counties. The spring that is the actual source is in a depression marked by a headstone. It is strange to think that these wild, open moors were forest-clad until prehistoric man cleared the trees. Grazing sheep have since prevented natural regeneration. There are evocative names hereabouts - Blackclough, Wolf Edge, Knar, Hawk's Nest, Wildboarclough. These moors, hills and valleys are attractive in summer, but in the grey light of winter with storm clouds on the horizon they are magnificent. It is said that in days gone by Flash was used as a refuge by criminals on the run. It was isolated and difficult to reach, especially in the winter, which deterred officers of the law from travelling here. Also, justice was traditionally handled at a local level, and if a wanted man crossed a county boundary his apprehension became legally complicated if not impossible. The position of Flash so close to the junction of three

Flash, Three Shire Heads.

counties was thus attractive to the criminal. It is said also that forgers and coiners worked here — hence the term 'Flash money', meaning it was counterfeit. Flash Bottom, 0·5m. SSW of Flash, lies in a valley and the ground here was marshy. *(See Swythamley).*

FORTON *1·5m. NE of Newport.*
The village lies on the A519 Newport to Eccleshall road. Just to the north of this road, and visible from it, is The Monument, a stone cone-shaped building, now in ruins. The story is that there was once a water mill on the nearby stream but the water failed and so the landowner built his miller a windmill on the ridge. This then fell into disuse and was partly demolished. What was left was

Forton, the Monument.

converted into a monument, or folly, by the addition of a conical cap and large stone ball which has since disappeared. At the crossroads are some houses and the Swan pub. The lane south from here leads to Forton Hall, a handsome brick house of 1665 with gables and mullioned windows. Close by the Hall is the church of All Saints. It has a square tower, the lower part of which is of the 13th Century and the upper part Perpendicular with a crown of 8 pinnacles. The 13th Century chancel has a Norman window in the north wall and a Victorian window in the east wall. The nave arcade and the south nave are of the restoration of 1723. The north nave is medieval. There is a font of the restoration and part of a Norman font with a Celtic design. The alabaster monument to

Forton, Meredale House.

Thomas Skrymsher, died 1633, is by Garrat Hollemans of Burton and is well documented. In the churchyard is an old yew tree with a girth of some 18ft. Lower down, in the valley, are several good houses in the same style as the Hall and a stone bridge with arches askew which carries the road (and the course of the old canal) over the River Meese. The Meese flows on to Aqualate Mere 0·75m to the NW. The road continues on to the hamlet of Meretown where there is a horse breeding establishment. Aqualate Hall lies 1·5m. SE of Forton. The entrance is off the Newport to Stafford road — not the main entrance with wrought iron gates for these are permanently locked, but the dirt road entrance 1m. E near Coley Mill farm. In the park there are deer. These used to roam in the field alongside the road, but there were several car accidents caused by drivers looking at the deer rather than the road, so the animals are now kept out of sight. Aqualate Hall is approached along the track that leads through the adjacent farm. The Hall was built by Edwin Skrymsher in the early 17th Century. Sir George Boughey bought the house in the late 18th Century and commissioned John Nash to rebuild it. The result was a spectacular, castle-like Gothic mansion. Unfortunately, this was burned down in 1910 and in 1927 a much smaller house was built by W.D. Caroe. An original Nash range with gables joins the new house to the 18th Century brick stable. Ownership of the Hall and the estate changed hands recently. In the grounds

Forton, Aqualate Mere.

155

Forton, Aqualate Hall.

there is a red brick house with stepped gables and a castle-like tower and there are two attractive Gothic lodges, probably by Nash, which are in a state of disrepair. The outlook from the Hall over the deer park and the great lake is truly beautiful. It was landscaped by Repton about 1800 but looks totally natural. The lake is surrounded by wetland plants, meadows and woods. The aspect is open and the country scene presented is idyllic. The mere is 1m. long and 0·25m. wide, which makes it the largest natural lake in Staffordshire. There is a heronry here and also a mermaid. Legend has it that when the Vivary Pool at Newport became silted up the mermaid who lived there came to Aqualate. She is a gentle creature and her only concern is to prevent the destruction of her new home. On one occasion, long ago, some workmen were dredging part of the mere when the mermaid appeared. She feared that they were attempting to drain the lake and gave this

Forton, Aqualate Mere.

warning:

'If this Mere you do let dry,

Newport and Meretown I will destroy'.

The mermaid has been seen many times and legend has it that whenever she is sighted calamity befalls the world. She was seen before the last two world wars.

FOXT *1m. NE of Froghall, which is 3m. NNE of Cheadle.*

A substantial but spread-about village of stone and brick houses. Pleasant enough but by no means pretty. There is a pub, the Fox and Goose, and close by is the charming Rose Cottage. The attractive simple little church has lancet windows and was built in 1838. The machiolated tower is a feature. The country around is moorland and stone walls abound. About 1m. N of Foxt, on the road to Ipstones, is Hope Stones Farm. It lies on a hillock adjacent to a tall natural rock outcrop - a most picturesque sight.

Foxt, the church.

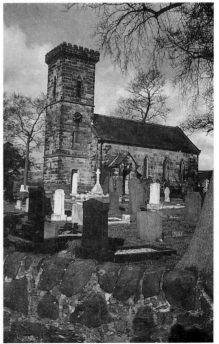

Foxt, Hopestones Farm.

FRADSWELL *8m. NE of Stafford and 3m. NNE of Weston.*

A small village with an early 19th Century Hall. The church of St. James the Less is attractively set amongst trees. It has a 13th Century chancel, Victorian nave, purple brick tower of 1764, stained glass windows by Wailes and a monument to Jane, daughter of the 4th Lord Cromwell.

FREEFORD *1m. S of Lichfield.*

Freeford Manor was the home of the Dyott family. The 5-bay house is of at least 16th Century origin, but most of what we see today is early 19th Century Georgian. Sir Richard Dyott was the Royalist commander of the Lichfield garrison during the Civil War. On 2nd March 1643 Lord Brooke, the Roundhead general, was standing at the cathedral end of Dam Street in Lichfield when he was shot dead by 'Dumb Dyott', the mute son (or nephew), of Sir Richard. Charles I granted the wish of Dumb Dyott, that when Dyott died his body should be taken by torch-light procession from Freeford to Lichfield for midnight burial. Some 200 years later this custom was revived on the death of General William Dyott. He lies in the Dyott chapel at St. Mary's, Lichfield.

FROGHALL *3m. NNE of Cheadle.*

Froghall is totally dominated by the huge Bolton's brass and copper works which were established here in 1890. They lie in the lovely Churnet Valley, but though often criticised do little to disturb the countryside.

Froghall, Bolton's works.

Froghall, wharf on Caldon canal.

The valley is very steep and narrow so the works are hidden to all but travellers on the main road, the A52. There is little more here than the works car parks, the bridge over the river and the Railway Inn. However, on the east bank is a turning to the north (B5053) which leads to Froghall Wharf. Here the Caldon Canal (1780) came to an end. It runs for 17·5m. and joins the Trent and Mersey Canal at Etruria (Hanley, Stoke-on-Trent). It was called the Caldon because its purpose was to convey the limestone quarried at Cauldon Lowe, 4m. away and high in the hills (649ft. higher). A plate-way connected the mines with the canal. The plate-way was gravity operated. The full tubs travelling downwards hauled the empty tubs back up. (Note: The essential difference between a plate-way and a railway is that the wheels of the waggon used on a plate-way had their flanges on the outside edge). The wharves here were busy places. Old photographs show throngs of men, horses and narrow boats, and piles of stone. The old buildings have been restored, and there is a restaurant, a battery of lime-kilns and a picnic place. Horse-drawn narrow boats operate from here in the summer.

FULFORD *4m. NE of Stone*
It lies high in the wooded hills to the north-east of Stone. Pleasant modern houses line

Fulford, the church of St. Nicholas.

the main road and cluster not so pleasantly in estates on the side turnings. They swamp the old, small village but the attractive red brick Gothic church of St. Nicholas (1825), and the Old Hall, now a farmhouse, lie at the top of the hill away from the recent developments in landlordly isolation. The upper side windows of the Hall have been ill-treated by blocking and butchering.

GAILEY *7·5m. N of Wolverhampton.*
A busy crossroads where the A5 and A449 intersect. The hamlet was mentioned in Domesday Book and is not just a modern crossroads development as one might have thought. There were a couple of farms, a Post Office/corner shop, an AA Control point, a large caravan company and an excellent craft centre that has taken over the church as a pottery and the school as a display warehouse. The church was designed by G.T. Robinson and built in 1849 with a chancel of 1874. Gailey wharf lies 0·5m. E along the A5. A Gothic Georgian house and a circular battlemented tower face each other

Gailey, sailing on M6-A5 junction reservoir.

across the Staffordshire and Worcestershire Canal. The wharfs are most attractive with colourful narrow boats tied up to stone quays, and lawns and trees completing a most picturesque scene. Life here is peaceful and slow, yet only yards away lorries and cars flash by in frantic haste. The Roman city of Pennocrucium lay astride Watling Street, 1m. E of Gailey Island at Stretton Mill (on the right if you are travelling westwards). There is nothing left to see of the Roman occupation. *(For a further note on Pennocrucium see Penkridge).* One and a half miles *Gailey Wharf on A5.*

further on is the ornamental black and white painted aquaduct that carries the Shropshire Union Canal over the road. It was built by Thomas Telford in 1832.

GAYTON *5·5m. NE of Stafford.*
A pleasant little village with a well-known pub, The Gayton Hotel, a church of the 18th and 19th Centuries but with a Norman chancel arch, some good houses and an old blacksmith's shop with a complete set of tools (now locked up and privately owned). There are several dead-end lanes. The charming Gayton Brook is crossed by a ford at one place and a bridge at another before meandering off across the gentle meadows. South of the churchyard is Moat Farm with a rectangular moat 260ft. by 180ft. At the NE of the village, down a short track and close to the stream, is a building next to a small pool which has a water course leading from it. This would appear to be the site of a mill. In 1066 Gayton and nearby Amerton were held by Aelmar and Alric. After the Conquest they were given to the great Earl Roger de

159

Montgomery, King William's right-hand man.

GENTLESHAW *See Cannock Wood.*

GLASCOTE *1·5m. SE of Tamworth.*
It is a part of Tamworth, an industrial suburb to the SE of the town centre. The name would suggest that glass was once made here. The brick built church of St. George was designed by Basil Champneys in 1880. It has a large, low saddleback roof, a round stair turret and stained glass windows by Burne-Jones.

GNOSALL *7m. W of Stafford.*
The name is pronounced Nose-ul. It is reputed to have the longest High Street in the county at just over 1m. However, there are really two villages, Gnosall and Gnosall Heath, joined by the A518 Stafford to Newport road. In recent years there have been many new houses built here but, for the most part, they are tucked away in medium-sized estates well out of sight of the main road, and the old village centre remains unscathed. The Shropshire Union Canal passes to the West of Gnosall Heath. This stretch of water in known to boatmen as being particularly attractive with pleasant country, deep dramatic cuttings, a tunnel, some delightful private moorings and several popular canalside pubs. On the 21st January 1879 a labourer was walking by the main road canal bridge when he was attacked by a man-

Gnosall, the church of St. Lawrence.

monkey who had great, white luminous eyes. A local policeman had heard of similar events and said that the apparition had began to appear shortly after the death of a man who had drowned in the canal. In the main village there is an old timber-framed and thatched house, now a shop and newly restored. However, the great attraction here is the church of St. Lawrence, thought by many to be one of the finest in the county. It is a large cruciform church with transepts and a crossing tower. It was a 'Royal Free Chapel' — a Collegiate church with a dean and 4 canons controlled by the King. This status brought great privileges. There were

Gnosall, alabaster knight, and stone child.

only 13 in the whole country and as these churches were richly endowed with land, they were financial forces to be reckoned with. St. Lawrence is essentially a Norman church but has been partly altered and partly rebuilt at various times since. The crossing arches, south transept, blank arcading and triforium of twin openings with straight heads are some of the finest Norman work in the county. The aisles were added in the 13th Century and the porch is by Lynam of 1893. The overall external style is Perpendicular. Gnosall is essentially a dormitory town for Stafford but it did have some local industry. There were stone quarries here in the Middle Ages and these were re-opened for a time when the canal was being constructed. In the early 19th Century Stafford shoe manufacturers sent out cut leather pieces for stitching and making up to cottage workers in several

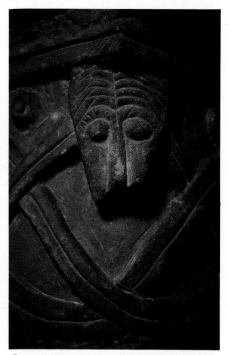

Gnosall, the old mill, bridge and canal.
Gnosall, canalside moorings.

Gnosall, Norman carving in church.

villages around the county town, including Gnosall. There is a moated site 0·5m. S of the village on the road to Haughton. It is rectangular and measures 170ft. by 180ft. Between 1836 and 1865 there was organized horse racing at Gnosall. On the main road at the entrance to the lane that leads to the church is a reconstructed stone lock-up. A railway once passed through Gnosall Heath but that fell victim to the cuts made by Mr. Beeching and is now dismantled.

GORNAL *4m. S of Wolverhampton.*

The Gornals — there are 3 of them — lie on the western boundary of the Black Country. Upper Gornal lies on the ridge that is followed by the A459 Wolverhampton to Dudley road. Lower Gornal lies 0·5m. SW and Gornal Wood 1m. SW. This is the traditional home of Aynuk and Ayli, the mythical characters who are the butt of so much local humour. It is here that a man placed his pig on a wall to watch the band go by. Most of the men used to work in the coal mines and their womenfolk were known all over the Black Country as purveyors of salt, which they sold as blocks from carts drawn by donkeys. Sand was quarried locally. It was very finely crushed and used as a scouring powder. This too was sold by Gornal women from carts drawn by donkeys. The area of Ruiton is deepest Gornal. It is also the name of the street where stand the remains of a windmill. There were two mills here at one time, it is said, but one was taken down

Gornal, the old Windmill at Ruiton.

because there was not enough wind for both of them! The windmill and the attached Windmill House are on an open green space. Around the green are several stone houses. It is easy to visualize the old country village it once was. The people here are most friendly. Pigeon racing and Nonconformity are the religions of Gornal. There are many chapels

Gornal, the Glynne Arms near Hilton.

of many denominations, but many more pigeon lofts. The last of the mines closed in the late 1960's and new housing estates have been built on reclaimed land. Ellowes Comprehensive School preserves the name of Ellowes Hall, demolished in 1964, which was the residence of the local ironmasters for some 150 years. Less than 0·5m. west of Lower Gornal, down a lane off the road to Himley, is the Glynne Arms. At the road junction is a little colour-washed toll house. The Glynne Arms is better known locally as the Crooked House (or Siden House). The south end has subsided considerably, due to settlement of the ground below caused by coalmining. All the doors and windows lie at strange angles and coins or marbles placed on a table apparently roll uphill. It has become quite a tourist attraction. The name Glynne is that of the family who previously owned the estate on which it stands. Their manor house was Oak House Farm, now demolished. This was the centre of an iron working and coal mining development in the mid 19th Century, owned by Sir Stephen Glynne, the 9th and last baronet. He became a brother-in-law to William Ewart Gladstone when the future Prime Minister married his sister, Catherine. The industrial venture failed in 1875, despite assistance from Gladstone, and the estate was sold. The area is still one of industrial dereliction and there is a waste disposal site nearby. Surprisingly, the locality is quite well-wooded.

GRATWICH 4m. WSW of Uttoxeter.

A hamlet in the lanes, amongst rolling country, north of the Stafford to Uttoxeter road. Gratwich is mentioned in Domesday Book when it belonged to Robert of Stafford and was a village of reasonable size for the time. The little brick church of St. Mary was built in 1775. It has Gothic windows and a bellcote, but the chancel is believed to be of the early 17th Century, a very early date for the use of brick in a religious house. Possibly the chancel originally belonged to a secular building now demolished. The River Blithe flows by just to the east and there were once 6 sluices to let water onto the meadows of King's Field. A mile down stream where the river passes beneath the bridge that carries the A518 Stafford to Uttoxeter road is

Gratwich, Burnhurst Mill on A158.

Burndhurst Mill. This old watermill was grinding animal feed until the 1950's. It is also known locally as Burnthurst and Blunderhurst.

GREAT BARR 3m. NE of West Bromwich.

Amongst what is now a suburban sea, but which used to be an idyllic setting, the Gothic Great Barr Hall, built for Joseph Scott in 1777, still survives, though changed

for the worse. It lies in a valley at the back of St. Margaret's Hospital and is used by the hospital as office accommodation. At one time the estate belonged to Handsworth Lodge, on the main road a little to the west. This also has a Gothic-style facade. Further along in the same direction is Fairyfield House, Gothic yet again. The church of St. Margaret is of 13th Century style by W.D. Griffin, 1860, with a steeple of 1890. The Scott Arms is named after the Scott family who were the squires of Great Barr from 1618 to 1911. The town is divided into 4 sections by 2 modern roads — the M6 and the A34 — which have an intersection here. About 1·5m. north of the Hospital is Barr Beacon, a hill of 700ft. which, as its name suggests, was used as a place to build fires as warnings or celebratory beacons. There is a peace memorial, beech trees, good views and a car park. About 1m. W at Grove Vale on the A4041 is Bishop Asbury's Cottage.

GREAT HAYWOOD 4·5m. E of Stafford.

There are two villages: Great Haywood and Little Haywood. They both lie close to the Trent and both turn their backs to the river. The long wall that runs between the two villages marks the eastern boundary of Shugborough Park, which extends over the river, though it only encloses a narrow strip of this eastern bank. Much of Great Haywood used to lie on the other side of the river close to Shugborough Hall, but from 1737 Thomas Anson began demolishing cottages as his tenants leases came to an end. He wished to improve the view from the Hall, and the villagers were first moved to another part of the estate and then moved over the river. Some of the new cottages built by the Lords of Shugborough still stand on the lane that leads to the Essex Bridge. This handsome structure was built in the late 16th Century by the Earl of Essex who lived in Chartley Hall about 3m. to the north. Its purpose was to provide passage over the River Trent to Cannock Chase for his huntsmen, horses and dogs. It is a narrow bridge, only 4ft. wide, but most strongly built. There are 14 arches with cut waters on both sides, though is is said that there were originally 40 arches. The river is most attractive here with sandbanks where swans sleep and high trees at the water's edge. A few yards north of the bridge the River Sow joins the Trent. A third 'river' at this confluence (the most westerly) is actually a branch of the River Sow which joins its mother stream after flowing over a weir. A little further north still is the Great Haywood canal basin and junction where the Trent and Mersey Canal is joined by the Staffordshire and Worcestershire Canal. The latter was completed by James Brindley in 1772 and crosses the River Trent here by a noteworthy aquaduct. Altogether, Great Haywood has a 'meeting of the waters'. The Staffordshire Way, a long distance footpath, passes through Shugborough Park and over the Essex Bridge. There are three churches in the village. St. Stepehen's is of 1840 by T. Trubshaw, enlarged at a later date by H.J. Stevens. St. John the Baptist is Roman Catholic, of 1828, by Joseph Ireland and was originally at Tixall. It was brought here in 1845 when Tixall passed to an Anglican

Great Haywood, Trent and Mersey canal.

Great Haywood, the Essex Bridge.

Squire. The style of the church is largely Perpendicular. There is also a Non-conformist chapel in the village. The main line railway from Stone to Colwich and Rugeley follows the Trent valley and runs parallel to, and within yards of, the Trent and Mersey Canal. Reggie Smith, a landlord of the Coach and Horses at Great Haywood, commited suicide by hanging himself in the loft of the pub. Ever since then there have been reports of motorists swerving to avoid a man walking in the road, only to find that it was a phantom. In 1976 a girl reported that she had knocked a man down but no body was ever found. In 1066 Great Haywood was part of the ecclesiastical estate of St. Chad's, Lichfield. After the Conquest it passed to the Bishop of Chester, who also controlled Lichfield. In 1086 there were 9 villagers, 5 smallholders and their families, a priest and a mill. The name Haywood probably means 'an enclosure (a "hay") of woodland', but could also mean a 'field surrounded (and so enclosed) by woodland'. **Little Haywood** lies 0·5m. SE of Great Haywood. It has subst-antial older houses with mature gardens, but consists for the most part of modern estates. The Lamb and Flag pub was home to one of the country's earliest revival folksong clubs (circa 1960). In the 19th Century the pub had its own brewery and 3-storey malthouse. The

village of Colwich adjoins Little Haywood to the south-west.

GREAT WYRLEY *1m. SE of Cannock.*

The name Wyrley means 'the bog myrtle glade'. The settlement lies just south of Watling street and today is very much a modern place of estate housing surrounded by old clay pits and coal mines. The parish church of St. Mark was built by T. Johnson in 1845 and lies hidden amongst the houses. Adjacent to the churchyard is the Rectory. There is little more to say about Wyrley except to mention the Wyrley Gang affair which remains a mystery to this day. In the last quarter of the last century the vicar of Great Wyrley was the Rev. Shapurji Edalji, a Parsee converted to Christianity who was married to an English woman. They had a

Great Wyreley, the church of St. Luke.

son called George who was studying to be a lawyer in Birmingham. Between 1888 and 1892 the family received abusive anonymous letters and had hoaxes played on them. It is likely that racial prejudice was the root cause of their problems. In 1902 a horse was found disembowelled in a field. The day after the killing George Edalji was suspected by police even though he had an alibi. Letters arrived threatening more killings. These were signed by G.H. Darby, Captain of the Wyrley Gang. The police accused Edalji of being the author and he was arrested and charged with maiming and killing a horse. Another horse was killed whilst he was under arrest but this was dismissed by the Stafford Police, who investigated the affair, as being the work of his accomplices. What is more, one John Henry Green confessed to the crimes but was never charged. In October 1903 Edalji was tried and found guilty at Stafford Quarter Sessions and sentenced to 7 years in prison. The press believed that there had been an injustice and campaigned for an enquiry. Sir Arthur Conan-Doyle, creator of Sherlock Holmes, investigated the case and concluded that Edalji was innocent. He wrote to this effect in the Daily Telegraph and shortly after an enquiry was held that resulted in Edalji receiving a free pardon, though he did not receive compensation for the 3 years he had been imprisoned. *(For Little Wyrley see Norton Canes).*

GRINDON *3m. N of Waterhouses, which is on the A523, 7m. SE of Leek.*
In 1066 Wulfgeat held it but it was taken from him and given to Robert of Stafford. At the time of Domesday it was waste and no-one

Manifold Valley W of Weag's Bridge.

Grindon, horses on the road to Butterton.

lived there. This is not altogether surprising for it is wild moorland country which may charm the summer visitor but can be a hard place in the winter. In 1947 six RAF men and two press photographers were killed when their aircraft crashed shortly after they had dropped food and other supplies by parachute to the villages of Grindon, Wetton, Onecote and Butterton, which had been cut off for many days by snow, ice and blizzards. Grindon is a sizeable village built on a sloping hill near the top of which is the church of All Saints. This was constructed in 1845 by the Francis brothers. It has a screen of sycamores and is beautifully situated. The font is Norman and there is a memorial to the RAF men who died here. The spire is a landmark for many miles around. Mycock is a very common name in the Grindon area. There are burial mounds in the hills and copper and lead were mined near the village. Less then 1m. E is Weag's Bridge in the

Manifold valley, where the motorist can park and walk along the now surfaced track of the

Grindon, a stone barn.

old railway. Half a mile north up the valley is the famous Thor's Cave. There are steps up to the cave from here but it is a very stiff climb. There is a much easier route from Wetton.

HALES *2·5m. E of Market Drayton.*

The hamlet of Hales lies on the northern slopes of the delightful Coal Brook valley. There is an air of timelessness here. The church of St. Mary is outwardly most impressive. It was built by George Gilbert Scott in 1856. The style is Middle Pointed (late 13th, early 14th Century). On the opposite side of the road, hidden by trees, is the old rectory. Down the lane that leads eastwards is Hales Hall and the Home Farm. The track continues past the farm and in the west laneside corner of the second field, to the south, is the site of a Roman Villa

Hales, the church of St. Mary.

(SJ.722.337). It lies on a slope above a stream. The villa has been excavated and revealed a small 2nd Century house with a portico and a separate bath-house. Between Hales and Almington (1m. NW) the road passes through sand and gravel quarries. To the north are disused pits and to the south the large ARC workings, still very much a going concern as the inhabitants of Almington, who have to but up with enormous lorries thundering past their houses, will all to volubly inform you. Ready-mixed concrete is also sold from here. Blore Heath lies 1m. north of Hales. This was the site of the Battle of Blore Heath, the second battle of the War of the Roses, which took place on 23rd September 1459. The Lancastrian forces under Lord Audley were defeated and Audley was killed. A cross marks the spot where he fell (SJ.716.353). It is best approached from the A53 Market Drayton to Loggerheads road. It lies in a

Hales, Audley's Cross.

167

Hales, Tyreley Locks.

cornfield almost due south of Audley's Cross Farm. It cannot be seen from the road because of the way the land falls. From Almington a lane runs due south, past the entrance to the quarries to Old Spring's Hall about a mile away. This is an attractive early 19th Century ashlar house of 5 bays with a pillared porch. It lies at the end of a long drive in a small well-kept park and is the registered office of Benfield, the house builders. From here a lane runs to Tyrley Locks on the Shropshire Union Canal, which here marks the boundary between Shropshire and Staffordshire. There are 5 locks, covering a rise of 33ft., a small souvenir shop and a few cottages. In the summer it is quite busy here. The bridge was constructed by Thomas Telford. One mile north of Tyreley Locks is Peatswood Hall. The black and white house has a large park and a handsome brick stable block of 7 bays and 2 storeys, with a central pediment, domed cupola and 3-part doorway.

Hales, Bishop's Wood from near Chipnall.

HALMER END *4m. NW of Newcastle-under-Lyme.*

A small mining village on the B5367. It lies on the edge of a bluff and looks down on coal mines old and new. There is little in the way of a centre, but terraced houses abound, many of which have been affected by settlement. Lately a new problem arose with earth tremours caused by blasting at the huge new open-cast coal pits at the Bateswood site which adjoins the built-up area. It was an underground explosion at the Minnie Pit on 12th January 1918 that put Halmer End on the front pages of the national press. The Malloch (death roll) was 155 men and boys. It was, and still is, the worst mining disaster to have occured in the North Staffordshire Coalfield. Wilfred Owen wrote a poem:

"And I saw white bones in the cinder-shard
Bones without number;
For many hearts with coal were charred
And few remember....".

Actually the tragedy is well remembered with plaques in most of the local churches and a monument by the pit-head mound that caps the old shaft. The mound itself is a memorial and is fenced around. To reach the site leave Halmer End on the road to Shraley Brook. At the bottom of the hill the road bears left past the Railway pub, through the brick abutments of the now demolished railway bridge, past the station masters' house (on the right of the bridge), and about 100 yards down the road there is a dirt road to the left. The Minnie Pit shaft mound is about 50yds. down this road on the left. Opposite are spoil banks and the brick foundations of the steam engine house, and behind them is the engine pool. Behind the shaft-pit-mound and stone memorial, and running parallel with the dirt track (which is itself an old mineral tramway route), is the embankment of the disused branch line. On the other side of this is part of the open-cast workings of the Bateswood Pit. This will probably be worked out by 1990. Podmore Lane (which starts opposite the rendered Methodist church of

1867), leads to a Nature Reserve, which incorporates the spoil banks of the old Podmore Colliery. The photograph of the open-cast pit was taken from the end of this lane. The main road to Shraley Brook passes a brick built Congregational Chapel of 1900 that is being used as a hay barn. **Shraley Brook** consists of little more than the Rising Sun pub and a handfull of cottages. The hamlet was devastated by the Minnie Pit explosion because most of the men and boys who lived there worked at the pit and many were killed. Two whole generations were virtually wiped out in a few minutes.

HAMMERWICH *1·5m. NE of Brownhills and 3·5m. SW of Lichfield.*

A most pleasant village close to the depressing estates of Brownhills and Burntwood, but still very rural. The church of St. John the Baptist stands on a hill. It was built in 1872 of red sandstone, but there has been a church here for over a thousand years. There are good views from the churchyard over rich

Halmer End, the Minnie Pit memorial.
Halmer End, Bateswood open cast pit.

169

Hammerwich, the windmill.

arable farmland in one direction and over part of the village and a white embattled windmill, now converted into a dwelling, in the other. To the south-east of the church is a lane called The Lion's Den. We have come across this unusual name in several places but can find no satisfactory explanation as to its origin. There is a duck pond here and another lane runs from this junction to a very substantial and very ugly footbridge over the railway that leads to a field. Someone, it seems, insisted that their right of way be honoured come hell or high water. There are new houses in Hammerwich but they have been very carefully integrated. The village is undoubtedly of ancient origin, and the Lichfield Morrismen perform an old dance called the Vandals of Hammerwich to a very good and brisk tune. This is also used for another dance called The Lichfield Green-hill Bower Processional. There is a cottage hospital here named after Thomas Barber Wright, the originator of Hospital Sunday.

HAMSTALL RIDWARE *See Ridware.*

HANBURY *7m. ESE of Uttoxeter and 2·5m. WSW of Tutbury.*
From the Uttoxeter to Tutbury road in the Dove valley the village of Hanbury looks splendid, set on a bluff beyond emerald green fields. One drives up the hill with great expectations only to meet with disenchantment. The village must once have been a charming place. The venerable church has ancient yews and several old buildings set

around it, including a good black and white cottage. The colour-washed water tower vies with the church for dominancy of the skyline, and from some angles gains the day. That is acceptable; what is not is the mass of tidy, orthodox but oh so ordinary modern housing that has destroyed the ancientness of the place. The Victorian School of 1848 is neo-Tudor with a quaint turret, and though not an attraction does little harm. (Queen Victoria made a personal contribution to the cost of building it). The church of St. Werburgh is beautifully positioned on the edge of the bluff that overlooks the broad

Hanbury, the church from the Dove valley.

plain of the River Dove. It has several treasures including three fragments of 14th Century glass by Coventry craftsmen displayed in the south aisle window. The centre piece depicts Christ crucified and wearing a purple robe. There is a fine monument to Sir John de Hanbury, believed to have died in 1303. If the tomb sculpture was made shortly after his death this would make it the oldest alabaster figure in England. The crossed legs indicate that the knight had been on a crusade to the Holy Land, and the dog at his feet shows that he died in peace. In the sanctuary, to the left of the altar, is a tomb to Ralph Adderly, Knight, who died in 1595. His likeness is engraved in line on the top slab, along with that of his two wives, and on the sides are sculptures of their children. Opposite is a monument to Sir Charles Egerton, Axe Bearer in the Forest of Needwood, who died in 1624. He reclines on one elbow, dressed in armour, for he was a soldier and commanded Queen Elizabeth's armies in Ireland. In the north-east corner of the Sanctuary, above the vicar's desk, are the stern busts of two Puritan Ladies in typical dress. They are Katherine Agard, died 1628, and her daughter Anne Woollocke, died 1657. Statues of Puritans are rare because they normally despised such imagery. Sir John Egerton, son of Sir Charles, is buried at the east end of the north aisle. He died in 1662 and wished to be buried in the chancel, but legend has it that his sister could not bear the thought of him lying within the gaze of Puritan Ladies, and so had his tomb placed around the corner out of their sight. St. Werburgh, to whom the church is dedicated, was the daughter of Wulfere, King of Mercia (657-74). The King was pagan but his Queen, Erminhilde, was Christian and she brought up her children as Christians. After the King's death Werburgh became a nun. At the request of King Ethelred she founded 4 monasteries - at Trentham, Repton, Weedon and Hanbury. The nunnery at Hanbury, founded in 680, was her favourite and it was here that she requested to be buried. She actually died at Trentham and the nuns there wished to keep her body. However, legend has it that they were overcome by a deep sleep and the nuns from Hanbury stole the body back. Hanbury became a place of pilgrimage. The well behind the church is still called the Pilgrim's Well and miracles were said to occur at Hanbury. At the end of

Hanbury, the Fauld crater from the air.

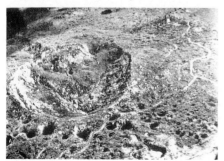

the 9th Century the Danes invaded the area. The saint's remains were removed to Chester for safety and her shrine is in the Cathedral to this day. In 875 the Danes looted and burned both the church and the monastery at Hanbury — both were probably made of wood — and there are now no

Hanbury, medieval stained glass

remains of either building. The church we see today was begun by the Normans. The massive columns of the north arcade, the slender columns of the south arcade and the base of the tower are of about 1100, but the church was virtually rebuilt in the 14th Century with further alterations and additions in the 15th and 19th Centuries. The chancel was rebuilt in 1862. There is much decoration around the altar. The walls have painted scenes and the ceiling is intricately patterned. The reredos, font and pulpit are all of alabaster, as are the central floor tiles. The 14th Century glass already mentioned was dedicated as a memorial to

Hanbury, Sir John de Hanbury's tomb.

those who died as a result of the Great Hanbury Explosion. During the Second World War bombs were stored in the disused underground workings of the Fauld gypsum mine, 0·5m. to the east of Hanbury. In November 1944 there was terrible explosion when part of the ammunition stored there was accidentally detonated. The village suffered considerable damage and 62 people were killed. The huge crater is still there (SK.183.278). Tutbury alabaster is well known, but in fact most of the workings are closer to Hanbury. There has been a long history of gypsum and alabaster mining in the area. The relationship of gypsum to alabaster is this: anhydrite plus water creates gypsum; gypsum plus more water creates alabaster and even more water dissolves the alabaster away i.e. the beds are 'washed out'. Alabaster is hard, fine grained, takes a polish and can be easily carved and is usually found near the surface. Small open-cast pits were worked from at least the 14th Century. In 1374 John of Gaunt ordered 6 cartloads from his quarry at Castle Hayes Park, 1·25m. ESE of *Hanbury, the British Gypsum mine at Fauld.*

Hanbury. (He wanted it for the building of his wife's tomb at St. Paul's Cathedral in London.) The quarry was extensively worked during the 15th Century and was described by Dr. Plot as 'incomparably the best'. Alabaster was quarried right up to the late 19th Century when, about 1880, mining with a shaft and tunnels commenced. Today the only mine operating in the area is that of British Gypsum at Fauld. The blue sheds (SK.182.286) that cover the surface machinery and the processing works can be seen quite clearly from the Uttoxeter to Tutbury road. What is not evident is the extent of the workings which cover an area of 10 square miles, mainly in the south of the mine-head. The rock is blasted and moved by mechanical diggers. Pillars about 20 ft. square are left to support the ground above. They represent a quarter of the seam — three quarters is extracted. It is a huge concern with an output of between 500,000 tons and 750,000 tons per year. The gypsum is used almost wholly for the manufacture of plaster. There are still a very few areas, mostly near

173

the surface, where alabaster grade gypsum can still be extracted, but these are nearly worked out. Alabaster is cut by sawing. It is not an economically viable business and there is only one local customer, who has an occasional block specially cut for him on request. At the entrance to the mine is a red brick house with stone dressings, leaded lights and black and white gables. This is known locally as The Manor and was built in 1903 by the owner of the nearby Manor Farm. Some of the roof timbers are of 1680, but where they came from is not known. The

Hanbury, the Manor at Fauld.

drive is lined with pieces of gypsum rock. A quarter of a mile east of the mine is a large red brick farmhouse with a half-timbered jettied gable and porch, and good brick barns of 1875. There are moated sites at Moat Farm 2m. NNE on the A515 Sudbury road (fragmentary 240ft. x 210ft.), and at Woodend, 1m. S of Hanbury (rectangular 190ft. x 210ft.). Both are marked on the 1·25 inch Ordnance Survey map. One mile SW of Hanbury is New Lodge where both George III and William IV were frequent guests. Here also, in 1849, died George Edward Anson, Keeper of the Privy Purse to Queen Victoria.

HANLEY *2·75m. ENE of Newcastle under Lyme.*

Waterloo Road at Cobridge on the outskirts of Hanley has some large Victorian houses, the old homes of master potters and businessmen, though today they are mostly in a bad way. Many of the houses have been sub-divided into bedsits and rented out to students and the unemployed; others stand empty and derelict. From the crossroads at Cobridge there is a good view of Hanley, standing atop its hill with skyscraper flats and other tall buildings, pronouncing that this is now the unchallenged centre of the Potteries. The name Hanley is Anglo-Saxon and means 'the clearing in the high wood'. Today it is a bright, modern shopping centre. As well as the usual chain stores there is a department store (very much a dying breed) and many individual, privately owned shops. The central area is now largely pedestrianised and adjoining it is a huge new shopping centre in the course of construction. The shops dominate the town. many a visitor must have come and gone and never seen the churches, the local government offices or the handsome new art gallery and museum. The Victoria Hall, which adjoins the back of the

Hanley, terraced houses in Ogden Street.

174

Hanley, the Upper Market Square.

Town hall, is known throughout the North Midlands as a concert hall. Delius, Elgar and Beecham have appeared here but in recent years it has become a place at which you are more likely to see popular singers and rock groups. The Hall was designed by the

Hanley, canal marina at Etruria.

borough surveyor, Mr. Joseph Lobley, and opened in 1888. The Town Hall itself was originally built as a hotel – the Queens Hotel – in 1869 to a design by Robert Scrivener. It is in a French style, built of brick with stone dressings. The modern block of Unity House is the present centre of administration. Hanley has been so much redeveloped that there is very little that is old, and even less that is especially attractive. There is very little evidence of the pottery industry that flourished here. In the centre the only buildings one feels obliged to mention are the Old Library of 1818 in Pall Mall, that used to be the British School and Art School, with an unusual attic storey added in 1880; the

new library which is truly awful; the new museum and art gallery which is superb both as a building and as a museum – the spitfire museum is here also; the Post Office in Tontine Street of 1906 by John Rutherford, a good, old-fashioned classical building; the Market Hall, also in Tontine Street, smoke blackened and unfriendly; the Italianate Bethesda Chapel of 1819 in Albion Street with a facade of 1859; the brick parish church of St. John in Tower Road of 1790 with a polygonal apse of 1872 and pedimented doorways with Tuscan columns; and, finally, St. Mark's in Snow Hill, of 1832, which is possibly the largest and finest Commissioner's church in Staffordshire. Near the church, at the corner of Hope Street and Hanover Street, is the Five Towns Restaurant, the birthplace of Arnold Bennett. Also born in Hanley was John Smith, the Commander of the ill-fated 'Titanic'. In 1910 Lady Scott, the wife of Captain Scott of the Antartic, made a bronze sculpture of John Smith and offered it to the town of Hanley. It was refused and now stands in the Museum Gardens in Lichfield. In recent years the Commanders' family have endeavoured, without success, to obtain the bronze for Hanley. Sir Stanley Mathews, in his time the greatest footballer in the world, was the son of a Hanley barber. He played first-class professional football for 38 years! In 1987 he unveiled a statue of himself in the pedestrianised area of the town, at the top of the hill near the BHS and Boots stores. Perhaps Hanley's most famous

Hanley, Etruria Hall.

son was not born here but was adopted. Josiah Wedgwood came to the town in 1769. The Trent and Mersey Canal was in the course of construction and to take advantage of it he built a large new factory and a large new house for himself in what was then a rural area on the edge of the town. The house stood on the hill, overlooking the works and the cottages he built for his workers. The house still stands. He sited the factory at the point where the newly turnpiked Leek to Newcastle-under-Lyme road crossed the course of the canal. Wedgwood had been chief advocate of the canal and it was he who drummed up enough support to make it possible. He was a major investor and also the treasurer of the canal company. The Grand Trunk Canal, as it was originally called, joined the River Trent at Wilden Ferry, near Burton on Trent, crossed the county and left through the Harecastle tunnel to the Cheshire plain and thence to the River Mersey. Wedgwood had already been largely responsible for the turnpiking of several roads in North Staffordshire and

through his energetic championing of improvements in transport became the accepted leader of the Master Potters. Wedgwood called his new canal-side industrial estate Etruria after the classical Etruscan pottery that he so admired. The house was called Etruria Hall. It still stands, a 5-bay, pedimented mansion with wings added at later date, designed by Joseph Pickford. The new factory was something of a landmark because it was the first large, modern factory dedicated to the production of quality prestige ware. Wedgwood himself was an extremely industrious man, full of ideas, both technical and commercial. For example, he invented new glazes (several of which involved the use of poisons such as lead and chlorine and which killed many of his workers) and had a London showroom in Greek Street, Soho run by his friend Thomas Bentley. After many successful years at Etruria the company moved to another green-field site at Barlaston in 1939. The Etruria factory was sold to the Shelton Iron and Steel Company which later became a part

Hanley, canal scene.

Hanley, a Spitfire at the museum.

Hanley, evangelists in Piccadilly.

of British Steel. British Steel demolished Wedgwood's works in the 1960's without any objection from the local council. All that remains is the enigmatic Roundhouse — no-one knows what purpose it served. Ironically, the steel works was closed a few years later and has retracted to a small rolling mill sitting amidst a vast acreage of unused ground. Some of this was cleared and landscaped in the 1980's and in 1986 the National Garden Festival was held there. Millions of pounds were spent on the venture and most of these millions were not recovered because attendances were so low. Etruria Hall and the steel mill lie just NE of the junction of the A500 (Queensway) and the A53 Hanley to Newcastle-under-Lyme road. Most of the ruins there are of the conveyor belt system which was used to bring in coal from the colliery on the other side of the A500. Between the Shelton works and the centre of Hanley are the new offices

of the Evening Sentinel, and past them the handsome canal marina around which have been built some good brick houses, a pub and a waterways office. Hanley has 2 parks. South of the town is the orthodox Victorian park of 1894 by T.H. Mawson, with a pavilion by Dan Gibson, and N of the town is Central Forest Park of 1971. The latter was created out of 80 acres of derelict colliery workings and 15 acres of old clay pits (called marl pits locally). The park will need some time to mature but it is a brave effort. At the entrance is the winding wheel of the Deep Pit. Other reclaimation schemes include the 49 acres of Monks-Neil Park at Fegg Hayes and the Grange Scheme which stretches from Etruria to Burslem.

HARLASTON *7m. E of Lichfield.*
Harlaston lies in the gentle green valley of the meandering River Mease. There are some good houses in the main street. The Manor House is a timber-framed building of about 1600. It stands close to the church which has an early 18th Century marble tablet to Anne, Lady Egerton. The jewel in Harlaston's crown is Haselour Hall, 0·5m. WSW of the village. In fact, the exterior front, with the exception of the small, central 'old porch' gable, was restored-rebuilt in 1885. The core of the house is original and is dated at about 1600. The large mullioned and transomed windows, the elaborate but not uniform decoration in the studding, and the maze of chimneys give this mansion great

charm. It stands at the end of a drive in park-like grounds with oak trees before and a small wood beyond. To the right and rear and attached to the house, is a medieval stone chapel of about 1370 though the thin turret and spire are of an earlier 13th Century style. On the roadside is an entrance lodge of the late 19th Century by Sir Edwin Luytens. Haselour Hall had many owners in the Middle Ages. The house passed to the Ardenes, the Stanleys, the Smythes, the Huddlestones, and the Brookes who took possession in 1557. It was probably the Brookes who built the Hall that we now see today. In the 16th Century it had a double moat, now filled in, and a guard house, now demolished. By the 18th Century it had become a farmhouse and the chapel was used as a cowshed. In the early 19th Century Thomas Neville began to restore the Hall and this was completed in the 1880's by a Mr. A.H. Trafford. At this time the left-hand gable was added and the chapel richly restored in high Victorian Roman Catholic style. At the time of Domesday Book Harleston was a substantial village with 21 families, 2 serfs and 2 mills. Before the Norman Conquest the manor had belonged to Earl Algar (or Aelfgar). This was only one of several properties he owned in the county so perhaps a few words about him would not be out of place. His father was Earl Leofric of Mercia. The House of Leofric was one of the 2 leading families in England. The other was the House of Godwine, Earls of Wessex, to which Earl Harold (who was to be killed at the Battle of Hastings) belonged. Algar was the Earl of East Anglia. In 1055 he was charged with treason and stripped of his title and lands by the Witan, the powerful 'Council to the King'. Exactly what he had done we do not know. Algar left England and went to Ireland where he raised 18 ships companies of Vikings. He then joined Grruffydd ap Llewelyn, the King of Gwynedd and Powys, the 2 largest kingdoms in North Wales. Together they raided and captured Hereford. Earl Harold was given 'the militia of all England' and drove the invaders to the Black Mountain. At a

Harleston, pollarded trees by the R. Mease.

meeting in the hills above the Wye a treaty was made and Algar was reinstated as Earl of East Anglia. In 1057 Algar's father, Leofric, died. Algar inherited his fathers estate but shortly after, in 1058, was outlawed for a second time. Again, for what reason we do not know. he returned to Wales and it was

Harleston, Haselour Hall.

probably at this time that his daughter, Aldith, married Gruffydd ap Llewellyn. Algar and Gruffydd then allied themselves with Harold Hardrada, the Viking chief from the north, and together they rampaged through England. Little is known of this attack but shortly after Algar was once again restored as Earl of East Anglia. Four years later, probably in 1062, he died. In 1063 Earl Harold and his brother, Tostig, attacked Wales and won many victories. Gruffydd was killed by his own men and his head given to Harold, who in turn gave it to King Edward. Harold was now the first nobleman of England and began to seriously consider his claim to the throne.

HATHERTON *1·25m. W of Cannock.*
The hamlet lies north of the part half-timbered and part red brick pub called the Four Crosses at Four Crosses on the A5. Hatherton Hall is set beside the lake in its small park. It is a late Georgian stuccoed house of 1817 in Tudor Gothic style of 5 bays with an ornate central porch. It was the home of the Walhouse family one of whom married the Littleton heiress of Pillaton and

Teddesley (both near Penkridge 3 miles away) and who became Lord Hatherton.

HAUGHTON *4m. WSW of Stafford.*
The village lies along the A518 Stafford to Newport road. There is a lay-by with a small shopping centre, a village hall and a garage. The church of St. Giles has a 13th Century tower, north wall and NE chantry. The rest was mostly rebuilt in 1887 by J. L. Pearson at the behest of the vicar, the Rev. G.T. Royds. There is a stained glass window in memory of Clement Fletcher Royds, an RAF fighter pilot, who was killed in action in 1945. Four Royds have been vicars here. Engraved in alabaster is the likeness of The Rev. Nicholas Graviner, died 1520. Close to the church, on the main road, is Haughton Old Hall, a delightfully lopsided black and white house of the 16th Century. Nearby, on the other side of the road, there used to be another very good timber-framed house but this was burned down several years ago. The owner had applied for permission to demolish the listed building on several occasions and had been turned down. His dog died in the fire. On the edge of the village, in the Newport direction, is a tiny cruck cottage. This has been very much restored and a large new bungalow attached. The whole is quite acceptable. Almost all the new development in the village has taken place on the north side, where considerable numbers of middle-

Haughton Hall.

market dwellings provide accommodation for commuters to the county town.

HAWKSMOOR 1·5m. ENE of Cheadle.

Hawksmoor is not a village. It is a National Trust Nature Reserve of 250 acres and lies adjacent to the B417 between Cheadle and Oakamoor. On the Bunter pebble beds and sandstone there are bilberry, dwarf oaks, bracken, scrub and birch as well as Forestry Commission plantations of sycamore, beech, pine, fir cypress and hemlock. The Crabtree coal seam outcrops near the River Churnet. In Lightoaks Wood, just SW of Oakamoor, in a hut which was once the home of 'Charcoal Jack', one of several charcoal-burners who were employed right up to the end of the last century by Bolton's copper works. At East Wall Farm (SK.036.448) iron slag has been unearthed, which suggests the there was probably a furnace here. East Wall was called Heystiswell in the 12th Century. There are three nature trails, of 2·5m., 1·5m. and 1·5m.

HEDNESFORD 1·5m. NE of Cannock.

Hednesford (pronounced Hensford) is a place of old coal pits and miners' terraced houses; yet in the centre of the town is the Anglesey Hotel. This most attractive house was built in 1831 by Edmund Peel of the Fazeley family that produced the Prime Minister, Sir Robert Peel. He used it as a summer residence and trained his race horses on the Hednesford Hills. (Race horses are still trained at Upper Longdon, 3m. to the NE.) It is very doubtful that anyone would build a holiday home in Hednesford these

Hednesford, the Anglesey Hotel.

Hednesford, the grotto at the R.C. church.

days, but at that time it was a little country village in the foothills of Cannock Chase, and no-one could forsee that from about 1850 onwards it would be vandalised both above and below ground. The parish church

Hednesford, iron foundry at Rawnsley.

of St. Peter is of 1868 by T.H. Rushworth, but without the tower he meant it to have. Today the parish church is upstaged by the dramatic lines of the Roman Catholic church of Our Lady of Lourdes, designed by G.B. Cox of Birmingham and built between 1927-33. Architects are scathing but it certainly jollys up the place a bit. The style is very Continental, a feeling enhanced by the tall pine trees to the front and the grotto to the side. In the evening sunlight the stone fairly glows. The Cross Keys Inn at Old Hednesford is timber-framed and dated 1746. To the NE by 0·5m., high in the Hednesford Hills, is Hednesford Raceway. Here a large circular water reservoir (built in 1878 and abandoned because of settlement fractures in 1916) has buildings, caravans and a motley array of fences which have been erected to protect a venue now devoted to stock car racing. The area around is a heathland common with long views over violated landscapes. Cock-fighting was practised at Cockpit Hill, and prize fights took place here. There was a horse-race

Hednesford, view from Littleworth looking N.

track and several stables operated locally. Three Grand National winners, Ereman 1907, Jenkinstown 1910, and Grakle 1913 were trained by Thomas Coulthwaite at Hazelslade. In 1873 a vast army excercise was held between Etching Hill at Rugeley and the Hednesford Hills which was watched by some 150,00 spectators assembled on Rawnsley Hill.

HIGH OFFLEY *See Offley.*

HILDERSTONE *3·5m. E of Stone.*
A linear village in attractive undulating country north of the county town. In 1762 an alternative road from Stafford to

Hilderstone, the church of Christ.

Manchester, by way of Sandon and Hilderstone, was turnpiked — that is, was greatly improved and paid for by the charging of a toll. The charming church of 1827, by Thomas Trubshaw, is set in a most attractive church yard with clipped yews and a variety of other trees. It is built of stone with lancet windows and a short spire. There are monuments to the Bourne family who paid for the church and who lived at Hilderstone Hall, a rendered Georgian house set in a small park. Just south of the Hall, by a wood with 2 small pools, is a moated site. It is rectangular, 400ft. x 320ft., with an extra bank on the north side and altered on the south side. The Manor House lies by the road 0·25m. NE of the Hall. Most of the village cottages are of red brick and lie on a hill at the bottom of which is Lower Farm, an 18th Century 4-bay house. At the back of the farm are fields laid to pasture. One of the meadows covers a gentle rise and here are some of the best preserved medieval field strips one could ever hope to find. They can be seen quite clearly from the road. In fact the Sandon/Hilderstone area is well known as an area where the old 3 field strip system lingered long, even into the 19th Century.

HILL CHORLTON *See Chapel Chorlton.*

HILL RIDWARE *See Ridware.*

HILTON *(near Wolverhampton) 5·5m. NE of Wolverhampton.*
Hilton is best known today for the Hilton Park Service Station on the M6 motorway which was built in the well-wooded grounds of Hilton Park Hall. There is no village here. The Hall stands to the east of the suburban areas of Featherstone (where there is an open prison) and Shareshill, both of which lie on the Cannock road NE of Wolverhampton. It is a very large and very fine house built in the early 18th Century of brick with stone quoins and dressings. The main front faces the lake. It has a 5-bay recessed

181

centre with 2 wings of 3 bays, all of 2 storeys with an attic storey. The pediment is curved and decorated with vases, scrolls and garlands. The modern entrance is at the side through an impressive coach porch which was installed by the Victorians. The interior is very fine with panelled rooms and an excellent staircase. The manors of Hilton and Essington belonged to the Swynnerton family in the Middle Ages. In 1562 they passed by marriage to the Vernons. It was Henry Vernon who built the present Hall. On raised ground 0·5m. S of the house is Portobello Tower, a battlemented folly that commemorates Admiral Vernon's capture of Portobello in 1739. Closer to the house, amongst trees, is a moat, the site of the early manor house, for Hilton is an ancient settlement that had an ancient custom. The Lord of Essington owed homage to the greater Lord of Hilton. Every New Year's Day the Lord of Hilton filled with water a

Hilton Hall, near Featherstone.

brass figurine in the shape of a man who had an enlarged symbol of his manhood. The figure, called Jack O'Hylton, was placed on a fire and steam issued through his mouth. This fanned the fire and made it burn more brightly. The Lord of Essington then brought in a goose which was driven 3 times around the fire before being killed, cooked and dressed. The bird was then served to the Lord of Hilton, by either the Lord of Essington or his bailiff, and the Lord of Hilton duly granted the lesser Lord a further year's tenancy. On the authority of Dr. Plot we know that the ceremony was being performed at least as early as 1650. Hilton Hall remained in the posession of the Vernon family until some 40 years ago when it was sold. Jack O'Hylton is now with a senior member of the family in a village near Kington, Herefordshire. The Hall was taken over by a religious order and became a kind of Catholic guest house. In recent times it was sold again and has been acquired by Tarmac Construction Ltd., who have renovated the Hall, the grounds and the outbuildings, and have established their Head Office here.It is to be hoped that they might one day replace the hideous green corrugated fence that surrounds the park. One mile SW of the Hall, close to the main road, is the site of Hilton Main Colliery.

HIMLEY *5m. SSW of Wolverhampton.*
The small village lies on the A499 Wolverhampton to Kidderminster road. Himley House Hotel is the building that catches the eyes. It was built as the dower house for Himley Hall, the entrance to which is off the B4176 to Dudley. Himley is an ancient manor but it is as the home of the Lords of Dudley that it achieved a degree of fame. After a fire had destroyed their house at Dudley Castle in 1750 the family moved to Himley. Dud Dudley, the illegitimate son of the 5th Lord, had operated one of the first iron furnaces in the country to be fuelled by coal at Himley some 100 years before. On taking residence at Himley the family set

182

Himley Hall.

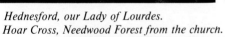

Hednesford, our Lady of Lourdes.
Hoar Cross, Needwood Forest from the church.

Hilderstone, old fields at Lower Farm.

183

Himley, the church of St. Michael.

the long 9-bay south facade and its giant Ionic portico. The grounds were at least partly landscaped by Lancelot Brown who dammed the stream to create 5 pools. The Great Pool is a major feature of the gardens around the house, now the haunt of fishermen. In 1836 Sir Stephen Glynn, Gladstone's brother-in-law, opened his Oak Farm ironworks within a mile to the SW of the Hall which was soon 'rendered uninhabitable' by the smoke and fumes. The Dudleys were getting a taste of their own medicine. The family decided to move and bought Witley Court in Worcestershire in 1845 which they turned into a veritable palace. In 1937 the Duke of Kent and Princess Marina stayed at Himley for their honeymoon. The Hall was finally sold in 1947 to the national Coal Board who used it to house their Regional Offices. In the 1960's they moved out and the Hall was bought jointly by the Borough Councils of Wolverhampton and Dudley who used it as an extension of the Wolverhampton Polytechnic, as a Teachers' Resource Centre (not training college) and as a library book store. Today the Hall is empty. In the grounds is a country park and a golf course, and in the high walled garden is a nodel village and a miniature railway. Public events are often held in the grounds which remain an oasis of green surrounded on almost all sides by the industry and suburban housing of Kingswinford, Gornal, Sedgley, Gospel End and Wombourne. The church of St. Michael (1764) has been spoiled externally by the application of cement rendering, but still looks well standing amongst the clipped yew trees in the churchyard. Inside is a lovely curved parapet on the west gallery and a monument to Rosemary, Viscountess Ednam, who was killed in an air crash at Meopham, Kent. On the right-hand side of Himley Hall Hotel, is a private Garden of Remberance. It is a secret garden wih a stream, a small stone temple with plain columns and a hipped roof, and 4 gravestones by Eric Gill to John Jeremy

about exploiting the countryside around. Between 1776 and 1807 the Wards of Dudley promoted 5 Enclosure Acts by which they obtained over 2,000 acres, supposedly for agricultural improvement but in practice carefully chosen for their mineral wealth — ironstone, coal, limestone, fire-clay and glass house pot-clay. What is more, these Acts enabled the family to avoid paying compensation for settlement damage caused by underground mining operations. Much to their shame they continued to shun their responsibilities into the present century. Unbelievable when you consider that William Dudley, 11th Lord Ward, later to become the 1st Earl of Dudley (1860), was the second richest (some say the richest) nobleman in England. Himley Hall had been rebuilt about 1720. Of this time is the west front of 7 bays and a tall central pediment. The 3-bay wings of this facade were added in 1824-7 by William Atkinson who also built

Ward (died 1929 aged 9), Georgina Countess of Dudley, Rosemary Viscountess Ednam (both of whom died in 1930) and the 2nd Earl of Dudley, died 1932. In 1987 the body of the 2nd Earl, William Humble Ward, was brought back from Paris where he had died and been buried. He was interred in the garden here. If he been brought back any earlier Death Duties would have been payable. The 2nd Earl had been Viceroy of Ireland (1902) and Governor-General of Australia (1908). In 1918 he divorced his wife, Rachel, and 2 years later she drowned whilst swimming in County Galway. In 1924 the 2nd Earl married the musical comedy star Gertie Millar, widow of popular composer Lionel Monckton. They lived mostly in their villa at Le Touquet. The Earl died in 1932 and 20 years later his widow passed away. She was buried at Himley but her grave was desecrated by thieves searching for the Countesses' jewels which they believed had been interred with her. The Glynne Arms, better known as the Crooked House, can be found down a lane off the road from Himley to Dudley. About 0·75m. S of Himley House Hotel (on the left-hand side if heading south), is Holbeche (or Holbeache) House, an early 17th Century brick house much altered in the 19th Century. Here lived the Catholic recusant, Stephen Littleton, and here on the 17th November 1605 Guy Fawkes' fellow conspirators, Catesby, Winter, Digby et al, were besieged. Some were shot dead and others captured, taken to London and executed.

HINTS 2·5m. WSW of Tamworth.

The village lies 0·25m. S of Watling Street (the A5). It is a charming and ancient place set amongst rolling timber-clad hills. The name is Celtic, derived from 'hynt' meaning a road. The lane to the village leads downhill and forks right and left at a large farm. The right fork, which has 'no access' signs, is the old road to Canwell. It leads down to a ford across the Bourne Brook, which upstream from here is called the Black Brook. On the

Hints, the village from the A5.

right-hand side of the lane, at its junction with the stream, is an area of very much disturbed ground. Here are the remains and waterfalls of the old Hints Hall water gardens. The old Hall was pulled down after the Second World War and has been replaced by a more modest modern villa. Just uphill from the rough ground, at the bottom of the adjacent field is an area in which Roman coins have been found by the local metal detecting club. This is the likely site of a Roman hostelry or mansio. Downstream is the site of a late medieval ironworks and forge that was powered by a water mill (SK.167.023). There was another forge in Rookery Lane (SK.155.029). Local people have noticed that the tracks near Bangley

Hints, circle of trees on low mound.

Farm are magnetic; they were partly constructed with material taken from the furnace slag heaps which still contained quantities of iron. A pasture at the site of the forge is called Hammer Mill Close. Iron was worked at Hints from the end of the 16th

185

Century to at least the middle of the 18th Century. The left-hand fork of the lane from the A5 leads to the village. Here are a variety of houses, both old and new, and the church. there is no pub and no shop. The present church of St. Bartholomew was built by Oldrid Scott in 1832. It is of yellow stone with red stone dressings and has lancet windows. Inside there are monuments to Sir Thomas Lawley, died 1779, Robert Lawley (Lord Warlock), died 1834 and Sir Francis Lawley, died 1851, all of Canwell Hall, which stood 1·5m. SSW of Hints. Below the church the lane comes to an end at the bridge over the brook that leads to a farm. The valley is

Hints, the old road to Canwell.

delightful here. Sheep graze in meadows surrounded by wooded hills. Joining the stream by the bridge is an overgrown drainage channel. This was dug out by Italian prisoners of war. In the grounds of the old Hall are some very superior modern houses. It is little wonder that this charming spot has

been inhabited since Iron Age times. There is a large circular prehistoric burial mound called the Gold's Clump (60yds. in diameter) on the land of Elford Low Farm, close to the A5 just west of the lane that leads to Hints, and in the hills around are likely sites for others. South-west of the ford at SK.147.026 is a circular clump of trees on a hill ridge. Such features were often deliberately cultivated in more recent times as route landmarks for livestock drovers, but they can also indicate ancient burial places or areas of religious significance. Even though the trees in such groupings may only be some 100 years old farmers and local people often plant new trees when the old ones die and so keep such living memorials alive for many centuries. One mile NE of Hints on the road to Hopwas is the quarry from which the stone for Tamworth church was taken. It is now embowered in trees and is called The Devil's Dressing Room.

HIXON *2m. SE of Weston, which is 5m. NE of Stafford.*
A village on a hill east of the busy A51. In recent times the settlement has acquired much new housing mostly occupied by commuters to the county town. There is a scruffy industrial estate and a church of 1848 by Gilbert Scott. Between the village and the main road is a disused wartime aerodrome, the old buildings of which are used as warehouses. To the SW of the village are two delightfully named farm-hamlets: Swansmoor and Tolldish.

HOAR CROSS *2·5m. ESE of Abbots Bromley and 10m. N of Lichfield.*
There is no village at Hoar Cross, only scattered cottages and farms. The area lay in the medieval Forest of Needwood and is still well-wooded. It has been suggested that the cross in the name may refer to an old boundary marker between the parishes of Yoxall and Ridware. The Hall belonged to the Talbots, Earls of Shrewsbury, but was purchased by the Meynells who rebuilt it in

186

1862-71 to a design by Henry Clutton. It is a large house built of brick in Jacobean style. The front has a symmetrical main block with a coach porch to the right and a chapel to the left. The garden side has 3 gables and big mullioned and transomed windows. Medieval banquets are held at the Hall on a commercial basis and it is sometimes rented out for antique fairs and the like. There are woods and formal gardens in the grounds. However, it is the church of Holy Angels which is the great attraction at Hoar Cross. It is a lavish Roman Catholic extravaganza, commissioned by the widow of Hugo Francis Meynell Ingram of Hoar Cross Hall as a memorial to her husband who died in 1871. The architect was G.F. Bodley and he was

Hoar Cross, the Hall Lodge.

Hoar Cross, the church of Holy Angels.

given a free hand with no financial restrictions. Work began in 1872 and the church was dedicated in 1876. At a later date the nave was extended by one bay and the chapels added. The church has nave, chancel, transepts, central tower and chapels in Decorated style. It is oppressively dark inside, more like a mausoleum than a church. This is largely due to the stained glass windows by Bullison and Grylls. It is the sumptuousness of the decoration and the furnishings that is so remarkable. Outstanding amongst these are the carvings of the Stations of the Cross, by the Dutch carvers, Wint and Boeck of Antwerp. They must be priceless. The money spent here was phenomenal — the marble floors, intricately carved walls, the statues of the saints, the

embroidery and vestments (which include a Chasuble said to have belonged to Pope Gregory XI, died 1378), and the lavish tombs and monuments to the Meynell family. Most of the furnishings and decorations were also designed by Bodley and this church is one of his two most highly thought of works. The key to the church is held at the cottages opposite. There are good views of the surrounding country from here. The Parsonage, north of the church, was also probably designed by Bodley.

HOLLINGTON *4m. NW of Uttoxeter.*
Hollington lies on the southern hills of the Staffordshire Moorlands and is famous for its stone quarries. The sandstone obtained from here is soft and easily shaped when freshly quarried, but quickly hardens and becomes very durable on contact with the air. There are 3 varieties of stone, red, white and mottled, and it has been used in the construction of many notable buildings,

Hollington, Ground Hollow Masonry works.

187

Hollington, Great Gate Valley.

such as the medieval Croxden Abbey, 1m. NE of Hollington; the Town Hall, Derby (1828); Drayton Manor (1835); Trentham Hall (1838); the County Buildings, Stafford (1895); the Town Hall, Walsall (1904); and Coventry Cathedral (1962). It has also been used for restoration work on the Cathedrals at Worcester, Hereford and Lichfield. The quarries still operate. At the Ground Hollow Masonry Works the stone is cut and shaped. Hollington village church is St. John's, of 1859-61 by Street. He tried hard here and the

church has several original features. A Roman road leads to the village from Rocester, 3m. to the east. From the village a steep lane leads down to the Raddle Inn and on to the hamlet of Great Gate which lies in a lonely valley with woods and meadows and in the hills beyond are the red and white cliffs of old stone quarries. Time stands still in such places.

HOLLINSCLOUGH *6m. S of Buxton and 2m. NW of Longnor.*

A stone-built hamlet in magnificent Moorland country with hills all around. The River Dove flows by less than 0·25m. to the north and here marks the boundary between Staffordshire and Derbyshire. The church of St. Agnes is attached to a house — as at Lordshill, Snailbeach in Shropshire — and has curious obelisk ornaments on the chancel and porch. There is a prehistoric burial ground 0·25m. SW, near Coatestown on Hollinsclough Moor. On the other side of the Dove are the distinctive limestone outcrops of Chrome Hill (the larger one) and

Hollinsclough, Dowall Dale.

Hollinsclough, Parkhouse Hill.

Parkhouse Hill (the smaller, conically shaped one). Together these are known locally as the Dragon's Back. Between them runs a track to Dowall Hall. The track continues up a rocky valley at the entrance to which is a pre-historic burial cave. This is a narrow fissure in which were found the remains of 10 people ranging in age from a baby to a old man. Buried with them were flints and pottery fragments and the bones of

Hollinsclough, cave in Dowall Dale.

domesticated animals including those of sheep (or goat), pig and the headless body of a dog. These were early Neolithic farmers, and a lovlier spot they could not have found. A spring issues forth from the rocks and gently meanders across the level meadows which are encircled by the hills. The entrance to this delightful, hidden place is at Glutton Bridge on the road between Longnor and Buxton, the B5053. If heading northwards, turn left immediately after having crossed the River Dove. All of this, of course, in Derbyshire but we make no apology for mentioning this enchanting spot.

HOPTON *3m. NE of Stafford.*
Hopton is mentioned in Domesday Book of 1086 when there was a village of at least 13 families. The village is most attractive despite the large number of modern houses. It is spread about on irregular sloping ground. Some houses are on the sandstone edge and have long views to Wales, whilst others shelter in little nooks. Deep lanes and rock outcrops add to the charm, and the village church is notable for having been adapted from an old brick barn in 1876. Hopton Heath lies on the ridge 0·25m. NE. Here is a mobile home park, some scattered cottages and warehouses belonging to the enormous and extensive RAF supply depot that virtually surrounds the village of Hopton. The Battle of Hopton Heath took place on 19th March 1643 and was the only major Civil War battle to be fought in Staffordshire. Canon-balls and musket-shot still occasionally turn up in the fields hereabouts. The Royalist army, under the Earl of Northampton (who was killed), defeated the parliamentary forces under Sir John Gell and Sir William Brereton. The dead of both side were buried at the churches of Sandon and Weston (on Trent).

HOPWAS *3m. W of Tamworth.*
The village lies beside the River Tame on the road to Lichfield, just beyond the westerly

Century. Pottery of the Beaker People and Food Vessel periods were found amongst the grave goods. On Ilam Tops are disused mine shafts and quarries.

INGESTRE *5m. ENE of Stafford.*
Ingestre is an estate that contains an estate village. It lies on a flat promontory with water on 3 sides – the River Sow to the south and the River Trent to the north and east. To the west is the high ground of Beacon Hill, Hopton Heath and Weston Bank. The Chetwynd family built the Hall, but in 1767 it passed by marriage to a junior branch of the

Talbots who took the name Chetwynd-Talbot when they became Earls Talbot in 1784. In 1856 they became Earls of Shrewsbury. The magnificent south front of Ingestre hall was built by Sir Walter Chetwynd (died 1638). The Hall must be the finest brick house in the county and is certainly the finest Jacobean brick house. The south front has 2 shaped gables and a recessed centre with projecting porch capped by a cupola, all of 2 storeys with mullioned and transomed windows. In 1882 there was a fire and the interior of the house was destroyed. John Birch was employed to

Ingestre Hall.

Keele Hall.

Sneyds were Royalist. In the 18th Century they made further fortunes in coal mining and iron manufacture, and in 1856-61 Keele Hall was rebuilt for them by Salvin. (The stables had been rebuilt some 20 years earlier by Blore. Today they are known as the Clock House). Salvin's Hall is of red sandstone with mullioned and transomed windows and gabled roofs in Jacobean style. It is 'L' shaped with a staircase tower at the junction of the wings. The garden sides to the south and east are also built for show. In keeping with the old house that preceded it there is a Great Hall. The ornate State Rooms are most attractive with their columns and carvings, 18th Century chimney pieces and beautiful views over the gardens and laurel-shrouded lakes. The front entrance faces a courtyard close to high ground. This courtyard is today used as a car park, thus destroying the ambience created by the splendid buildings. The fortunes of the Sneyd family declined, and for 10 years in the early part of this century the Hall was rented out to the Grand Duke Michael of Russia. In 1901 he was visited here by Edward VII. After the First World War the house was empty for some years, and during the Second World War it was occupied by the Army. In 1947 Colonel Ralph Sneyd sold the Hall and 154 acres, and 2 years later the University College of North

Keele University.

Staffordshire was established. In that same year, 1949, the Colonel died and with him the senior line of the Sneyd family. (Apparently, it was Colonel Sneyd, as DAPM in Paris during World War One, who arrested the notorious female spy Mati Hari.) The Hall has survived and is well cared for; not so the Park, which has been littered with such an ill-assorted collection of buildings that they need to be seen to be believed. Individually some have undoubted merit, but together they are an unholy mess. The early college had literally been housed in Nissen huts and other old army buildings. They were ugly but at least they were commercially worthless and easily removed. What Keele has today cost enormous sums of money and are therefore here for many years yet. These buildings include the plate-glass Library by Sir Howard Robinson, which clashes very nicely with the blue engineering brick chapel by G.G. Pace and red brick box dedicated to Walter Moberley and designed by J. A. Pickavance. The rest are best forgotten. Note: in 1962 the University College of North Staffordshire was upgraded and became Keele University.

KIDSGROVE *5m. NNW of Hanley (in the Potteries).*

From the railway station at Kidsgrove a path leads down steps to the murky orange water of the Trent and Mersey Canal, which emerges here from the Harecastle tunnels. The small tunnel (2,880 yds. long) was constructed by James Brindley in 1766-77 but is no longer used. The larger tunnel (2,920 yds. long) is the work of Thomas Telford, built in 1824-7 and is still very much in use. The Harecastle Railway tunnel of

Kidsgrove, the Harecastle tunnels.

1848 (accessed from Boathouse Lane) has been by-passed. The town is in an old coal-mining and industrial area with rows of dull Victorian terraced houses and estates of modern houses. The blue brick church of St. Thomas was built in 1837 and is said to have been designed by Mrs. Kinnersley of Clough Hall. The chancel was added in 1853 by Sir George Gilbert Scott. There are monuments to the Kinnersleys. Close to the church is a remnant of the Park of Clough Hall, which was pulled down between the Great Wars. East of the church, on the hill above the railway, is an 18th Century stone tower folly. The Victorian Hall in Liverpool Road is of 1897. It has a steep pediment, short columns, a portal arch and was designed by Wood and Hutchings. If the desire comes upon you to escape all this, Mow Cop beckons 2m. to the NE with the promise of fresh air and distant views. It lies on the border between Staffordshire and Cheshire. Before leaving Kidsgrove though, mention should be made of the Kidsgrove Boggart. This is the head-less apparition of a woman murdered in one of the canal tunnels by the narrow-boat man with whom she was travelling. Her shrieks of anguish have brought terror to many who have walked in the woods hereabouts.

KING'S BROMLEY *5m. N of Lichfield.*

One of the most beautiful cottages in the county is Old Thatch in Manor Road, King's Bromley. Originally 2 dwellings it has recently been made into one. The walls are white-washed and the thatched roof hangs low over and around the upper storey windows. The gardens too are beautiful and a credit to their owner. The old Manor House used to stand nearby but it is long gone. All that remains is a 4-storey brick tower, probably of Victorian origin, and a hexagonal garden house. The Manor House used to be the home of the Lane family, descendants of Colonel John Lane, Protector of King Charles II. They had moved here from Bentley Hall in Wolverhampton during the 18th Century.

Kinver, Holy Austin Rock.

Kings Bromley, Old Thatch Cottage.

199

The village has charming areas but is spoilt by the relatively heavy traffic on the A513 and its position at a road junction. The church of All Saints is mostly Decorated but has a Perpendicular tower and clerestory, and a handsome Victorian porch. The lower part of the south nave wall is all that remains of the original Norman church. The 'King' in King's Bromley means what it says. The manor was originaly owned by the Kings of Mercia and after the Conquest by King William. Bromley is derived from broom (a yellow flowering shrub found on poorish sandy soil) and 'ley' (meaning a field or clearing). The name probably means 'a field made by clearing broom'.

KINGSLEY *6m. E of Hanley.*

A stone built village on the relatively busy A52 Hanley (Stoke on Trent) to Ashbourne road. It is on rising ground and has good views over the surrounding country. There is a back road here well worth the diversion. It leads from the centre of the village northwards to Hazelcross. At Hazelcross turn right and the lane leads back to the main road along a lovely stretch of the Churnet valley. There are superb views over the river and the Caldon Canal to the Ruelow Woods. There is a bungalow on the right hand side of the road that stands on the site of an old lemonade works. It has its own private spring of water. The church of St. Werburgh at Kingsley has a tower which is 13th Century in its lower part. The rest was much rebuilt in 1820 by James Trubshaw junior, and in 1886 by Lynham who remade the chancel.

KINGSTONE *3.5m. SW of Uttoxeter.*

The village has been very much developed in recent years and the school is most unfortunately sited on what should be the village green. The church of St. John (1861) looks somewhat severe. It stands on a rise facing the village over the road and a small stream. This could have been a quaint place but is not. The red brick ivy-clad Hall, with its 2 large projecting gables of applied plaster

and timber facings in mock-Tudor style, stands with its large red brick barn along the lane that leads SW past the church. This lane comes to a dead end at the edge of Kingstone Wood. Near the top of the hill is the Shrewsbury Arms and opposite is the old black and white Manor Farm. Near here is the village shop with an approach road that takes one through a housing estate. One wonders about the name Kingstone. Does it perhaps refer to an old boundary marker or perhaps a monolith from an ancient burial mound? To the south are the forests of Kingstone Wood and Bagot's Wood, modern coniferous re-plantings of the medieval Needwood Forest. To the south-west by 1m. is The Blythe, a tiny hamlet on the River Blithe (sic). Here, at the end of a short lane to the north, and protected by a pack of howling dogs, is a delightful tumble-down red brick mill and the black and white mill-house. They stand amidst a tangle of

Kingstone, Blythe Mill, The Blythe.

overgrown stream-side trees and bushes. The river meanders around the meadows hereabouts in a wide stony bed. The fields are laid to pasture but the old, probably medieval, plough marks can be seen quite clearly. The area has a timeless feel to it despite the unexpected vehicle workshop at the crossroads. The Blythe Inn, a little ways south, is owned by the youngest landlady in England; at least she was a couple of years ago.

KINGSWINFORD *3.5m. WSW of Dudley.*

Kingswinford is the first entry in the Staffordshire Domesday Book. There it is called Swinford, though even before the

Kingswinford, The Village.

conquest it had belonged to King Edward. After the Conquest the manor passed to King William and sometime after 1086 it acquired the prefix 'King' to differentiate it from other Swinfords, much in the same way that many of the Astons and Actons were qualified by the addition of the name of their new Norman Lord. Swinford means 'swine-ford', in this case presumably the ford across the stream that runs through the old village centre near the church. Part of the old centre still remains, and it comes as something of a surprise to find a village green, a row of cottages, an old pub and a high grey house with Gothic windows astride a busy main road (the A4101) in the middle of surburbia. The medieval church of St. Mary has a Norman tympanum carving of St. Michael slaying the dragon and a Norman Tower, restored in the 17th Century. The building was much enlarged in the late 18th Century. It has a Breeches Bible — which has Adam and Eve fashioning breeches from leaves to protect their modesty — and a font with a gilded canopy by Sir Ninian Cowper. There are monuments from the 16th and 17th Centuries to the Corbyn family. The church

had a large parish in the Middle Ages, but in the 18th and 19th Centuries it lost much of its territory to the new parishes which were created in response to the great population increase that came with industrialisation. In the churchyard is a stone pillar believed to be the shaft of a medieval preaching cross. At this cross the decisions and sentences made and passed by the Court Leet at the Old Court House were publicly announced. The Old Court House is on the other side of the main road (A4101) and is now a pub of the same name. Just west of the Old Court House, along the A4101, is the Pesnett Trading estate, at the entrance to which is an old pit head winding gear scaffold. *(See Pensnett.)* Scattered around the town are some of the elegant villas built by the 18th Century glassmakers and ironmasters, such as Somerhill House, of 1756, in Somerhill Road. This is a brick mansion of 5 bays and 2.5 storeys with a grand facade. It is now a hotel and the front garden has been turned into a car park. Broadfield House in Compton Drive is another large house of the period — again brick of 5 bays and 2.5 storeys with a porch of Ionic columns and a 3-part lunette window. This now houses a museum of glass, which has exhibits from all over the world as well as examples of ware from local manufacturers. For the rest, Kingswinford is very much a modern place with acres of estate houses and shopping precincts. New houses have even intruded into the large gardens of the few old houses that are left.

Kingswinford, M.E.B. Accounting Unit.

The new centre of the town of Kingswinford is at the crossroads of the A491 and the A4101. Here is The Cross pub, the circular concrete dome of the M.E.B. showroom and many shops. In Standhills Road is the monstrous white concrete building with pink pillars that houses the Central Accounting Unit of the M.E.B. The 16th Century timber-framed Bradley Hall was dismantled in 1924 and rebuilt at Stratford upon Avon. Kingswinford could ill afford such a loss. The modern Bradley Hall is an old person's home and is on a different site. One mile NW of the town is Holbeche House, a 17th Century house with secret priest holes that has a 19th Century brick facade. This is where Guy Fawkes' accomplices were killed and captured. *(See Himley.)*

KINVER *3m. W of Stourbridge.*

The name Kinver is one of the oldest place names in the Midlands and is probably of Celtic origin. Prior to 1066 Earl Algar owned Kinver and its two mills, but they were taken from his estate and kept by King William. In 1086 there were 24 families, a priest and 2 slaves in the village. King William either created or extended the Forest of Kinver, that is he fixed the boundaries. Even today the area is quite heavily wooded and from a distance the settlement looks to be surrounded by forest. Kinver Edge, rocky and tree-clad, stands high above the village. Today it is a country park of some 300 acres, owned and maintained by the National Trust. Here is the 7-acre hill fort constructed by prehistoric settlers and lower down are the caves of other early peoples. These caves were hewn out of the red sandstone and at a later date were extended by the addition of brick fronts. Indeed, they were occupied as houses into the early years of this century. The best known and most easily accessible are on Holy Austin Rock. From the top of this bare, rocky, red crag are superb views over the forests. The highest cave house reminds one of an American Indian desert dwelling. The village of Kinver was an ancient borough but has not had a market for many years. The long winding High Street is

Kinver, the Old School House.

202

Kinver, the church of St. Peter.

16th Century Whittington Inn and south of the Inn is Whittington Farm, an 18th Century brick house of 7 bays, 2 storeys and a parapet. At Greensforge 3 Roman forts have been identified from aerial photographs. The most important measures 550 ft. by 450 ft. and has a turf rampart and 2 ditches. South of this is a larger fort of a different date enclosed by a single ditch. These forts were occupied in the 1st Century. A large marching camp of 35 acres lies 1m. NW. The following metal working sites are known in the parish of Kinver. They are all in the valley of the River Stour. Kinver Water Mill (SO.848.833), probably the site of a medieval mill which produced iron and steel wire in 1868. Now it is part of a pumping station. The site of Walke Mill Ironworks (SO.851.843), pre 1600 and reputedly the first rolling and slitting mill for nails in England. In 1628 a new mill was built here by Richard Foley which was closed by 1919. The site of Prestwood Wire

Kinver, the town from Holy Austin Rock.

quite charming with its half-timbered cottages, old pubs, Georgian houses and a variety of shops. In Dark Lane is the 16th Century timber-framed Old Grammar School, a most handsome building now converted to a house. The church of St. Peter stands high above the village of Kinver Edge. There has probably been a church here since Saxon times but most of the present building is of the 14th and 15th Centuries. The north aisle was rebuilt in 1856 by Thomas Smith. Inside there is a Norman rood staircase, which is very rare, a 14th Century font and a 17th Century pulpit. In the south chapel is the altar tomb of Sir Edward Grey of Enville, died 1528, who has for company his 2 wives, 7 sons and 10 daughters. In the north chapel is the effigy of John Hampton of Stourton Castle and monuments to the Foleys of Prestwood. The east window glass is by Wailes of about 1853. One mile east of the village at Whittington is the timber-framed

Mill at SO.868.861, about 3m. NE of Kinver, may also be the site of Halfcot Mill. The site of Gothersley Mill (SO.862.870), about 3m. NE of Kinver which was a blade mill until about 1743, then possibly a forge, then a slitting mill before 1790 and which finally closed in the 1870's. The site of the Old Hinksford Mill (SO.867.900), about 3·5m. NNE of Kinver, a blade mill from about 1650. There is another mill known by this name.

KNIGHTLEY *3m. NNW of Gnosall, which is 7m. W of Stafford.*
A small scattered hamlet with a strange little yellow brick church of 1840 by Thomas Trubshaw which has a stained glass window by Kempe of 1900. Knightley Grange lies 1m. S of the church. It is a red brick mansion with stone dressings in a neo-Elizabethan style. The house stands on a bluff and has superb views over the white painted Gamekeeper's Cottage towards the Wrekin. In the park there is a deer farm surrounded by high wire-netting. Half-a-mile SE of the Grange is Knightley Dale, a hamlet with a substantial

Knightley, view W from Knightley Grange.

Knightley, deer in the Grange park.

moated site in the field just north of the junction of the lanes. Down a track at the foot of Prospect Hill is Knightley Hall which has an enormous chimney stack and a large yellow brick barn. The Knightley family now live at Fawsley, Northamptonshire.

KNIGHTON *See Adbaston.*
KNUTTON *See Newcastle under Lyme.*

KNYPERSLEY *6m. N of Hanley on the A527.*
A dour southern suburb of Biddulph which like the country around it bears the scars of

its industrial history. The smoke-blackened church of St. John the Evangelist was built in 1848-51 and paid for by James Bateman, who also financed the large neo-Jacobean parsonage, complete with stables and coach-house, and the school of 1850. All were the work of the architect, R.C. Hussey. James's father, John, had lived at Knypersley Hall and James kept the walled garden in which he cultivated plants for his famous gardens at Biddulph Grange, 1·25m. to the north. Most of the ground of the old Knypersley Hall

Knypersley, Greenway Country Park.

have ben sold and built upon, but the back garden remains and is now, fittingly, a garden centre. One mile to the south-east is the Greenway Bank Country Park which includes the last 110 acres of the 19th Century landscaped park of Greenway Bank Hall which was demolished in the early 1970's. There are dramatic stone outcrops, an arboretum of native British trees and two pools. The Serpentine Pool is set in a delightful wooded valley where there is much bird life, including redstart, kingfisher and dipper. In the wetland areas are many species of plants, such as marsh marigold, marsh violet and water avens. The other pool is the Knypersley Reservoir, a canal feeder reservoir, at the southern tip of which is the source of the River Trent, one of England's longest rivers. In the spring the azaleas and rhododendrons flower in profusion. There are public toilets and a car park, for which a charge is made.

LAPLEY *3·5m. WSW of Penkridge.*
An intriguing little village with a lot of character that lies just off the old Roman road that ran from Stretton (Pennocrucium) to Whitchurch. In the late 11th or early 12th Centuries a Benedictine Priory was founded here, possibly on the site of an existing Saxon monastery. The Priory buildings are now all gone, with only a few fragments incorporated into the farm buildings of the Hall, but the church of All Saints survives. It is an imposing building with a high, strong central tower which is Norman in its lower part and Perpendicular above, with a parapet and 8 pinnacles. The nave and chancel masonry is also Norman, with a perfect Norman window in the south chancel wall. There are 2 Perpendicular windows in the north nave. Next to the church is an attractive old house with good gardens. South of the church is Park House, a large, pleasing building with crenellated walls and

Lapley, Park House.

Lapley, the church of All Saints.

a turreted gatehouse. It dates partly from the 18th Century and partly from about 1867. Across the fields is Fort St. George.

LEEK *11m. NE of Hanley (in the Potteries).*
Leek was one of the many important manors owned by the great Saxon Earl Algar whose estate was dispossessed after the Norman Conquest. As with most of his lands Leek was usurped by the new king. The old borough lay at the top of the hill around the Market Place and the parish church. It was the creation of Earl Ranulph de Blunderville of Chester, and his grid pattern of streets is still evident. Later, the borough was developed by the Abbots of Dieulacres Abbey which lay 1m. N of the town. At the centre of Leek, roads from Buxton, Ashbourne, Uttoxeter and Stone, Burslem and the Potteries, and Macclesfield all meet. Around the town is the magnificent countryside of the Staffordshire Moorlands – their hills and dales, rivers and reservoirs. The old stone market town began its transformation to a place of industry in the

18th Century when silk spinning and weaving, ribbon weaving and button making became substantial cottage industries. In 1762 the road between Stockport, Macclesfield, Leek and Ashbourne was turnpiked and improved, so providing the town with easy transport to the major markets of the south and the north. The first silk weaving factory, the Wellington Mill in Strangman Street, was not built until 1853 and even then the cottage industry continued in purpose-built houses, such as the early 19th Century 3-storyed terraced houses with their long top-storey windows, that still survive in London Street. In 1860 the huge 6-storey mill of Wardle and Davenport was built in Mill Street, one of many similar factories that brought great prosperity to Leek. The waters of the River Churnet, which curve around Leek in a large meander, were found to be suitable for silk dyeing and this trade flourished as a complimentary industry to the weaving process. During the 19th Century much of the town was either built or rebuilt. There

206

are comparatively few early buildings. Amongst them are the timber-framed and gabled Roebuck Inn of about 1626; the Ash Almshouses in Broad St. of 1676, stuccoed and recently renovated (1987), making a pretty sight; and several 18th Century houses such as the Vicarage, Foxlowe (east of the church), the former Grammar School at Overton Bank, and in the Market Place the Red Lion. The second half of the 19th Century in Leek was dominated by a local architect, William Sugden (died 1892) and his son, William Larner Sugden (died 1901). One of their most notable buildings is the red brick Nicholson Institute of 1882-4 which houses the School of Art, the museum and the library. It lies largely hidden behind the splendid 18th Century stone house called Greyfriars in Stockwell St. Together they make a delightful group. The Sugdens built many of the public buildings: the County Police Station; the former Black's Head, now Woolworths; the District Bank, one of their best; the Memorial Hospital in Stockwell St; the Congregational Chapel in Decorated style; and many, many more public and private works. They did not, however, have a hand in constructing the parish church of St. Edward the Confessor, a large, but not very attractive, stone building which was rebuilt after a fire in 1297. In 1556 and 1593 the south

Leek, Greystones and the Library.

and north aisles were removed and irregular windows inserted in the new walls. The porch is of 1670. The chancel was rebuilt again and furnished by G.E. Street in 1865.

There are some good examples of the Leek School of Embroidery, founded by Lady Wardle in the 1870's and a stained glass window by Morris in the Lady Chapel. In the west of the nave is a striking 18th Century gallery of many tiers. The monuments include a brass plaque to John Ashenhurst, died 1597, and a memorial to William Trafford of Swythamley, died 1697. In the churchyard are 2 Saxon crosses probably of the 11th Century. There can be little doubt that a Saxon church preceded that of the Normans, and there are records of carved Saxon stones being seen inside the church early in this century. On the 20th, 21st and 22nd June it is possible, weather permitting, to see a double sunset from Doctor's Corner (where 8 doctors are buried) in the churchyard. The sun sets over Bosley Cloud 7m. NW beyond Lake Rudyard, disappears and re-emerges to set a second time over the Cheshire plain. All in all, Leek is a most

Leek, the Wardle and Davenport Mill.

Leek, the market.

The witch had a neighbour who had noticed that whenever the witch's cat came near to her her baking turned out badly. One day the neighbour threw a hot oatcake at the cat and chased it into the witch's house. Inside the house she found no sign of the cat but the witch was howling in agony from the pain of a bad burn on her back. One mile north of the town at Abbey Farm (SJ.982.578) are the remains of Dieulacres Abbey which was founded by the Earl of Chester in 1214. It was a Cistercian house that moved here from Poulton in Cheshire. Very little remains of the Abbey. The Early English bases of the crossing piers of the church are in situ and there are many fragments of sculpture built into the outbuildings and walls of the farm. The best pieces are in the garden arch, attached to the house at the end of the entrance drive, and include a fine mid-14th Century king. The farmhouse itself is black and white on a stone base, dated at 1625. The

Leek, weaver's houses in London Road.

pleasant town. It has a variety of buildings, a good selection of shops, a flourishing market, a busy atmosphere and a superb situation. However, it has very few specific tourist attractions. About the only place that could be so called is the James Brindley Mill at the bottom of Mill Street, which was probably built by the great canal engineer in 1752 and now houses a small museum. However, Leek is the ideal centre from which to explore the Staffordshire Moorlands. The suburb of Compton has some early 19th Century areas, such as King Street and Albion Street, where there are 3-storeys weavers' cottages and the impressive churches of All Saints (1885-7) by Norman Shaw, and St. Mary (Roman Catholic, 1886) by Albert Vicars. Before leaving Leek perhaps we should mention at least one of the town's witches. At Gettliffe's Yard in Derby Street there is reputed to have lived an old crone who owned a black cat.

Leek, Abbey Farm out buildings.

stone archway at the back, with tracery in the spandrels, almost certainly belongs to part of the original Abbey buildings. The house was built by the Rudyard family who had acquired the Abbey soon after the Dissolution of the Monasteries. The stone outbuildings have Gothic doorways and the windows were built about 1820. One mile W of Leek by the River Churnet is Westwood Hall, a large neo-Elizabethan gabled

Leek, Abbey Farm, medieval sculpture.

mansion of 1850-3, built by John Davenport of the pottery manufacturing family. The south and east fronts are of red sandstone but the rest is brick. The house is pleasantly irregular but has not been well treated; one of the 2 original courtyards has gone, as have many of the leaded glass windows, and the chimneys have been drastically reduced in height. In the grounds is an attractive modern Summer House, the Old Stables and an Entrance Lodge with a large arch. Two miles NE of Leek is Lake Rudyard, a large and long-established reservoir after which Rudyard Kipling was named. It can be seen to its best advantage from the special lay-bys on the A523 Leek to Macclesfield road. At Tittesworth, 1·25m. NNE of Leek, in the fields of Tittesworth Farm, are the remains of Prehistoric Camps. The old packhorse salt road from Cheshire passed through Meerbrook (at the northern end of the Tittesworth reservoir), and then to Middle Hulme, Blackshaw Moor, Stonycliff and on to Blackmere House (now called The Mermaid Inn) on Morridge Hill.

LICHFIELD *12m. SE of Stafford.*
Lichfield is the only Cathedral in the country that has maintained its medieval outline. Its 3 spires — the 'Ladies of the Vale' — are unique, instantly recognisable and a landmark on every approach to the city. The town itself is handsome and largely unspoiled, though very little is left of the medieval settlement and much of what we see today is Georgian. Its early history is loosely connected with that of the Roman town of Letocetum, less than 1m. to the SW at Wall on Watling Street (the A5). Indeed, the name Lichfield means 'open land near Letocetum'. (The root of the Roman name is Celtic.) The Lichfield coats of arms include one which depicts 3 British kings lying dead killed in battle with the Romans. They are said to lie in the burial mound on Borrowcop Hill to the south of the town. An alternative derivation of the name Lichfield is death's field from 'lych' meaning death, a reference

Leek, evening view looking NE.

Lichfield, Dam Street.
Lichfield, the Cathedral and Minster Pool.

Lichfield, the town centre.

210

to the legend that Christian's were slaughtered here by the Romans on an order from the Emperor Diocletian. There was a Christian settlement at Lichfield by at least the early 600's and in 655 a local prince called Morfael of Luitcoet joined with the great British prince, Cynddylan, and won a victory over the invading pagan Angles at Caer Luitcoet, which was either Lichfield or close to it. Shortly after, however, Cynddylan was killed, Morfael fled to Somerset and the Angles took Lichfield, though they had in the meantime become Christian's themselves. About 670 Lichfield and a large estate around it were given to St. Chad. He established a Ministry here, a large church from which priests went out and preached under trees (often yew trees because of the all-year-round shelter they provided), at specially erected preaching crosses and not infrequently in the old pagan temples. The ordinary people had largely become Christian because their King decreed it, not because they believed in the new gospel, and for many years they worshipped the old gods along with the new. In 672 St. Chad died and in 700 the first 'cathedral of all Mercia' was built at Lichfield, and the remains of St. Chad were buried there. The Cathedral, probably made of wood, became a place of pilgrimage and in the 9th Century became, for a short time, the seat of an Archbishopric. By late Anglo-Saxon times the Diocese stretched from Warwickshire to the Ribble — a huge area. At the time of Domesday the church at Lichfield owned 2 extensive estates: one around Lichfield that stretched from Norton Canes in the SW to Hints in the SE, and to Rowley and Yoxall in the N; and the other around Eccleshall that stretched from Doxey near Stafford westwards to the Shropshire border. These properties were probably Anglian, or even possibly Romano-British estates which had been handed over intact to the church. After the Conquest the Normans transferred the seat of the diocese to Chester (1075). It then went to Coventry, and then to Coventry and Lichfield jointly.

The church chapter was reconstituted by Roger de Clinton in 1130, and at about this time the Cathedral was rebuilt. It had a nave, choir and apse. Roger de Clinton also fortified the Close around the Cathedral and cut a moat around the settlement. About 1220 the third and last and largest Cathedral was begun and was substantially complete by about 1330 when the great apse at the east end was finished. In 1290 the estates of the Bishopric were greatly extended by the acquisition of Cannock Chase from the King. The Cathedral was savagely mutilated during the Civil War and was besieged 3 times by the Roundheads. In 1646 a spire collapsed and badly damaged the building. It was rebuilt by Bishop Hacket in 1661-69 and re-consecrated in 1670. In the 18th Century there was further substantial rebuilding, both inside and out, and again in the 19th Century when from 1857 to 1901 Sir George Gilbert Scott and his son, John Odrid Scott, created much of what we see today. How much was faithful restoration or accurate replacement of older work is not known. The great sandstone west front is quite spectacular. The mass of ornament is bewildering - statues, cinqfoils, quatre-foils, trefoils, arcading and carved porches. The interior is equally impressive and finely wrought. Amongst the monuments are busts of Samuel Johnson and David Garrick by Westmacott; Bishop Ryder by Chantry; Bishop Woods in bronze by Epstein; and Bishop Lonsdale by G.F. Watts. Perhaps the most outstanding feature of the Cathedral is the Lady Chapel, begun about 1320, with its 9 huge traceried windows, its arcaded wall and the 19th Century Oberammergau triptych alter piece. The Cathedral is fronted by a lawn and surrounded by a charming close. This was the cultural and social centre of the town, even the county. Stafford was the administrative centre of the shire but it was to Lichfield that men who cared for more than business tended to gravitate. Paradoxically, the Bishops, the figureheads of sophisticated life, lived not in Lichfield

Longton, Town Hall and town centre.

actually a part of the main road, and a busy bottle-neck junction, which is here crossed by a huge, ugly railway bridge. On one side of the Square is the Town Hall and on the other was the church. The Town Hall was rebuilt in 1836 to a design by Burril. It is of ashlar, in Classical style and has 13 bays with coach-porch and pediments. The extension is of 1912. Today it is unused and the windows boarded up - quite shameful. The Market

Longton, Gladstone Museum.

Hall lies behind - a great barn of a place, ill-lit and inelegant. The front facade is dirt-blackened and the rear, which faces a street, is very dull. The church of St. John the Baptist was built in 1761 and paid for by John Bourne. However, mining settlement caused structural damage and it was rebuilt in 1792-5. It was further restored in 1889 and finally demolished in 1985 because the settlement could not be halted. The church stood on the green mound adjacent to the red brick Crown Hotel. The shopping centre lies on the hill beyond Times Square. It is a brisk, busy place, and there is a new shopping precinct, named after Arnold Bennet and opened in 1965. There are more pottery works in Longton than in any other town in the Potteries and more china factories than in the other 5 towns put together. There are no dynasties of famous manufacturers but there are a number of firms who were established in the late 19th Century and are still in business. Several of the works exhibit variations of the Classic Georgian facade of central arch surmounted with a Venetian window and pediment. The Portland Works (Aynsley Pottery) in Sutherland Road has exactly this arrangement and was built as late as 1861. The remarkable 19th Century townscape of the Potteries has now long gone. The thousands of graceful bottle-shaped brick kilns have almost totally vanished. A few more slender versions are still used for calcining flint, but as furnaces for firing

Longton, Victorian cottage interior at Gladstone Museum.

Madeley, the old manor house in 1686.

probably part of an earlier defensive structure. The moats are thought to have been largely ornamental. The stream was once dammed and formed a lake between the

Madeley, remains of the old manor house.

mansion and the road. The Manor House was the home of John Offley, to whom Izaak Walton dedicated 'The Compleat Angler'. They were good friends and Walton often fished in the lake. The estate passed to the

Madeley, moat by the old manor house.

Crewe family and they held it until this century. At **Heighley,** 1.25m. N of Madeley, are the meagre ruins of Heighley Castle (SJ.773.467). The Castle stands on a high hill and a section of red sandstone walling can be seen from the main A531, about 0·25m. W of the motorway bridge. The access lane dips steeply downhill to the north, off the main road. It passes Castle Farm and is joined by a forestry track on which is a sign marking the entrance route to the Castle. The Castle was once a very substantial and strong place and the 'moat' was hacked out of the rock. Today only one small piece of walling still stands. The hill is totally overgrown and very rough underfoot, with old logs and stones covered in brush making the going very hard. We nearly came to a nasty end up here, victims of a precipice that was hidden by man-high nettles and ferns. There seems to be quite a lot of stonework in the undergrowth. There are superb views from the castle, but it is

Madeley, view over M6 from Heighley Castle.

a dangerous place. This was the home of the Audley family in the Middle Ages *(See Audley)* and was later held by the Gerards. The Castle was pulled down after the Civil War. At **Wrinehill,** 1m. further along the A531 towards Betley, is the Summerhouse of about 1710. It only has 3 bays but nevertheless displays a grand facade with giant pilasters, pediments and segmental headed windows.

MAER *6·25m. SW of Newcastle-under-Lyme.* Between Stableford and Blackbrook the A51 passes through a beautiful valley of curving wooded hills. These are the Maer Hills. Half a mile west of Hill Chorlton the road bends around the tree-clad Berth Hill, on which are the single ditch and bank earthen defences of a 9-acre prehistoric fort. The road is joined here by a lane that leads south to the village of Maer. At this junction is a War Memorial and a lodge. From the lodge a parallel grand entrance drive leads to Maer Hall. The approach to the village is quite dramatic. The lane passes through a deep sandstone-lined cutting and a small bridge to the stable block with its imposing 18th Century gatehouse. The church is perched on rocks high above. Further along the red brick village appears, largely unspoiled. All in all, a delightful little place. The Jacobean Hall was built by the Bowyer family, then passed to Josiah Wedgwood II and then to the Harrisons, a shipping family from Liverpool. The Harrisons added large Victorian wings but these were pulled down about 10 years ago and the Hall restored to its original size. The house is very handsome and has a superb hall. The long gravelled approach drive from the main road passes through the well-kept and well-wooded park, (in which is situated the village cricket field), skirts the large lake and brings one to the gabled front of the Hall. The church of St. Peter has a south porch of about 1200 and most of the rest is early 17th Century restored by the Victorians. There is some modern stained glass by Shrigley and Hunt, and in the chancel are the effigies of Sir John Bowyer, died 1604, and his wife. In the churchyard are yew trees and sycamores.

Maer Hall, Charles Darwin knew it well.

222

The monuments include the effigy of a cross-legged knight (meaning he had been on a crusade), believed to have been either Ralph Butcher, died about 1310, or Ralph Butcher, died 1342; several unknown effigies; Lady Hawys Botiller, late 14th Century; Ralph Botiller; and a wall monument to Rupert Skrymsher, whose father was Adjutant General to Prince Rupert. Norbury is best known for the canal junction that lies 1m. SE from the village. It is a junction no longer, the Newport canal being long disused and the locks concreted over, but Norbury Junction is still a busy place. A holiday hire boat company operates from here and there is a British Waterways Maintenance Yard. It is a place of great character with a small inland dock, a chandlers, a pub and a few cottages. The road to Gnosall from here passes through 2 tunnels under the huge embankment that carries the canal. Half a mile NE of Norbury Junction is the southern entrance to the 1·25m. Grub St. cutting. Quite dramatic canal country. Three quarters of a mile NW of Norbury village is Loynton house of about 1800 with 5 bays, a doorway with columns and a pediment. Half a mile W of Loynton House (but more easily approached from Weston Jones) is an ancient burial mound called Gregory. It is oval, 180 ft. by 150 ft. and 8 ft. high, and lies near a stream. There is another burial mound 1·25m. NNE of Norbury village church. A quarter of a mile NNE of Norbury Junction, in a wood adjacent to the track that leads on to Knightley Grange, is a square moat.

NORTON CANES 2m. NW of Brownhills and 3m. SE of Cannock.

In 1086 it belonged to the Bishop of Chester, as part of his Lichfield estate, but was described as waste, i.e. no-one lived there and the land was uncultivated. The village stands on rising ground just north of Watling Street (A5), with good views over countryside blighted by old collieries and industrial housing. The church of St. James has parts of

Norton Canes, Little Wyreley Hall.

1832 but was rebuilt in 1888 after a fire. It is of dirty black stone with a red tiled roof. There are monuments to the Fowke and Hussey families of Little Wyrley Hall which stands 1·25m. S of Norton Canes. The Hall is a Tudor house that has been encased in brick. A long service wing was added to the west about 1660 and extended again on the E side in 1691. It has good gables and dormer windows, some of which date from 1820 as does the staircase and stairwell with balconies below the cupola. The door furniture of the first floor rooms is highly ornate and is of 1691. With only one exception ownership of the manor of Little Wyrley has passed by inheritance from Norman times to the present. In 1691 Dr. Phineas Fowke inherited the manor and the current owner Mrs. Frank Wallace is directly descended from him. Her husband was a big game hunter and had a huge collection of trophies. He was also an artist and an author, somewhat more worthy occupations. Little

Norton Canes, sailing on Chasewater.

245

Wyreley was surrounded by coal mines, a railway and a canal. Only the canal, a spur of the Essington and Wyreley Canal, remains, but within a mile or so in every direction the housing estates are watching, with avaricious eyes. One mile to the E of Norton Canes is the huge Chasewater reservoir, a Railway Museum and a Raceway. Chasewater is used for many water sports — speed boat racing, sailing, canoeing, water skiing and sailboarding.

OAKAMOOR 2·5m. ENE of Cheadle.

Oakamoor is in the lovely Churnet valley 2m. NW of Alton, from which it can be reached by a lane that runs along the banks of the river. The village is a most pleasant place, surrounded by woods and steep hillsides. there is a pub, a Post Office and long walks by the river. Strange to think that until recently there was a factory and a railway here. In fact, there was industry at Oakamoor from at

Oakamoor, the weir on the R. Churnet.

least 1572 when George, Earl of Shrewsbury, built an iron refining forge. This had ceased production by 1590 but in 1592 Sir Francis Willoughby built a furnace and a forge, selling the iron produced at Newcastle-under-Lyme and Leek amongst other places. By 1692 there was a slitting mill in the valley and 1717 a forge is recorded as being here. Most of these forges and furnaces are believed to have been in the vicinity of Ordnance Survey map ref.SK.053,452. In 1777 a tinplate works was built at Oakamoor, the only such 18th Century mill in Staffordshire. It consisted of a water-driven rolling mill in which iron bars were rolled into sheets, and a tinhouse where the sheets were coated in tin by being dipped into a series of baths. The mill had probably ceased tin production by 1800 and converted to copper manufacture. In 1857 the copper wire for the first transatlantic underwater communications cable between Valencia and Newfoundland was made at Oakamoor. Sad to say it broke several times. The first succeessful cable was laid 7 years later in 1864. The Oakamoor works (SK.053.446) were closed in 1962 and the building demolished. Production was then concentrated in the company's Froghall works, 3m. to the NW, which had been opened in 1890. The firm of Thomas Bolton and Sons is still very much in business there. In 1868 the firm owned a silk mill in Oakamoor but little is known about this works. The attractive barge-boarded and gabled house called Lightoakes was home to one of the Bolton brothers. The other lived at the gabled neo-Jacobean Moor Court. There is a Bolton Memorial chapel of 1878, and a Free Church designed by Edward Clarke. The church of Holy Trinity is of 1832, by J.P. Pritchett, and is built on very steep ground. An unusual feature are the 3-light straight-headed Perpendicular windows. *(See Hawksmoor).*

OFFLEYBROOK *See Offley.*

246

OFFLEY HAY *See Offley.*

OFFLEY MARSH *See Offley.*

OFFLEY ROCK *See Offley.*

OFFLEY *3·25m. W of Eccleshall.*
Offley is an Anglo-Saxon name and probably means Offa's field. About 1·75m. N of High Offley are Bishop's Offley, Offleyrock, Offleymarsh, Offleybrook, and Offley Hay. Whether this Offa was the great King himself, a relation or simply an Anglo-Saxon with the same name we shall probably never know. Many of the place names in this area are of Anglo-Saxon origin — Horsley, 'Horsa's farm': Tunstall, 'Tuna's nook'; Garmelow, 'Garma's grave'; Copmere, 'Coppa's lake'. The brook called Lonco, like most river names, is probably an earlier Celtic name. **Bishop's Offley** would have belonged to the Lichfield Cathedral estate which, for some years after the Norman Conquest, was transferred to Chester. **High Offley** lies on a hill about 1m. NW of Woodseaves, which is on the Eccleshall to Newport road. When approached from the W it has the appearance of a medieval hill town with the church a landmark for several miles around. The village is small and well preserved. We could see no new housing, only farms, brick cottages, the old manor house, the pub and a school now up for sale, with permission for it to be converted to a dwelling. The medieval church of St. Mary

High Offley

High Offley, the church of St. Mary.

has a porch dated at about 1200. Most of the rest of the building is of the 12th and 13th Centuries except for the upper part of the tower which was rebuilt in 1667. Inside there are monuments to the Skrymsher family. On a hill to the S of the churchyard at High

High Offley, the old Manor House.

Offley Roman finds have been made, including in large numbers tiles, armour and pottery. These are reported by Pitt in his History of Staffordshire (p.319). They probably mark the site of a villa or small settlement, though Pitt suggests that High Offley may be the location of the lost Roman town of Mediolanum. The Royal Oak has been most unsympathetically modernised and looks incongruous, positioned as it is next to the charming old church and opposite the faded and run-down but characterful Manor House. The latter is of rendered red brick with 3 clusters of tall chimneys with 3 in each group. The porch has a crusader cross slit window and unusual lintels. It is now a farmhouse with a large red brick farm building in something of a decline. Grub Street lies 0·5m. S of High Offley. The hamlet clusters around the bridge that carries the Offley to Norbury road over the Shropshire Union Canal which emerges from a deep wooded cutting here. This stretch of the canal is well known to both boatmen and fishermen. The northern Offleys are set in most attractive country — rolling, wooded and well-watered. The River Sow is dammed in several places creating small lakes, the largest of which is Copmere, 1·5m. from Eccleshall. There is a maze of lanes joining scattered cottages, a feature of late medieval forest clearance. At **Offleybrook,** on the lovely lane to Outlands, is a working mill (SJ.782.301) which is not

Offley Mill at Offley Brook.

marked on the 1·25 inch Ordnance Survey map. It is used to grind and mix animal foods and the owner has just installed a new water-wheel. The old one is still in place but has not been used for many years. The wheels cannot be seen from the road. At **Offley Hay** is the delightfully positioned Walkmill House with lawns that run down to the large mill pool. On the opposite side of the road is a derelict corn mill with most of the original machinery. Sadly, it has been badly neglected and the roof and floors have collapsed. The machinery lies all-a-jumble but there are plans to restore it. Adjacent to the mill is a long, low, single-storey brick building. This was part of the mill which, though originally used to grind corn, became a fulling mill. In this building was a long table

Offley, Walkmill, the pool

on which was placed urine-soaked woollen cloth, which was then literally walked on to remove the oils from the wool. In an adjacent farmyard there was a pit with stone steps which contained the urine, and a series of rods above on which were hung the cloth pieces to be soaked. The farm building near the 'T' junction is partly of stone, and this is believed to be the remains of an earlier mill, possibly the one known to have been here in the 15th Century. The long, low shed previously mentioned has stone lower parts and was probably part of the earlier mill also. Above the doorway to the shed is a stone lintel which seems to have been inserted after the building had been completed. This lintel came from Gerard's Bromley Hall, the magnificent stone house described by Dr. Plot as one of the finest in the county. On the lintel are the initials 'J. D.' and the date 1830. 'J. D.' is Josiah Deakin who used to live at Walkmill House, and presumably 1830 is the date he inserted the lintel into the fulling

Offley, Walkmill, fulling shed to fore.

Offley, The Tunstalls, near High Offley.

Onecote, the R. Hamps and the Jervis Arms.

249

Offley, cottage opposite Walkmill House.

shed. In Offley Hay there is a sycamore tree which is said to have grown from the stake that was driven through the body of a giant in an attempt to keep him down. Between Bishop's Offley and High Offley is the hamlet of **Tunstall.** Here is a farm house called The Tunstalls which catches the eye. It is of brick painted white and has 4 bays, 2 storeys and a hipped roof, as well as two tall 'spider trees'. From here there is a very good view over land to High Offley on its hill.

OKEOVER *1·5m. NW of Ashbourne.*
Two miles south of the Dove Dale gorge the River Dove flows in a broader valley. On its western bank the oak trees of Okeover Park still stand as they and their forebears have stood for centuries, longer even than the lords of Okeover Hall and they have been there in unbroken line for 800 years. The Okeovers of Okeover (the family took its name from the manor) are one of very few families in the country to have maintained a presence at their ancestral home from early Norman times to the present day. The estate was passed from eldest son to eldest son until 1955 when Mr. Haughton Ealdred Okeover died, without having produced a male heir. However, Mr. Okeover's nephew, Sir Ian Walker-Okeover, succeeded to the property and so the family presence continues. There was a village here from before Domesday, though today the church and Hall stand all alone. At some time the village became deserted and there are now no obvious signs

that it ever existed. The first Hall was a moated manor house, possibly the one depicted by Dr. Plot in his 'History of Staffordshire' (1686), though that may have replaced an even earlier house. In 1745 Leak Okeover started to rebuild the Hall in brick but his plans were never fulfilled. He built the 9-bay west wing, with its handsomely carved pediment, the north wall of the east wing and the imposing stable block, but only made a start on the higher south range and the rest of the east wing. These were finished 200 years later by Marshall Sisson (between 1953-60), who restored and completed the house in the fashion intended by Leak Okeover. Inside are some good plastered ceilings and a very fine wrought iron staircase rail. There are 3 sets of iron gates — the outer (with obelisks) and inner entrance gates and those between the house and the church. In the garden is The Temple of Pomona inside which is a white marble statue by Giuseppe Gorganzoli of a young girl with a rosebud at her breast called The Dawn of Love. There is also a lavatory called the Necessary House with an arched entrance and a broken pediment. In the Park is an old tree called the 'Wishing Oak', which has the girth of some 30ft. The medieval church of All Saints stands a mere 30yds. or so from the Hall. The tower is Perpendicular but the rest is Decorated with a restoration by Sir George Gilbert Scott in 1856-8. In the chancel window are figures and fragments of the original 14th Century stained glass. The Victorian glass in the nave is by William Warrington. There are monuments to Humphrey Okeover, died 1538; Leak Okeover, died 1765, and his wife Mary, died 1764, by Joseph Wilton, which are especially beautiful; and a palimpest (a brass plate re-used by engraving on the back) of the wife of William Lord Zouch, of about 1447.

ONECOTE *8m. NNE of Cheadle.*
It lies on the B5063 between Cheadle and Longnor, a tiny place in the high moorlands on the banks of the River Hamps, which here

is little more than a stream. Our memory of the place is of the colourful sunshades in the riverside garden of the Jervis Arms. To the N is Butterton Moor. To the E is Grindon Moor, stone wall country, and the few trees here remind us that bleak though it may be in winter, these hills were once forest-clad. The church of St. Luke is of 1753-5. It has a tower, a nave and a low chancel with a Venetian east window. At the west end is a huge Commandment Board with painted figures. Folk-tales have lingered long in the Moorlands. One tells of an Onecote farmer who was returning from Leek market after nightfall when he was plucked from the ground by a headless horseman. He was taken for a terrifying ride with the horse flying through the air, leaping not just over hedges, but whole fields. He was deposited near his home and died a few days later. Another farmer saw the phantom horseman and though he lived, his horse and dog died shortly after. The horseman is said to be one of 4 evil spirits cast out of heaven to await the 'crack of doom'.

Onecote, horses in the moors at evening.

An unassuming but most pleasant village which has not been helped by the 20th Century houses; neither, however, has it been ruined. It lies on a hill just to the W of the delightful Moddershall Valley. At the heart of the settlement is St. Mary's Abbey which is a Benedictine convent for nuns. It was founded in Ghent in the 17th Century 'for young English Ladies of Catholic families' and moved to England in 1794. The Abbey buildings are based around an early 19th Century brick house, but the chapel was built in 1854 by Pugin who was only 19 years old at the time and had just taken over his famous father's business. It is large and the style is Decorated. Inside is a good iron screen. The chapter house, sacristy and presbytery are all of 1892. The church of St. John the Evangelist lies on the edge of the village, down a lane that leads on to the Moddershall Valley. It is rock-faced, with bellcote and lancet windows, and was designed by R. Scrivener and Son (1894).

251

Just north of the village is Kibblestone Camp for Scouts.

PATSHULL *2m. S of Albrighton, which is 8m. W of Wolverhampton.*

Some large, old country houses have an air of melancholy. They were designed for perfect summer evenings - any self respecting squire went abroad for the winter - to be filled with light and laughter, to be the scene of the hunt balls and the weekend retreats of visiting gentry. When they become hotels, homes for the elderly or company headquarters, and accumulate cheap and unsympathetic satellite buildings, they almost physically wilt. Although one regrets the demolition of so many of our great houses one can be consoled by remembering that there are fates worse than death. Patshull was owned first by the Astleys, then the Pigots (who bought it on the proceeds of the sale of the famous Pigot diamond) and then by the Earls of Dartmouth. Today it is an orthopaedic hospital. The Hall was built about 1750 by James Gibbs for Sir John Astley, 2nd

Patshull Hall, now a hospital.

Patshull, the pool in the park of the Hall.

baronet, and altered and enlarged in the 1880's for the 5th Earl of Dartmouth by William Burn. The approach was designed to impress — gate posts, a large forecourt with two pedimented gateways, a substantial gatehouse of 5 bays with giant pilasters, and an archway with Tuscan columns and a central cupola. Beyond all this is a second forecourt with 2 arches. The front facade is of 7 bays with a 3-bay pediment and angle towers. The land falls away from the front of the house and this has been terraced with steps down to the gardens. The church lies

some 200yds. from the house, in the direction of the lakes, down a track along which we passed droves of young people hobbling on crutches – somewhat nervously for the ground was pretty rough. The lane is wooded as is the churchyard. St. Mary's was also designed by James Gibbs and built in 1743. In 1874 the north aisle was added. It is ashlar with a west tower, a Victorian cupola and a Venetian east window. There are monuments to Sir John Astley, died 1532; Sir Richard Astley, died 1687; Lord Pigot, died 1795; Sir Robert Pigot, died 1796; and others to the Earls of Dartmouth. In the churchyard, against the north wall, is the statue of a man in armour with long curly hair. This is thought to be the Duke of Monmouth, brought here form Sandwell Park (West Bromwich), the former home of the Earls of Dartmouth. The Park is largely to the S of the Hall. In recent years it has been developed as a sports and leisure centre by a company that has no connection with the hospital. There is a golf course, a hotel and fishing in the Great Pool. The setting is splendid and the facilities excellent. The entrance to Patshull Pool, as it is known locally, is from the south, 1·5m. W of the village of Pattingham.

PATTINGHAM *7m. W of Wolverhampton.*
To the W of Wolverhampton is a new housing development at Perton. The old, small hamlet is now called Old Perton, which is near Wightwick Manor. From Old Perton a lane leads westwards along Perton Ridge to Pattingham. Here are many fine and very expensive modern villas, largely owned by the well-to-do of Wolverhampton. Pattingham is an old village, once owned by the great Anglo-Saxon thane, Earl Algar, and after 1066 by King William. It is a compact, nucleated settlement with some good Georgian houses, one of which is the large brick built Vicarage. It has 5 bays and 3 storeys with large angle pilasters and wooded gardens. The pub near the church is one of the most popular in the area. The church of

St. Chad has a fine Early English (restored) south arcade and a large tower of the 14th Century. The stained glass is by Kempe, and Kempe and Tower and the reredos is by Oldrid Scott. The church was restored by Gilbert Scott in 1871 and the spire dates from then. His son, Oldrid, later added the pinnacles and flying buttresses. The Shropshire border lies 0·5m. to the SW. Near Nurton, 1m. E of Pattingham, the Staffordshire Way long-distance footpath crosses the Old Perton to Tettenhall road. The country all around is pleasantly agricultural.

PELSALL *3m. N of Walsall centre.*
A northern suburb of Walsall, full of modern houses and large unexpected greens. The church of St. Michael is a Commissioners' Church of 1843 with a tower of 1875 and a chancel of 1889. Pelsall is an Anglo-Saxon name. The 'all' ending means a 'nook', a

Pelsall, St. Michael's church.

secluded place in the country. How times change. Today the settlement is bounded by the Wyreley and Essington Canal to the north and a railway line to the west. It lies on the edge of the Cannock coalfield and from the 18th Century until recently iron and coal were mined here. Up to about 1880 nails were made by 'sweated' labour in small forges attached to the workers' cottages. At Moat Farm there is a moat 168ft. by 80ft. To the south of Pelsall, at Heath End, is a large sewage works.

PENKRIDGE *6m. S of Stafford.*
In Anglo-Saxon times the manor belonged

to King Edward and after the Conquest it passed to King William. In 1086 it was a substantial village of at least 30 households and the manor also included land at Wolgarston, Drayton, Congreve, Dunston, Cowley and Beffcote. The name Penkridge is derived from the name of the river that flows through it - the River Penk - which is a very ancient Celtic name. Today there is a flourishing Wednesday general market and an important livestock market. In the late 17th and early 18th Centuries there was also a very famous horse-fair. In the 1720's Daniel Defoe attended it and said he thought that it was the 'greatest horse-fair in the world', and that 'an incredible number of gentlemen attended with their grooms to buy gallopers, or racehourses'. Horse races were also held here from about 1680 to 1734 and again in the 19th Century. The village flourished on several trades — brick making, stone quarrying (from the 13th Century until 1940) and iron working (at Slade Pool just S of Bednall in Teddsley Hay from at least 1585). It was well served by communications and

was a coaching station — see the huge white-painted Littleton Arms in the centre of the village on the A449, the main road between the Black Country and the Potteries. Here too, on the other side of the road, is the handsome timber-framed White Hart Inn, obviously restored but probably of 16th Century origin. Another good, old house is the Old Deanery, N of the church, of about 1600, with a stone-built centre and timber-framed wings. To the E the M6 sweeps by, surprisingly silent, probably because it is in a deep cutting. To the W is the main line railway and the trains clatter by, surprisingly noisily, probably because the line passes over a long, raised viaduct. This viaduct has 7 arches, each of a 30ft. span, and is 37ft. high. It is the most important engineering work on this line in Staffordshire. (It was built for the Grand Junction Railway which opened in 1837). The village centre is on the main road but there is another, much pleasanter and possibly older, centre at School Square which has some good houses and cottages in stone, brick and half-timber. The School-

Penkridge, St. Michael's church.

house itself is of brick with pointed windows, designed by Joseph Potter and built in 1818. Along the road to Cannock from this square are more good houses and the Haling Dean Centre. Just over the motorway bridge on the road to Cannock is the famous Veterinary Surgery of Eddie Straiton, one of the finest establishments of its kind in the country. Even though Mr. Straiton has now retired and lives in Minorca, he still writes and broadcasts on radio and television. The great Roman forts on Watling Street around Stretton Mill, 3m. SW of Penkridge, were collectively called Pennocruciam after the nearby village. From the ground there is nothing to see of the Roman camps and defences because they have been systematically ploughed out. Only in comparatively recent times have they been located by the study of aerial photographs. The church of St. Michael at Penkridge is of extreme antiquity. The present building was almost certainly preceded by an Anglo-Saxon church and that in turn preceded by a Celtic temple. In medieval times it was a 'royal free chapel', i.e. a Collegiate church, of which there were only 13 in the whole country. (Five of the others were also in Staffordshire, namely Wolverhampton, Tettenhall, Stafford, Gnosall and probably Tamworth.) A Collegiate church owed allegiance to the King alone, had great financial privileges and was usually endowed with extensive estates. St. Michael's lost its Collegiate status and was stripped of its lands in 1548 after the Reformation. The church is built of local red sandstone. The exterior is Perpendicular. The interior is earlier with the chancel of about 1225 and the nave of about 1250. The tower is Decorated below and Perpendicular above. It has a 14th Century E window, Early English arcades and overall is a high, spacious church with a most pleasant and inviting atmosphere. The fine chancel screen is Dutch wrought iron dated at 1789. (It had been used as a gate on a Boer farm in South Africa and was rescued by the Hon. William Littleton, who was aide

to the High Commissioner there). There are 6 misericords and 15th Century stalls, some with original carved fronts. The stained glass is mostly Victorian. The monuments include: an alabaster portrait group of William of Winnesbury, Chief Forester of Cannock, died 1502, and wife and daughter; an alabaster effigy of Sir Edward Littleton, died 1558; and memorials to Sir Edward Littleton, died 1574; Sir Edward, died 1610;

Penkridge, the White Hart Inn.

Sir Edward, died 1629; and Richard Littleton, died 1518. The Littleton family lived at Pillaton, 1·5m. ESE of Penkridge, and later at **Teddesley** Park, 2m. NE of Penkridge. At Teddesley they built a large brick Hall designed by William Baker. This 18th Century mansion was demolished after the Second World War. The Snetzler organ (1769) from Teddesley Hall is now at St. Andrew-by-the-Wardrobe in the City of London. The stable blocks still stand, large and handsome and, rather bizarely, in the middle of a field. They are now used for the

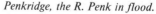

Penkridge, the R. Penk in flood.

Penkridge, Cuttlestone Bridge.

purposes of agriculture. The Home Farm still flourishes, and amongst the outbuildings is the largest diameter water-wheel in Staffordshire. It measures 38ft. by 2ft. 8ins. wide and has 13 arms. The mill was primarily designed to power a threshing machine and secondarily to power a sawmill, a kibbling machine and a cutting machine. It was made by James Bate of Himley and was installed in 1838. The main entrance to the Park is from the village of Bednall, 4m. NE of Penkridge, but there is another entrance off the Penkridge to Acton Trussell road just E of the motorway bridge. Parts of the Park have a distinctly medieval feel to them. In fact, Teddesley Hay was one of the 8 early medieval hays of Cannock Forest. (The others were Alrewas, Bentley, Cheslyn, Gailey, Hopwas, Ogley and Rugeley). Each Hay was in the control of a Forester and they were responsible to a Chief Forester, the first of whom was the son of a Saxon thane called Richard Chenven. The Chief Forester was

Penkridge, Synthetic Chemicals factory

appointed by the King. There is a surprising amount of information about the early forest and its foresters, obtained from Court and Inquisition records, and this is given at some length in the Victorian History of the County of Stafford, Volume II, pages 338-343. On the NE fringe of the village of Penkridge, between the road to Acton Trussell and the River Penk, is the Rolling Mill (SJ.925.145), an old water-mill that is now powered by electricity but which still grinds corn. The river used to flow close by the mill but has been diverted to its present course as part of a flood prevetion scheme, though the river still floods on occasion and makes a huge lake hereabouts. The name Rolling Mill refers to its previous use as a mill for rolling iron.

Penkridge, the Roller Mill.

Other metal working mills in the Penkridge area were at: Bangley Park (SJ.947.143), site of Hazel Mill - pond bay, mill pond, slag, brick building on stone base, iron wheel with hexagonal shaft; Wolgarston (SJ.937.144) site of Newtown Mill — marshy areas where mill pools were, stone dam, causeway between pools, iron slag mound to south, a mill here since 1532 at least, used for grinding bone in 19th Century and corn also; Congreve (SJ.904.132) - site of Congreve Mill on Manor Farm, was a forge until about 1830, then a cow shed and demolished in 1977 as part of a flood control scheme. Half a mile SW of Penkridge is the 18th Century Cuttlestone Bridge with 5 arches and cutwaters. Less than a mile SW of the bridge is the hamlet of **Congreve,** the old home of the Congreve

Penkridge, country adjacent to Congreve

family. The grand mansion has gone but the present attractive brick manor house is still quite old at about 1700. The family also owned Stretton. Of this family was William Congreve, the playwright, and in this century 2 of their number have received the Victoria Cross for gallantry. (They are commemorated at Stowe by Chartley church). Sir Geoffrey Congreve was created a baronet in honour of his father but was himself killed after having won the D.S.O. in World War Two. He is commemorated in Penkridge church. *(See Pillaton)*.

PENN *2m. SW of Wolverhampton town centre.* Penn is a Celtic name, one of the oldest in the county. There are 2 settlements - Upper and Lower. Upper Penn is a residential suburb of Wolverhampton that lies astride the A449 Wolverhampton to Kidderminster road, and Lower Penn is a small village, 1·25m. W, in open country close to the Staffordshire and Worcestershire Canal. In Domesday Book

Upper Penn, St. Bartholomew's.

both settlements have individual entries. Before 1066 Upper Penn was held by Earl Algar and Lower Penn by Lady Godiva, wife of Earl Leofric. Lady Godiva erected a Preaching Cross at which Christian services were held by the priests from Dudley Priory. After the Norman Conquest both manors passed to William, son of Anscuif, and both were included within the boundary of the Forest of Kinver. About 1200 Sir Hugh de Bushbury built the church of St. Bartholomew at Upper Penn. It lies on a hill, very probably the site of a pre-historic fort. Of the church we see today a blocked N window may be Norman; 2 bays of the N arcade are 13th Century and 2 bays W of these are Perpendicular; the tower is 15th Century encased in Gothic brick of 1765; the brick NW annexe is of 1826; the west half of the S side with lancet windows is of 1845; the ashlar-faced E end is of 1872 by Parley of Lancaster. The font is Perpendicular and there is a monument to John Marsh of 1802 by Flaxman. In the churchyard, against the S wall, is the base of the Godiva Preaching Cross which was found buried by the church in 1910. Penn Hall lies W of the church. It is a 17th Century house encased within 18th Century walls with 6 bays to the entrance side and a round-headed doorway above which is an Art Noveau sundial. On the garden side there are 7 bays with a central doorway surmounted by a pediment. Inside is some 17th Century panelling and plasterwork, and upstairs are some unusual doors with 1 large panel over 4 smaller panels. In the grounds there is a barn of 1779 and 2 summer houses. **Lower Penn** is a pleasant village that lies on the slope of a hill with a pub, the Greyhound, and a charming half-timbered cottage called Walnut Tree which is now attached to a boarding kennels for cats and dogs. Higher up the hill is the old forge, now a dwelling, and almost opposite is the rock-faced church. Higher still is the village green and the stuccoed Charlton House. Dirtyfoot Lane leads off the green and a few yards along is the good, mellow

257

The Greyhound and the Walnut Tree.

brick house called Lower Penn Farm. (The sign outside simply says The Farmhouse). This looks to be the most important building in the village and was probably the manor house. The brickwork is thought to date from the 1670's. It is an irregular building of 2 storeys, with 5 bays, 2 front-facing gables and extensions of a lower height to the right-hand side. Together with the farm buildings it forms one side of a 'U'-shaped courtyard. To the left-hand side of the house is a mature yew tree. At the very top of the hill are some fine modern villas, one of which is The

Ridgeway, a neo-Elizabethan timber-framed house with herringbone masonry on a superb wooded site with far-ranging views over the surrounding countryside. The road follows the ridge SE to Spring Hill and the A449.

PENSNETT *2·5m. SW of Dudley and 1·25m. from Kingswinford.*

The name is Celtic and in the Middle Ages Pensnett Chase spread for several miles around the hamlet. In 1619 Dud Dudley, one of the eleven illegitimate children of the Earl of Dudley, came down from Oxford University to manage his father's furnace and 2 forges on Pensnett Chase. Soon after he was experimenting with coal as a fuel for smelting iron, There is some doubt as to whether he succeeded, but he certainly said that he had done so. In 1787 the Pensnett Chase Act was passed enclosing much of the Chase and giving the Lord of Dudley both agricultural and mining rights on the old common land. Not only was coal and iron

Pensnett, the claypit opposite the Trading Estate.

258

mined there but also were special clays used for the manufacture of fire-resistant tiles and pots. On the western edge of the village, on the A4101 Pensnett to Kingswinford road, is a large clay pit that is still quarried by Hinton, Perry and Davenhill who make Ketley Bricks and Dreadnought Tiles at their works in Dreadnought Road, Pensnett. The quarry lies on the opposite side of the road from the Pensnett Trading Estate, at the entrance to which is an old pit-head winding wheel and

Pensnett Trading Estate, old pit gear.

scaffold has been erected. North of the main road, and in the direction of Dudley, are the woods of Barrow Hill, one of the many unexpected green areas in the Black Country. Here is the large, almost imposing, church of St. Mark, designed by J. M. Derick and built in 1896-9. It is built of ashlar stone, has lancet windows, a high nave with clerestory and a high chancel. Between the church, and Gornal Wood and Lower Gornal to the NE, is a stretch of wasteland and poor pasture that has a great deal of character with donkeys grazing and huts made from old railway sleepers. The land rises up to the heights of Upper Gornal and the ridge road between Sedgley and Dudley.

PILLATON *1·24m. ESE of Penkridge.*
In the flat land W of Penkridge, over the motorway and on the edge of Cannock Chase, is the hamlet of Pillaton. A track to the south of the settlement leads past the old manor farm to Pillaton Hall. It is one of those unsung and largely unseen romantic relics of

which there are so many in England. The manor belonged to the Monastery of St. Mary and St. Modwena at Burton on Trent at the time of Domesday. It was then held by a succession of local lords until 1502 when William of Winnesbury died. He had been Chief Forester of Cannock Chase, and by virtue of that appointment was also Lord of Huntington and Teddesley. His heir was his daughter, Alice, and she married Richard Littleton (died 1518), a lawyer in Royal Service. The Hall and the chapel that we see today were built by the Littletons. Originally, it had 4 ranges forming a quadrangle. Today all that remains is the front gatehouse block and the chapel, a little brickwork of the east range, a chimney of the west range and the stone base of a fire-place of the main hall range. The gatehouse has 4 round angle turrets and an arched entrance. On either side are wings with mullioned and transomed windows, probably inserted later in the Jacobean period. The moat still exists. In 1488 the stone chapel of St, Modwena was mostly rebuilt and is still well maintained

Pillaton Hall.

and well furnished. Amongst the furnishings is a very rare, Early English, carved wood statue of a seated saint, probably of the late 13th Century *(See Penkridge).*

PIPE RIDWARE *See Ridware.*

RANGEMOOR *5m. W of Burton upon Trent.*
A small village in Needwood Forest with oaks in the hedgerows and ferns by the

259

Rangemoor, Needwood Manor Hotel.

mile east of Rangemoor on the road to Tatenhill, is Needwood Manor Hotel, a red brick Gothic house in the style of a Scottish Baronial castle.

RANTON 4m. E of Stafford.

The village is most easily approached by a lane leading S off the B5405, the Woodseaves to Great Bridgeford road. It is a scattered settlement with a small nucleus of old cottages and a small medieval church. All Saints is 13th Century Early English with mainly Perpendicular windows. The chancel is of brick and is of 1753. In the village there has been some new development in recent

roadside. Many of the roads are long and straight, a sign of post-medieval enclosure of waste and common land by big landowners whose field boundaries were fixed by lines drawn on maps and not governed by the lie of the land. Most of the village is Victorian with a church, club, school and cottages built by the Bass brewing family, Lords of Burton. The Church of All Saints was designed by Butterfield and built in 1866 with a south aisle of 1886 and a no-expense-spared chancel by Bodley of 1895. Byrkley Park lies 1·75m. NW of the village. Here was the house, now demolished, of Lord Burton's brother. It is now a garden centre. Lord Burton lived at Rangemoor Hall, now Needwood School, 0·5m. SW of Rangemoor. The original small Georgian house was greatly enlarged by the architect R.W. Edis in 1879 and further extended in 1900. It is part ashlar and part rendered and though large, has little character. The gardens however, are most attractive. They lie in a hollow to the E of the house with pools, lawns and trees and even the Drakelow power station looks quite in place in the far distance. At the time of writing the Hall had just been sold by the County Council and was in the process of being renovated. There is a stable block of 1895 and a large brick-lined ice-house, 18ft. deep, approached through a long tunnel. The East Lodge, 1m. N, is a 5 bay Georgian house of ashlar with a Tuscan column porch and Grecian decoration to the window pediments. Half a

Ranton, the grotesquely overgrown ruins of Ranton Abbey, the house.

years, mainly large detached houses, desirable in themselves, perhaps, but totally incongruous to their surroundings. They benefit from the country but give nothing in return. There is a village hall in which local rock groups practice. In the country around here there are 3 moated sites: at Hextall (SJ.858.250), just over 0·5m. N of Ranton – 3 sides remain 230ft. by 210ft.; at Ranton Hall (SJ.846.244), 0·5m. NW of the village – rectangular remains 340ft. by 280ft.; and at Ranton Abbey (SJ.839.243). Ranton Abbey was founded by Robert and Celestia Noel of Ellenhall about 1150 for Augustinian cannons from Haughmond. In 1820 the 1st Earl of Lichfield built a large house, a hunting lodge or weekend retreat, adjacent to the Abbey. Time has not treated either building very well. All that remains of the Abbey is the large, imposing tower (of the

Ranton, the tower of the Abbey Church.

15th Century) and a little of the nave wall with a Norman doorway decorated with roll moulding. The house, also called Ranton Abbey, is now in ruins though most of the exterior walls are still standing. It was accidentally burned down in 1942, during the Second World War, when troops of Queen Wilhelmina's bodyguard were quartered here. The timbers and water tanks lie as they fell. The amazing feature today is the ivy growth which has enshrouded the building. From a distance the house is invisible in its cloak of green. From a further distance its presence is revealed by the chimney stacks. It is an eerie place and there are tales of witchcraft being practiced here. It is even said that the medieval monks were involved in far-from-Christian rites, and torch light processions at midnight have been seen in recent years. The agricultural park is most attractive and well wooded. Game birds were once bred in the outbuildings of the house. It was owned for many years by the Wedgwood pottery company, but in 1987 Patrick, Earl of Lichfield, bought the estate

and plans to restore the abbey tower, rebuild the house and re-make the lake which has been drained and planted with trees. There are 2 entrances to the Abbey off the B5405 Woodseaves to Great Bridgeford road. At one entrance is a delightful lodge. The Hall and Abbey lie at the end of the track, 0·33m. long, embowered by trees, but the top of the church tower is usually visible from the road. One mile east of Ranton is Vicarage Farmhouse, a timber-framed house with close-set vertical studs, inside is some good Jacobean wall panelling.

REAPS MOOR *2m. S of Longnor.*

A hamlet in the North Staffordshire Moorlands; a scatter of small farms with small fields enclosed by stone walls, a pub and a church-come-house-come-village hall, all under the same roof. This kind of eminently practical arrangement is occasionally found in remote country places. The village hall is on the ground floor and above it is the church of St. John (1842). The house is attached to the end.

RIDWARE *2-4m. E of Rugeley.*

There are 4 Ridwares: Hamstall Ridware, Pipe Ridware, Mavesyn Ridware and Hill Ridware. They lie between the River Blithe to the east and the River Trent to the west, close to their confluence. The name Ridware has Celtic and Anglo-Saxon roots and is interpreted as 'dwellers by the ford' and also as 'river folk'. It is thought that the original settlement was at the ford of Hamstall Ridware. Hamstall means 'home farm' or 'homestead' and was added to the name Ridware when the later daughter settlements were established. The dedication of the church at Hamstall Ridware is to St. Michael, often a sign of antiquity. It is suspected that the territory of the Ridwara (who were Angles) extended beyond these 4 villages and probably included Yoxall, 2m. E of Hamstall Ridware, and Hoar Cross, 2·5m. to the N. The country of the Ridwares is flat and agricultural, but the cooling towers and chimneys of Rugeley power station dominate the skyline.

Hamstall Ridware   4m. E of Rugeley as the

Hampstall Ridware, the old manor gate towers.

crow flies. A place of some character. The village lies just to the west of the River Blythe, close by the bridge. Meadows stretch to the waters' edge. The Hall and church lie on higher ground to the north. Today the Hall is in ruins but the quadrangular outbuildings have been developed as an arts and crafts centre, and a very good one too, with a wide variety of quality merchandise and a coffee shop. The old Hall is built of brick with stone dressings and lies behind the coffee shop, which is adjacent to the

Hampstall Ridware, over the R. Blythe.

farmhouse. The Hall was also based on a quadrangle. It was a manor house of the Fitzherberts, built in the 16th Century. The gatehouse is more or less complete, with its twin capped turrets and an arch built between and decorated on top with stone strapwork (interlaced ornament similar to fretwork). The watch-tower is in ruins but substantial. There are many walls still standing, some of which are incorporated into the coffee shop and the farmhouse. Inside the farmhouse are some reset linenfold panelling and some medallions of about 1530-40. The path from the farm courtyard passes another part of the old Hall, a quaint recessed stone colonnade and balcony with strapwork. This is a delightful little structure that really ought to be

Hampstall Ridware, the Great Barn.

preserved. Ruins can be most attractive but when they degenerate beyond a certain point they can become shapeless, ugly and dangerous. This loggia faces what is now a large walled vegetable and flower garden. A side door to the farmhouse is most attractively festooned with flowers in the summer. The church of St. Michael lies only yards away from the Hall and the farmhouse. Nothing of the Saxon church remains and almost all of the Norman work has been rebuilt: 14th Century chancel and north chapel; Perpendicular north aisle and clerestory; 18th Century north chapel walls; 14th Century tower, small and squat. There is a Norman font and part of the upper window in the west wall of the nave is

Norman also. There is a monument to Richard and John Cotton of 1502. The Fitzherbets acquired the manor of Hamstall Ridware from the Cotton family by marriage. There is also an inscription to Thomas Strongintharme, died 1778.

Pipe Ridware A lane leads south and then west from Hamstall Ridware to Pipe Ridware, a tiny hamlet close to the River

Pipe Ridware, three-storey farmhouse.

Trent. The church of St. James was built in 1840, probably on the site of an earlier church. The chancel was added by Oldrid Scott in 1899. Inside is an interesting stepped triple arcade separating the chancel from the nave. The font is genuine Norman; the front facade of the church neo-Norman.

Hill Ridware The largest of the Ridwares with houses, a pub and a Post Office. Here is the 18th Century brick Rectory of 5 bays. The church is in Mavesyn Ridware.

Mavesyn Ridware The name Mavesyn is a contraction of Mal-voisins, meaning dangerous neighbours, and there are snippets of history that seem to justify this description of the Norman lords who settled here. In 1403 Sir Robert Mavesyn rode out of his fortified manor to join Henry IV at Shrewsbury. A neighbouring lord, Sir William Handsacre, set out at the same time but to join the rival army of Harry Hotspur and Owain Glyndwr. The 2 knights met near Mavesyn Ridware at a place marked by 2 great oaks called Gog and Magog. They fought their own private battle and Sir William was killed. Sir Robert Mavesyn then

Mavesyn Ridware, the medieval Gatehouse.

continued on to Shrewsbury where at Battlefield he met his death in the Battle of Shrewsbury. The Hall from which he set out is now gone but the gatehouse remains and is in very good order. The original Hall and stables probably formed a quadrangle behind the gatehouse, which is stone in the lower front but for the rest is timber-framed, though this was enclosed in brick until about 1718. The gate arch has 14th Century mouldings and in the windows are loop holes. After the Battle of Shrewsbury the manor passed to the Cawardens and then to the Chadwick family. In 1718 the house was rebuilt by Charles Chadwick, a handsome place of brick, 5 bays, 2 storeys and a hipped roof. The church of St. Nicholas is something of a curiosity. In 1782 all but the Perpendicular tower and the Early English north aisle were pulled down and the large brick Mavesyn Chapel added. It is a very clumsy arrangement, curious but inelegant. The chapel houses the monuments to the

Mavesyn Ridware, the Tithe Barn.

dead of the families who owned the manor. These include 2 effigies of unamed knights, one of the 13th Century and one with his legs crossed (meaning he had been on a Holy Crusade); the tomb chest of Sir Robert Mavesyn; Thomas Cawarden, died 1477; Hugh Davenport, died 1473; and 3 small reliefs of recent origin depicting the Mavesyns at war. The village is small but most attractive and in the main street is a superb and beautifully preserved Tithe Barn. There is also a beautiful little thatched timber-framed cottage. To the south, by 400 yds is the High Bridge over the River Trent. It has a span of 140ft. and was made at Coalbrookdale in 1830.

ROACHES *See Upper Hulme.*

ROCESTER *3·25m. NNE of Uttoxeter.*
Rocester is pronounced 'Roaster'. The town

Rocester, excavation of a Roman fort.

lies between the River Churnet and the River Dove, about a mile N of their confluence. In a field to the NE of the church is the site of a fort which is in the process of being excavated. There have been many finds of pottery and a beautiful enamel broach depicting a man on horseback which is probably of Celtic origin. There are believed to be 4 forts here in all, the first dating from about 70 AD. Rocester is set in attractive country but the village is most disappointing. The western approach off the B5030 is pleasant enough with a weir on the River

Churnet, the modest stone mill and the bridge, but the town centre is spoiled by modern flats and there is no sense of a village centre. To the east, near to the River Dove, is the giant Tutbury Mill, built by Richard Arkwright about 1782 as a cotton mill. It is 4 storeys high and 24 bays long. Parts of the roadside entrance are stone-built. The church of St. Michael has a medieval fabric but was much rebuilt and restored in 1870 by Ewan Christian who added the spire to the tower. Inside there are polished marble columns and the east window is by William de Morgan who is renowned for his ceramic lustre tiles. In the churchyard is an extremely well preserved cross of at least the 13th Century. In the pasture field to the S of, and adjacent to, the church is much disturbed ground. Here stood an Augustinian Abbey founded about 1146 by Richard Bacon, the Earl of Chester's nephew. There is nothing above ground left to see today. Very visible though is the new factory of J.C. Bamford, the manufacturers of earth moving equipment with a worldwide reputation. The building is long, low, windowless and constructed of a green material. The grounds have been landscaped and small lakes created. If one must have a factory in the country this is the way to do it. All in all, it is very praiseworthy. It is a pity, however, that the smoked glass section was added in 1987. As a landlord and neighbour the firm has

Rocester, bridge and mill by the R. Churnet.

upset many local people. Old cottages stand empty and large tracts of land are used as

Rocester, the J.C.B. factory.

265

Rocester, the Tutbury Mill.

noisy testing and training grounds. Near the front of the factory is a raised helicopter landing pad. Banks farmhouse lies on a hill

Rocester, Banks Farmhouse (left)

0.5m. W of Rocester and can be seen clearly from the main road. It is a large 'L' shaped red brick folly of 2 storeys with a 5-sided tower, probably of about 1700. It was almost certainly designed as an 'eyecatcher' for Woodseat Hall which now lies in ruins a little to the south. Barrow Hill lies 1m. N of

Rocester, the barrow on Barrow Hill.

Rocester. The B5030 to Ellastone climbs the hill. On the left-hand side, heading north, is an ancient burial mound. The occupants of the nearby house (approached along the track that leads to the big white house) told us that when Birmingham University archaeologists examined the site earlier this century they found fertility figures that left little to the imagination. The barrow lies within a 6·75 acre camp of uncertain age but probably used in the Iron Age.

ROLLESTON *2·5m. N of Burton on Trent.*
From the 17th Century the Hall was the home of the Mosley family, a member of the which was Sir Oswald Mosley, founder of the British fascist party distinguished by the brown shirts they wore. The gabled Jacobean mansion was enlarged in Georgian style in the late 18th Century, damaged by fire in 1870 and rebuilt in 1871 in an Italianate style. Most of the Hall was demolished in the 1920's. The large village lies within half a mile of the River Dove. There are good older houses but there has also been much characterless modern development. The School is of patterned brick and is dated at about 1640. The almshouses are of single-storey brick with quoins and a broken pediment, dated at 1713. The church of St. Mary is a largely rebuilt Norman building. The south porch and room adjoining are 13th Century; the north aisle and south aisle are Decorated; the tower is 14th Century with a later spire; and the north chapel is of 1892 by Sir Arthur Blomfield. There is stained glass by Kempe and monuments to Bishop Sherburne of Chichester, died 1536; Thomas Caldwell, died 1554; Sir Edward Mosley, died 1638, and other Mosleys. In the churchyard is a very large Anglo-Saxon wheel-style Cross Head, believed to be of 9th Century origin and brought here from Tatenhill.

ROWLEY REGIS *0·66m. NW of Blackheath.*
It lies deep in the depths of the Black Country on the B4171 between Dudley and Blackheath; a high hillside place of housing

estates and derelict land with no obvious boundaries. The name Rowley is thought to derive from the Anglo-Saxon 'ruh-leah' meaning 'rough clearing' or 'a clearing in rough scrubland'. The Regis, meaning Royal, seems to have been added in the 14th Century, presumably to differentiate it from another Rowley. The Pipe Rolls show that in the 12th Century it did indeed belong to the king. (King Charles II had a horse called Rowley.) There used to be a borough of Rowley Regis and together with Tipton it returned a member of parliament, one of whom, Arthur Henderson, became first a cabinet minister and then Lord Rowley. The area is probably best known for the hard dolerite-basalt laccolith used as a road stone and known as Rowley Rag. It is still mined in 2 deep quarries. This stone was not worked until the 19th Century. Before that coal was mined here and nail making was an important local industry. The church of St. Giles was founded in 1199 as a chapel-of-ease to the church at Clent. The vicar, the Rev. George Barrs, described the church as 'a cold, damp, ruinous and gloomy dilapidated dungeon' and in 1849 he had it rebuilt.

Rudyard, the north end of the lake.

However, by 1900 it had become unsafe because of settlement caused by mining, and was rebuilt once again in 1904. Then it was destroyed by fire in 1913 and the Gothic red brick church we see today is of 1923. Rowley has a ghost, the distraught spirit of a girl called Elaine who fell in love with a young priest from Hales Abbey. The couple eloped but were caught and as punishment were imprisoned in the tunnel that led from Haden Hall to the monastery. The entrances to the tunnel were bricked up and they were left to die.

RUDYARD *2·5m. NW of Leek.*
Rudyard is famous for its lovely lake, the 'silver lake', which was greatly enlarged as a reservoir to feed the Caldon Canal. (Authority to make the reservoir was granted by Act of Parliament in 1797.) Today it looks totally natural and is most conveniently seen to its best advantage from lay-bys on the A523 Leek to Macclesfield road. Fishermen and sailors frequent its shores and silver waters. It is wooded all around and is a beautiful sight. The village of Rudyard lies at the south-western tip of the long (1·5m.), but narrow, reservoir. There are hotels and guest houses and it is a well attended resort in the summer. There is also a rather shabby shanty town of flimsy cabins tucked away on the western hillside, but along the lake are some more substantial houses and a yachting club house. A place of great character. It was whilst walking by the lake that Lockwood Kipling proposed marriage to Alice Macdonald, and when their son was born in India some time later they named him, Rudyard, after the place where they had become engaged. Rudyard Hall is a good 17th Century stone house of 2 storeys to a 'T' plan. It also has good gate piers and a barn with mullioned windows. Cliffe Park Hall lies above the west

Rudyard, a ship on the silver lake.

bank of the lake, a Gothic, ashlar house of about 1830 with turrets and battlements. It has a coach porch to the S side and facing the lake a symmetrical front with a bow. The name Rudyard may mean 'the place where rudd (a type of fish) are kept' or alternately, 'a lake near a garden in which rue is grown'.

RUGELEY 7·5m. ESE of Stafford.

The name means 'Red Pastures'. Rugeley was one of the many substantial manors owned by the Saxon thane, Earl Algar, which were usurped by King William after the Norman Conquest. Rugeley Hay was one of the eight Hays, or separate divisions, of the Royal Forest of Cannock. Rugeley is a small town, not a village, with a sizeable shopping centre which is now mostly pedestrianised. Without being busy it is quite a lively place and not altogether unpleasant. There are no buildings of special merit but there is a Victorian Gothic Town Hall and a Market hall in Market Square, both of 1878. On the edge of the town, on the road to Lichfield, are a couple of black and white cottages. The dominant buildings here though are the 2 emormous power stations (Rugeley 'A' and Rugeley 'B') and the adjacent Lea Hall Colliery, which lie to the NE of the town between the Trent and Mersey Canal and the River Trent. (The canal was constructed in 1777 and is 12 ft. wide at the bottom and 3 ft. deep. It was designed to take boats 70 ft. long carrying loads of 20 tons with a draft of 2 ft. 6 ins.) All that is left of the old medieval church of St. Augustine is the tower, chancel and north chapel, joined by the 4-bay north arcade of the ruined nave. The chancel is still in use and inside there is a monument to Thomas Lauder, died 1670, in his winding sheet, but looking as though he is in a hammock. The new church of St. Augustine is of 1822 by H.J. Underwood. It is large, with galleries, and has glass by Kempe in the east chancel window and the north chapel window. In Heron St. is the Catholic Church of St. Joseph and St. Ethelfleda of 1849, with a bizarre steeple, and St. Anthony's convent (R.C.) which was originally a house called Heron Court, of 1851 in brick, in a pretty Elizabethan style. The town has had a varied industrial history. From the Middle Ages to 1963 there was a leather tanning industry here. In the 14th Century there was a fulling mill and in 1418 John Glasman of Rugeley sold white glass to York Minster. In the 17th Century William, Thomas and Walter Chetwynd of Rugeley were renowned iron-

Rugeley, the main street.

268

Sandon, the church and the deserted village.

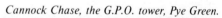
Cannock Chase, the G.P.O. tower, Pye Green.

masters with furnaces and forges on Cannock Chase and other places. In the 19th Century there was a plaster works and in the 20th Century shoes were made here (Lotus 1953). That is not to mention coal mining and brick making for which the local heavy clay is ideal. There is a modern industrial and trading estate on the road to Colton. As to transport, the town has a main line railway, a canal, a river and an old coaching road. On the north-western outskirts of Rugeley is Etchinghill, a place known to prehistoric men who built a large burial mound here. Here too there were regular horse race meetings between 1824-39 and 1848-60. Now, alas, it is smothered in countless rows of modern, and definitely not up-market houses. Just to the S of Etchinghill is **Slitting Mill,** a most pleasant little village carved out of a wooded corner of Cannock Chase. Here are some pleasant modern villas, properly spaced apart, and a large water pumping station (SK.029.171) tucked out of sight

Rugeley, the Waterworks at Slitting Mill.

down a lane by the pub. The pumping station stands on the site of the old iron slitting mill from which the village is named. (A slitting mill cut iron bars into thin rods from which nails were made.) The now dry mill-pond and pond bay still exist to the rear of the station and alongside the stream, the Rising Brook. There are also some overgrown brick culverts, brick walling and stone slabs by the ford across the stream. Half a mile west of Slitting Mill, in Birches Valley, is the Cannock Chase Forest Centre and Deer

Museum. All kinds of tourist and commercial information about the area can be obtained here. Nearby is a reconstructed Deer leap, an arrangement that allows deer to jump into an enclosure but stops them from jumping out again. These were very common in medieval times. The best way to describe a deer leap is to imagine a fence separating two fields. At the point where the leap is to be constructed the fence is lowered by about 2 feet and a mound of earth is raised against it so that the deer can walk up to the level of the top of the fence. On the other side of the fence is a shallow pit about 2 ft. deep. The deer can jump (or leap) into or over the pit and so into the adjoining field. However, they cannot jump back over the other way because the height of the fence, from the bottom of the pit to the top of the fence, is too great (at least 6ft.). Rugeley's most infamous son is William Palmer, the Rugeley Poisoner. He was born here in 1824 and educated at the grammar school. He became a doctor of medecine and lived in a house opposite the Talbot Arms. His practice did not earn him enough to live on and he took to gambling and forgery. In 1854 his wife died suddenly and he collected £13,000 from his insurance company, an enormous sum in those days. Within a year his brother also died, but the insurance company was suspicious and refused to pay. Palmer then poisoned a bookmaker to whom he was in debt. He administered the poison at Shrewsbury Races. The bookmaker fell ill and Palmer brought him back to Rugeley. He got him lodgings at the Talbot Arms so that he could look after him. That night the bookmaker died. A coroner's court accused him of murder and he was duly tried. It was suspected that he had poisoned many other people but he was only charged with the murder of the 3 people mentioned above. The case was of national and international interest. Although he was found guilty the prosecution never established which poison had been used. Palmer was hanged in public outside Stafford Gaol. It is said that the

Rugeley, dear leap between Wolseley park and Cannock Chase.

people of Rugeley were so upset at the bad reputation their town had gained that they petitioned the Prime Minister to have the town renamed. The Prime Minister

Rugeley, the power stations.

suggested that they might care to honour him, their national leader. He was Lord Palmerston.

RUSHALL *1·5m. NE of Walsall.*

In the Domesday Book Rushall is entered as an established manor, whereas Walsall is not even mentioned; but times change and today

Rushall is a suburb of Walsall. The residential areas are fringed with open land along the banks of the Rushall Canal. The church of St. Michael is by James Cranston and was built in 1856. It has a nave, chancel, transepts, and a tower. In 1867 it was lengthened and the spire was added. The font is 13th Century and the wall paintings in the transepts are by Reginald Frampton of 1905. Just to the SE of the church are the ruins of the 15th Century Hall with a high curtain wall. There are signs of fireplaces and

Rushall, the curtain wall of the old 'castle'

271

there is a crude gatehouse with segmental arches. The Hall was held for Parliament by Colonel Leigh at the beginning of the Civil War. In 1643 it was taken by Colonel Lane of Bentley for the Royalists, but was recaptured by Parliament the next year and was dismantled at the end of the war. The stone house that stands near the ruins was built in the 19th Century. The name Rushall means 'rush-nook' i.e. 'the isolated farm by the rushes'.

RUSHTON SPENCER 5·5m. NW of Leek.

The village lies along the A52 Leek to Macclesfield road, about 1m. N of the northern end of Rudyard Reservoir. The village is ordinary enough but overlooking it on the bluff to the W, and visible from the main road, is the 'Chapel in the Wilderness'. The church of St. Lawrence, to give it its more prosaic name, can be approached either from the village, by way of a lane that crosses the route of the now dismantled railway (past the old railway station, now a house) and up the hill of Rushton Bank, or from Ryecroft Gate by turning right at the pub on the top of the hill. The church is embowered in firs and yews at the end of a track that leads across a field, and has to be looked out for. The exterior is largely of stone and has a date of 1690 above the E window and one of 1713 above the S doorway. Within the stone walls and the mullioned windows, and below the weather-boarded bell-turret, is a much older timber-framed church, possibly of the 14th Century. It has low beams, oak piers and trusses, one of which carries the gallery. St. Lawrence is a very rare church. It is highly probable that the original village stood close to the church and moved down into the valley below when the road became important as a trade route. There are still a few houses on the high ground at Rushton Bank to the north of the church and by the pub and Rushton Hall to the south. In Domesday Book the manor is referred to simply as Rushton. It belonged to the King

and at that time was 'waste'. The hatchments in the church are of the Trafford and Brocklehurst families who lived at Swythamley Hall, 3m. NE of Rushton Spencer. Swythamley is set in lovely country, the landscape of the medieval romance, 'Sir

The Chapel in the Wilderness.

Gawain and the Green Knight'. The Staffordshire-Cheshire border is marked by the Dane River, which is crossed by the Hug Bridge, 0·75m. NE of Rushton Spencer on the A523. In 1620 this bridge was destroyed in a flood. Responsibilty for maintaining it was divided between Cheshire and Staffordshire. The Cheshire half was rebuilt in stone, but for some time the Staffordshire side consisted of 'long, tottering and loose poles'.

SALT 3·5m NE of Stafford.

Salt brine, from which salt is obtained by evaporation, has been obtained from natural springs and by pumping in Stafford (at Rickerscote and the Common) and at Shirleywich, near Weston on Trent (1·75m. SE of the village of Salt). However, there are no historical records or signs on the ground that salt was produced at, or close to, Salt itself. The name is at least as old as Domesday Book where it is called Selte, so one must presume that it had some ancient connection with the trade, if not as a producer then as a market place. The village is pleasantly situated on a minor road in the Trent valley opposite Sandon park. Modern houses now line the road on either side of the old centre which lies around the Holly Bush

272

Salt, an old cave near Tinker Borough. 536

pub. The church of St. James is on the eastern fringe of the settlement. It was built by Thomas Trubshaw in 1840-2 and paid for by Lord Talbot. The tall bellcote, the lofty nave, the high vaulted sanctuary, the large rose window and irregular nave windows delight some but are disparaged by others. Little known, even to locals, are the ruined cave houses on Salt Heath, 0·66m. S of the village on a wooded hillside (SJ.956.272). The public footpath from the village starts alongside a house called The Hollies. The

Salt, the old Ingestre estate water pumping engine house.

Salt, cave house ruins at Tinker Borough.

path is not defined on the ground but if one heads leftwards, towards a gap between 2 woods, the caves will be seen near the top of the bluff to the right. They are well camouflaged by undergrowth and have to be looked for. The caves were extended at the front by the addition of orthodox house fronts built of stone blocks. There is a path, like a small terrace, in front of them. The caves, fireplaces and stone blocks are now in ruins, but were lived in until the early part of this century by people who followed the tinkers' trade. The area is called Tinkerborough. A few yards NE, on the side of the hill facing the village, is another much older looking cave, made in the apparently softer rocks below a striking unconformity between the sandstone strata. One suspects that man may have lived in this area since prehistoric times, but as far as we know it has not been expertly investigated. Salt was very highly prized in ancient times, and the Romans even paid their soldiers' wages partly in salt — hence 'salary'. It is not unlikely that ancient man would choose to

live near the source of a mineral so useful in many ways and, indeed, necessary for life itself.

SANDON *4m. NNE of Stafford.*
The village lies along the A51 Rugeley to Stone road in the Trent valley. The centre of the settlement is at the junction with the road to Stafford and was rebuilt about 1905 in Arts and Crafts black and white by Sir E. Guy Dawber at the expense of Lord Harrowby. The pub, the Dog and Doublet, the village hall and a few cottages were all made to match — somewhat artificial but not unpleasing. A little further northwards there are some good brick houses, a Post Office and an old chapel now used as a furniture workshop. The Sandon we see today is a relatively new creation. The manor that Earl Algar owned in 1066, and which passed to the King after the Conquest, lay 0·33m. ENE of the new centre, between the church and the moat that marks the site of the medieval and Tudor manor houses. It was the fashion in the 16th and 17th

Sandon, the Park from the church.

Centuries to empark the land around the Hall or Manor House. Some landowners built themselves a new Hall away from the village and others chose to keep their old house and remove the village. At Sandon the lord chose the latter and the old village of Great Sandon was obliterated. The tenants presumably moved down to the hamlet of Little Sandon which had grown up along the

Sandon, the new main road village.

road, so the Sandon of today should really be called Little Sandon. The church and the moat of the old Hall are in Sandon Park whose woods line the main road. It is a large and beautiful estate, very little of which can be seen by the public, although the road from Sandon to Milwich passes through similar undulating and slightly mysterious country. The estate used to belong to the Erdeswick family, one of whom was Samson Erdeswick (died 1603), a local historian of some repute. His son sold the manor to George Digby, his half brother, whose daughter and heiress married Lord Gerard of Gerard's Bromley (near Ashley). His grand-daughter married the 4th Duke of Hamilton in 1698. The old manor house in which the lords had lived until then is that depicted in Dr. Plot's 'Natural History of Staffordshire' (1686). However, the 9th Duke of Hamilton, Lord Archibald, demolished the old manor and built a new classical house, designed by Joseph Pickford, 0·5m. further S, near the main road. The 9th Duke sold this house and the estate to the 1st Earl of Harrowby in 1777. In 1848 the house burned down and the 2nd

Earl commissioned William Burn to build another. The new stone-built Jacobean mansion with gables and turrets was complete by 1852. The entrance side has 9 bays, 2 storeys and a coach porch. Attached to the house is a fine Victorian Conservatory of 1864. In the grounds are an Ice House by the drive; the Italianate belvedere Tower Top from the dismantled Trentham Hall; the Perceval Shrine in memory of the murdered Prime Minister, Spencer Perceval (died 1812); the Pitt column, at the most southern tip of the Park near the road; a Doric pillar of 1806; and the Home Farm of 1777-80 in classical style of ashlar with low roofs by Samuel Wyatt. By the railway is the Sandon Estate Station, a delightful neo-Jacobean building of 1849, which contained private apartments for the Duke and a coach-porch for his carriage. The station can be seen quite clearly from the road to Stafford, near to the village centre. It had fallen into shameful disrepair but fortunately the Harrowby estate decided to sell it and the new owners have renovated the old building in a most excellent way. Just SW of the station and the railway line is the Trent and Mersey Canal which follows a parallel course to the River

Sandon Hall.

Trent. The church of All Saints now stands alone save for one little cottage at the back of the churchyard. There are lovely views across the Park from here. The oldest part of the church is the 13th Century south aisle, which was in fact the original church. To this was added the tower; then a north aisle; then,

Sandon, the church of All Saints.

about 1300, a new chancel; then a new nave was built in place of the north aisle; and lastly a new short north aisle was added in the 14th Century. The furniture and furnishings are very fine — bleached oak pews, pulpit and reredos, all of the 17th Century. There is a fragment of early 14th Century glass in the west window, heraldic glass of the 17th Century in the east window and glass by Wailes in the west window of 1845. The monuments include memorials to the Erdeswickes, George Digby and the Harrowbys. The north aisle became the Harrowby Chapel in 1851. The epitaph to the 5th Earl reads: 'He built the central layout of Sandon Village and many farms, small holdings and cottages, and planted some 100,000 trees. He loved every sod of soil on the Estate.' The present Earl, the 7th, is a banker. The family name is Coutts Ryder, of the same line that established Coutts & Company bankers to the Queen.

SEDGLEY *3m. S of Wolverhampton.*
In early medieval times Sedgley was a large parish and a large manor which had, prior to the Conquest, belonged to Earl Algar. It lies at the northern end of the high watershed ridge that runs from southern Wolverhampton to Dudley, and which divides the Black Country. From Beacon Hill there are wide views over Shropshire and Wales to the west and over the Black Country and Cannock Chase to the east. On top of the hill is a late 19th Century stone tower, built by Lord Wrottesley as an astrological observatory. The town centre of Sedgley is a thriving place though its northern fringes degenerate as Wolverhampton is approached. The actual centre is the Bull Ring, a reminder that blood sports were widely practiced in the area during the 18th and 19th Centuries. Here is the Red Lion, an old coaching inn. All around the town are modern housing estates. The medieval church of All Saints in Vicarage Street was rebuilt by Thomas Lee in 1826-9 at the expense of the 1st Earl of Dudley. It is an impressive Gothic building with a tall, recessed pinnacled spire, high aisles, long 2-light windows and no chancel arch. The ashlar Roman Catholic church of St. Chad and All Saints in Catholic Lane is of 1823, an early date for such a grand church because Catholics were only allowed to worship in public from 1829. The presence of the church is explained by the fact that there used to be a Roman Catholic college 1·5m. N of Sedgley town centre at what is now the Park Hall Hotel (technically now in Wolverhampton). The hall is approached along the Ednam Road off the A4039. It is probably of the early 18th Century and is of brick with 5 bays, 3 storeys, a centrepiece of various columns and a carved frieze in Jacobean style. On either side are long 2-storey wings. The gardens are largely given over to a tarmac car park. Park Hall was an old home of the Dudley family. In Ettingshall Lane, which used to be called Hell Lane, there lived a witch who could turn herself into a white rabbit which regularly snooped about the gardens and even the houses of her neighbours. About a mile W of Sedgley town centre, down Bush Bank, at Gospel End is the site of Baggeridge Colliery, the last large pit in the Black Country. The area has been landscaped and in 1983 the newly formed Country Park was opened by Princess Anne. Close by, signposted by tall chimneys, is Baggeridge Brickworks which is still a going concern. Between Gospel End and Wombourne is a

mile or more of open country. One mile SSE of Sedgley town centre is Cotwall End Nature Reserve, a Site of Special Scientific Interest, with a variety of plant and animal life — some in natural habitats, others in aviaries and freshwater pools. There is also a walled garden and a fox's lair, constructed so that it can be viewed through a window. Admission is free.

SEIGHFORD *2·5m. NW of Stafford.*

The old name of the village was Chesterford — Cesteforde in Domesday Book — which implies that there is an undiscovered Roman settlement hereabouts. The village consists of red brick cottages, farms, the half-timbered Church Farm, a pub and the village green, which lies between the school and the church. The 'ford' of the village's name is where the Gamesley Brook is crossed by the lane that leads off the village green, opposite the school. St. Chad's church has a 17th Century brick tower with Gothic details, buttresses and stone pinnacles of 1748 and a brick south wall. The north wall and chancel are medieval stone. Inside, the north arcade and chancel arch are Norman, probably of the late 12th Century. The south chancel window has 15th Century figures and fragments. The monuments include alabaster effigies of William Bowyer, died 1595, and wife, and an obelisk commemorating Francis Eld of 1777. The pulpit and communion rail are Jacobean and the Squire's pew is of 1748. It is a church which has great atmosphere. Seighford Hall lies 0·25m. NW of the village green. It is a large timber-framed house with a late 16th Century core and considerable late Victorian extensions which are very well done. The Hall was the home of the Eld family. In recent years it was a hotel but is now a home for old people. To the left of the house are the sizeable outbuildings. The brick church-like structure was the Gamekeeper's Cottage and the timber-framed stables have recently been renovated and converted into dwellings. Just to the NE of the Hall (on the

Seighford, the ford and the village beyond.

277

Seighford, the church of St. Chad.

Seighford Hall.

road to Great Bridgford) is Cooksland Hall Farm, and at the end of the track is a large timber-framed barn. Seighford Aerodrome lies 0·5m. W of the village. It is now very little used but the runways are still intact and relatively clear of undergrowth. A light aeroplane is stored in a hangar hidden by a wood. Close to the southern tip of the aerodrome is Coton Clanford Hall Farm, a good timber-framed house with a 3-storey brick porch. Coton Clanford is a hamlet 0·75m. S of the Hall. As one might suspect by the presence of the wartime aerodrome the land here is relatively flat. The scattered farms and cottages are joined by a maze of narrow, unsignposted winding lanes, many of which form rough circles, as not a few strangers have found to their fury.

SHARESHILL *4·5m. N of Wolverhampton.*
An old, pre-Norman settlement. The present village lies just beyond the suburbs of Wolverhampton but has been ensnared by motorways, with the M6 1m. to the E. (at junction 11) and the M54 just over 1m. to the S (at junction 1). A few of the older houses have survived but as always new housing has done little to enhance the townscape. The church of St. Luke has a stone tower, the lower part of which is 15th Century and the upper of about 1562 with a freize of saltire crosses below the crenellations. The rest is Georgian with stone dressings of about 1742. The windows have round heads and pilasters; the porch has Tuscan columns and the apse has a Venetian window. The furnishings are of the period — box pews, pulpit and altar rails. The alabaster figures are of Sir Humphrey Swynnerton, died 1562, and wife. William Havergal (died 1870), a respected composer of hymns and church music was a vicar here. Frances Ridley Havergal, also a writer of hymns, was his daughter. Little Sandon lies 0.25m. NE of Shareshill. Here is an old windmill and an old Hall. One mile SE of Shareshill is Hilton Hall.

SHEEN *2·5m. SSE of Longnor, which is 6m. SSE of Buxton.*

A remote village in the North Staffordshire Moorlands between the upper reaches of the River Dove to the E and the River Manifold to the W. The farms and cottages straggle along the road. There is a school, a Post Office and a church. St. Luke's was rebuilt in the 19th Century. The work was started by C.W. Burleigh but finished by William Butterfield who was appointed by Alexander Beresford Hope, the squire of Beresford Hall. (Beresford Hall was previously the home of Joseph Cotton of 'Compleat Angler' fame. It lay about 2m. to the SSE but has been demolished — see Dovedale.) Beresford Hope was a wealthy Anlgo-Catholic and a friend of the founders of the Camden Society to one of whom, namely Benjamin Webb, he gave the living of Sheen parish. All the stained glass in the church is of 1854 by O'Connor. The monuments include: a defaced effigy in the churchyard; a memorial to the Crichton family of about 1855, also in the churchyard; and tablets to Beresford Hope, died 1887, and Lady Mildred Beresford Hope, died 1881. The school is by Burleigh and the most excellent and interesting Parsonage is by Butterfield of 1852. It has varied roof lines, broad chimney stacks, a polygonal stair turret and pointed arch windows. About 1m. SSW of Sheen is Hulme End. Here is the Light Railway Hotel, a reminder that the narrow gauge (2' 6") Manifold Valley Light Railway operated between Hulme End and Waterhouses (where it connected with the normal gauge railway) between the years 1904 and 1934. When the line was dismantled the trackway was metalled and is now a footpath. To the E. of Sheen, by 0.5m., is Brund. Here is Brund Mill (SK.099.613), a 3-storey watermill which, though partly ruined, is of great interest because of the machinery and engineering technique used here for grinding. In the hills to the east of Brund are 2 ancient burial mounds.

SHENSTONE *4m. E of Brownhills and 3m. S of Lichfield.*

The village lies 1m. S off the busy junction of the A5, the A5127 and the A5148. It sits on a hill with 2 church towers making it easily identified. Shenstone has a history as old as history can be, for here was found an early stone hand axe made some 30,000 years B.C., before the last Ice Age. The Romans were busy hereabouts. Watling Street passes 0·33m. to the NE, Ryknild Street 0·25m. to the W and the Roman fort-settlement of Wall (Letocetum) is only 1·5m. NW. There can be little doubt that the Anglo-Saxons had a settlement at Shenstone from soon after the Roman departure. In 1066 the manor was held by Godwin who lost it to the great marcher lord Roger de Montgomery after the Conquest. In 1086 it was a settlement of some considerable size for its day with a population of at least 26 families. In Shenstone Park is an isolated rectangular

Shenstone Hall.

moat, presumably the site of an early timber-framed manor house. Shenstone Hall is 0·5m. NE of the village surrounded by high walls. The facade and forecourt facing the road is Jacobean with mullioned windows and 3 gables made Gothic at the end of the 18th Century. The garden facade is even more strongly Gothicized with an ornate porch and decorated gables — altogether an attractive house. Shenstone Court lay 0·5m. SE of the village but was pulled down before the Second World War. The church of St. John is surprisingly impressive though somewhat stern. It was built in 1852 by John Gibson — nave, aisles, tower, outer south chapel and large rose window. NW of the new church stands the tower and some walling with an Early English doorway of the old medieval church. Shenstone has such excellent road communications that it is attractive to commuters and is in danger of being spoiled by developers.

SHIRLEYWICH *0·75m. SE of Weston on Trent, which is 4m. NE of Stafford.*

The area was originally called Brinepits but at the end of the 17th Century Robert Shirley (Lord Ferrers) developed the salt workings here commercially and within a few years the name had changed to Shirleywich. The Earl dug new pits until he found a brine stream. The new brine pit was 27 ft. deep and 6 ft. square. The brine was evaporated in 3 iron pans 8 ft. by 5 ft. and it took 1 ton of coal and 16 hours to produce 14 bushels of salt. This was twice as long and twice as costly as anywhere else, but the quality was good and the product commanded a higher price. About 1700 a new, stronger brine stream was tapped and a new works was built. Production rose to about 800 tons a year. Demand then dropped and the works were leased to a local farmer, Preston Moore. In 1777 the Trent and Mersey Canal came within a few hundred yards of the works. During the Napoleonic Wars trade increased. There were now 8 pans and production had risen to 4,000 tons of salt a year. About 20 families, totalling about 100 people, lived in Shirleywich and all were employed at the works. By the 1830's production was 12,500 tons a year but by 1870 it was falling because the supply of brine was getting weaker. By the 1890's the works only operated inter-mittently and by 1901 they were closed. As the Shirleywich works closed so a new company began to expand at Stafford *(see Stafford)*. Today there is very little to see at Shirleywich. The brine pits were behind the 3 pairs of semi-detached houses opposite the Shirleywich Service Station. Next to them on the right, is an area of disturbed ground. There was a row of 13 cottages here. The people who lived in these houses grew to be very old and the local people think that it was the salt in the air that kept them fit and healthy.

SHUGBOROUGH *5m. ESE of Stafford.*

Shugborough is an estate, not a village. There was a village here once but it was removed by the Anson family between about 1750 and 1825 to improve the view from the Hall. Some of the dispossesed tenants were re-housed at Great Haywood near the Essex Bridge. The estate covers some 900 acres of Cannock Chase and the greater part lies on a promontory of low land S of the confluenece of the River Sow and the River Trent. It can be approached on foot from Great Haywood but the main entrance is off the A513 Stafford to Rugeley road at Milford Common.The square entrance lodges have pyramid roofs and pairs of columns. They were designed by the architect, Samuel Wyatt, who worked at Shugborough between 1790 and 1806. The drive passes through woods of tall trees. To the left is a marshy area with pools and dense under-growth. The road leaves the woodland and enters the agricultural Park. The main-line railway emerges from a tunnel here and it is a surprise to find such an intrusion. A little further along the Home Farm is passed on the right. Here are found: the Dairy where butter is made using 19th Century equipment; the Farmhouse Kitchen, restored and furnished as it was in 1805; the Scullery, with both washing facilities and a bread making oven; Noah's Park with Jacob sheep and poultry for young children to see at close quarters; shire horses; northern shorthorn cattle; longhorn cattle; white park cattle, an ancient 'Roman' breed; Tamworth pigs; Gloucestershire Old Spot pigs; bearded Bagot goats; and various breeds of sheep. The mill is being restored and will grind corn grown on the estate. The farm buildings were constructed about 1805.

Shugborough, a baby Bagot goat.

The entrance drive ends at the County Museum which is housed in the out-buildings of the Hall. These are arranged around a courtyard. There are recon-structions of domestic rooms, craft workshops, a school room and retail shops etc., together with a collection of coaches, the restored Estate Brewery and much more. The buildings have been painted in pale grey to match the painted brick Mansion. It is a surprise to find that the 8 giant columns which front the impressive portico of the Hall are a sham, being made of wood dressed in slate and painted. The history of the house is this: the centre is of 1693; the wings are of 1748, though originally only of 1 storey and heightened after 1768 by James Stuart; the columned portico was added by Wyatt in 1794, and at the same time the high centre block was lowered by removing the balustrade and placing it over the wings; the Saloon with convex front, a Drawing Room and other rooms at the rear were added in

Shugborough, a Tamworth Gilt pig.

281

1803-6. The rooms presently open to the public exhibit splendid plasterwork and decorative mouldings on ceilings, coveings, arches, friezes, columns and chimney pieces

Shugborough, a farmer's 'market cart'.

and are beautifully furnished with a collection of paintings, 18th Century ceramics, silver and French furniture. The house was bought by the Anson family in 1624. The man who made their name and their fortune was George Anson, died 1762. He was in turn Admiral, Commander-in-Chief and First Lord of the Admiralty. He died childless and his fortune passed to his elder brother, Thomas (1695-1773), and it was he who employed James Stuart to work on the house and the monuments in the grounds. When Thomas died he was succeeded by his sister's son, George, who changed his name to Anson. George's son was created Viscount Anson in 1806 and he employed Samuel Wyatt as architect at Shugborough after the death of James Stuart in 1788. The 2nd Viscount was created Earl of Lichfield in 1831. When the 4th Earl died in 1960 Shugborough passed to the National Trust and is now administered by them in conjunction with Staffordshire County Council. The present Earl of Lichfield is Patrick, the professional photographer. He has a private apartment in the S wing and stays there quite regularly. The Mansion, though handsome enough, is, by stately home standards, not especially noteworthy. It is for the Park Ornaments that Shugborough is famous. These are a collection of mostly Classically inspired buildings scattered around the grounds at strategic points, and whose purpose was simply to delight the eye. They include: the Lantern of Diogenes, 1764-71, a copy of the Choragic Monument by Lysikrates, probably by James (Athenian) Stuart; the Arch of Hadrian, a copy of the Roman original with busts of Admiral Lord Anson and his wife, to commemorate the Admiral's circumnavigation of the world in 1740-4, again by Stuart between 1764-71; the Tower of the Winds, yet another copy of a Classical original, made about 1765 and positioned near the site of the old village before it was demolished; the Doric Temple, with its 6 column front and a rear blank wall — a rather miserable affair but nevertheless of historical interest because it is the second earliest such work of the Greek revival in the world; the Chinese House of 1747, delightfully positioned in a wooded corner near the Mansion and set behind the iron Chinese Bridge of 1813; the Ruin, at the back of the house, an absurd concoction originally much larger and even more absurd; the Monument to a Cat, a pet of either Thomas Anson or the Admiral commemorated by an urn on a base to a height of about 20ft.; and the Shepherd's Monument, a highly acclaimed piece. Of functional purpose are: the Railway Bridge 0·75m. E of the tunnels, a rusticated arch with Ionic columns and good retaining walls; the Trent Lodge, an Italian-style house near the Essex Bridge; the Lichfield Drive Lodges, moved here in 1845, which lie hidden amongst trees on the road to Rugeley and are now used as dwellings as the drive is disused; the eastern Railway Tunnel Entrance (SJ.981.216), looking like a castle gatehouse with turrets and battlements by Livock, 1847; the western Railway Tunnel Entrance (SJ.988.215), looking somewhat Egyptian; and the Lichfield Drive Bridge (SJ.997.211), in Classical style to match the nearby monuments. During the summer various exhibitions, sporting events and fairs are held in the grounds and the Staffordshire

Shugborough Hall.

Shugborough, the Chinese Bridge and chalet.

County Police Dog Training School let their alsatians practice attacking human beings on fields here. Salon musical concerts are occasionally held in the Mansion house. The Staffordshire Way long-distance foot path cuts through the Park, entering at the SW near the farm and exiting at the Essex Bridge.

SLINDON 2m. N of Eccleshall, which is 7m. NW of Stafford

A sparse little hamlet on the road from Eccleshall to Newcastle. It consists of a few houses, a roadside fountain, a farm shop and the charming little church of St. Chad. The church is of 1894 by Basil Champneys and was commissioned by J.C. Salt, a Stafford banker. The overall style is Gothic with a central tower, nave chancel and short transepts. The stained glass windows are by Kempe of about 1900. It is a building which is well thought of. One mile NE is Millmeece (water) Pumping Station, still standing and

Slindon, Mill Meece pumping station.

in good order though not in service. At regular intervals the 2 large, horizontal tandem engines are fired for the benefit of enthusiasts. Millmeece was built in 1914 and

Slindon, the church and the village beyond
was designed by William Campbell of Hanley. Both the engine house and boiler house have semi-circular headed windows, and the hipped roofs have hand-made tiles. The chimney stack is 125ft. high.

SMALLTHORNE 1·25m. NE of Burslem on the B5051.

The main road (B5051) cuts across the valley. On the slopes is industrial suburbia but in the valley bottom is a small nature reserve. The stream regularly floods and recently caused a good deal of damage to the newly restored Ford Green Hall, a good 16th Century half-timbered yeoman farmer's house with a 2 bay 18th Century extension to the E side. The Hall is now a museum which is occasionally open to the public when it is not booked by school parties, which is most

Smallthorne, Ford Green Hall.

284

Edward Aston of Tixall, died 1568, and his wife. There is also a bust of Izaac Walton of 'Compleat Angler' fame who was born at Stafford in 1593. Adjacent to the church is the school of St. Mary, built of stone around 3 sides of a quadrangle by Gilbert Scott in 1856. It is now unused and in need of attention. St. Mary's Grove, on the other side of the church, has some good Georgian houses which have recently been beautifully restored as part of a town redevelopment scheme. This scheme has, however, become something of a farce, with the town council, the property developers and the market traders all at loggerheads. For the indefinite future the people of Stafford have been left with an enormous temporary car park close to the centre of the town. In Market Square is the handsome, ashlar-faced Shire Hall, designed by John Harvey and built in 1795-9. It presently houses the Crown Court. To the right of the Shire Hall is the Judge's House of about 1800, also ashlar-faced. Opposite is The Chains pub, a place that is not unknown to some of the judges' regular customers. Around the corner are the County Buildings in Martin Street by H.T. Hare of 1893-5. These are of brick with stone dressings and add considerably to a street of great character. The main staircase is a grand affair that leads up to some good panelled rooms, one of which has, horror of horrors, been smothered from head to toe in white paint. It is called the White Room. Martin Street joins Eastgate Street which, despite the new Magistrates' Court and Police Station, is one of the pleasanter streets in the town. Here is the Borough Hall of 1875-7 by Henry Ward, a slightly whimsical structure in 14th Century French Gothic which now houses an entertainment complex based around the Gatehouse Theatre. A modern glass bay window has been installed above the main entrance. On the corner of Eastgate Street and Martin Street is the most handsome Eastgate House which was built in 1683 by General John Dolphin. In the 18th Century it was given a new facade, the one we see

Morris dancer capering at Stafford Castle.

today, and in 1839 it was occupied by T.B. Elley, one of the town's leading shoemakers. The County Council bought the house in 1891 and it became the residence of the Chief Constable (see the letter box on the wall). It is now used as offices by the Registrar of Births and Deaths, and has been the backdrop for thousands of wedding photographs. The Registrar also occupies the handsome red brick and stone Tudor-style building next door. Close by, on the opposite side of the road, is the William Salt Library, which occupies an attractive house of about 1730-5. Here are kept the county historical archives, a treasure house of old books, papers, maps and records of all kinds. William Salt was a banker of the firm of Stevenson, Salt & Co., whose ashlar-faced premises, of about 1795, are now occupied by Lloyds Bank in Market Square. Next to the bank is the Old William Salt Library, which was previously the old Bank House, and now houses the Staffordshire Railway Building Society. In Greengate Street is the High House, a large timber-framed town house of 1595 (not 1555 as was previously thought), constructed of oak from Doxey Wood. It has four gables and overhangs on brackets and is, indeed, a high house. In recent years some one million pounds has been spent on restoring the building and yet it still has a large, incongruous plate glass window on the ground floor. In 1642, during the Civil War, Prince Rupert stayed for 3 days at the High House as a guest of Captain Richard Sneyd. The prince is reputed to have fired at the weathercock on the tower of St. Mary's church, either for target pactice or to demonstrate the merits of a newly introduced rifled pistol from the Continent. The house to the left of the High House is of a similar style and age but has been covered in stucco. Left of this, and also stuccoed, is the Swan Hotel which has some early interior features including a section of Jacobean staircase with unusual balusters and a vaulted stone cellar. It is now in the control of Berni Inns, which may not have pleased George Borrow who found the place full of individuality and character; but would not have surprised Charles Dickens who found it 'the extinct town inn, the Dodo'. In fact, Dickens did not like Stafford in general and was most scathing. The Swan Hotel was a coaching inn but only for the local trade between Wolverhampton and the Potteries. The great national coaching road passed through Sandon and Haywood to the W of *Stafford, the old windmill at Broad Eye.*

Greengate Street and the High House.

Stafford. Opposite the Swan Hotel is the little church of St. Chad. an architectural jewel. This was the town church built by the Lichfield Diocese, for we must remember that St. Mary's belonged to the King. St. Chad's is a Norman church with a Perpendicular crossing. It was called 'ruinous' as early as 1650 and there were shops between it and the street. In 1854 Henry Ward of Stafford began the restoration, which was completed in 1873 by Sir George Scott who entirely rebuilt the front and donated the statue of St. Chad. The Norman work is: 4-bay nave with sturdy round piers and 1-step arches; clerestory; crossing arches with 2 demi-shafts; and the blank arcading in the chancel. The octagonal tower is by Sir Charles Nicolson, the aisle walls are of 1874-5 and 1880 and the north transept is of 1886. Many of the carved Norman designs have an Eastern flavour, a feature that is explained by the tradition that

292

Stafford, Church Lane.

the workmen were Saracens captured in the Holy Land by medieval knights of the Biddulph family *(See Biddulph)*. Also in Greengate Street is Chetwynd House, a Queen Anne style house of 1740, of brick and stone with giant pilasters and moulded window surrounds. The paved forecourt is enclosed by good wrought iron gates and railings. This was the home of R.S. Sheridan, the playwright and M.P. for Stafford between 1780 and 1806. It is now the Head Post Office. Church Lane, which runs between Mill Street and St. Mary's church, is a delightful little throughfare and would be an attraction in any town with its Georgian brick and stucco shops and houses, and the quaint black and white Sheriff's Office. In Earl Street are the handsome Almshouses of about 1660 founded by Sir Martin Noel. There are 6 stone houses on either side of the Chapel which has a large ogee-shaped gable. Around the corner in Water Street is the Old Malthouse, which has been converted into a handsome terrace of shops. Opposite are some good modern flats in red brick with stone dressings. At the bottom of Water Street are the two water-wheels of the old Town Mill which was working until 1957. There has been a mill on the River Sow, at or near this site, since at least 1086. At Broad Eye is the windmill, built in 1796 with stones from the old Elizabethan Shire Hall which was demolished to make way for the building we see today. Around the town centre are some buildings that should be mentioned:

The Masonic Lodge, an abandoned methodist chapel of 1848 in Gaol Road: St. Georges Hospital, the old lunatic asylum, a vast place begun in 1814-18 with a frontage of 31 bays and numerous additional blocks; the General Hospital in Foregate St., of 1766-7, of which the long front of 1892-7 is by Aston Webb; the Lock-up, rebuilt adjacent to a part of the old town walls on the island at the end of the Lichfield Road; Forebridge Villa, in Lichfield Road, which is now incorporated into St. Joseph's Convent; The Shawms, a house at Radford Rise by T. Sandy in the style of Voysey, now converted to flats; the Borough Library of 1914 at the junction of the Lichfield and Newport road; St. Paul's, Lichfield Road, by Henry Ward of 1884 with a steeple of 1887 by Robert Griffiths; the Friends' Meeting house in Foregate Street, a tiny, hemmed-in brick building of 1730 with a good collection of original fitments, including the gallery, the elders' gallery, the

Stafford, St. Chad's church, Greengate Street.

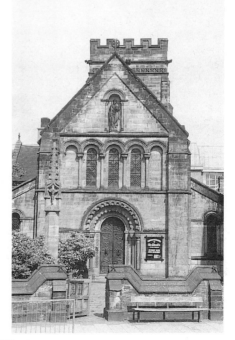

293

staircase, the overseer's bench and the panelling; Burton Hall in Burton Manor Road (at the S end of the town), a Gothic, gabled red brick mansion with blue and yellow brick ornament and pointed trefoiled window lights, built in 1855 by E.W. Pugin and now too close for comfort to the roar of the M6; Rowley Hall (SW of the town centre), of about 1817 by William Keen, an unimpressive ashlar building decorated with a colonnade and a bow of 3 bays with 6 detached Ionic columns, set in a small park and after having been abused as a kind of reform school is now a home for old people; the impressive row of ornate Victorian terraced houses in Lawn Road, a part of the Rowley Park housing development of the 1850's which was built on land severed from the estate of Rowley Hall; the Regimental Museum of the 16th the Queen's Lancers and the 5th Royal Irish Lancers housed in Kitchener House, Lammascote Road, an horrendous modern building but with a good small museum; and finally the Gaol in Gaol Road, of 1793 with extensions of 1852, which

Stafford and District General Hospital.

is one of our overcrowded Victorian prisons. It is not unusual to find companies of funeral directors located close to prisons. The reason, of course, is that they were a regular and reliable source of corpses. In former

Stafford Jail.

times public hangings were not uncommon and the scaffold was usually erected in front of the prison. In Stafford the undertaking firm of Emery's is situated opposite the main gate of the jail and the establishment of John Rose is within 100yds. of the prison. The town is surrounded by modern housing

Stafford, St. Patrick's R.C. church.

estates, Parkfields to the N, Western Downs to the W, Wildwood to the S and Kingston Hill to the E. Close to the windmill at Broad Eye is Castletown, a cluster of narrow streets and mean terraced houses which developed from about 1837 when the Grand Junction Railway was opened. There was a maintenance depot at Castletown and the new 'village' housed the workers. The middle management lived in Brunswick Terrace off the Newport Road. In 1876 Bagnall's manufactured locomotives and allied products at their Castle Town Works. This is now largely occupied by a company operating under the aegis of the Manpower Services Commission which runs training

Stafford, the R. Penk in flood.

schemes for the young unemployed. In Newport Road, at the town end, is the King Edward VII Grammar School (now called Chetwynd Middle School), a handsome Gothic brick building of 1862. The chapel was added in 1928. Further out, at the junction of West Way, is the flat-roofed

Edgar Wood house called 'Upmeads' of 1908 – interesting to architects but somewhat mundane to the layman and now spoiled completely by the planting of houses in its once extensive gardens. On the hill of Castlechurch is the church of St. Mary with a Perpendicular W tower and the rest by Scott and Moffatt of 1844, with a N aisle of 1898 by John Oldrid Scott. At the church is a stone slab with abstract designs that is a puzzle. Its purpose and age are unknown, except that it is probably at least Norman if not much

Stafford, brine pipe exit at Baswich.

older. An avenue of yew trees leads to the church. Of the many other churches and chapels in Stafford and its suburbs one other deserves mention, namely Holy Trinity in Baswich Lane, **Baswich**. The lower part of the tower is medieval, the upper of the 18th Century. The red brick nave and chancel are of 1740 and the transepts are of recent origin and not altogether sympathetic. Amongst the furnishings and fittings are the 18th Century W gallery and pulpit. There is a monument to Brian Fowler and wife of 1587. A little further down the road, by the railway bridge, is the 'Saltings' caravan Park which is on the site of the old Baswich salt works. There were 3 monasteries, or at least settlements of monks in Stafford. Outside the N walls of the town, in the area of Foregate, a community of Grey Friars (Franciscans) was established in 1297, and outside the S walls of the town, in the area of Forebridge, a community of Black Friars (Augustinians) was established in 1344. At

Stafford, St. Thomas' Abbey Baswich.

Baswich an even earlier Augustinian Priory was established in 1179. There are substantial remains of their Priory of St. Thomas (SJ.951.230) on the banks of the River Sow. The ruined walls and windows have been built up with bricks to make farm buildings. The area has never been properly excavated but a start has been made in the last year or so. The name Baswich is Anglo-Saxon and means 'Beorcal's dwelling'. It is not widely appreciated that today Stafford is a garrison town. Touching the north-eastern fringes is a mammoth RAF supply depot covering hundreds of acres. The warehouses, offices and accommodation stretch along the 5 miles of public roads that encircle the village of Hopton and Beacon Hill. It is a very sensitive establishment indeed and airforce personnel are ordered not to appear in the town in uniform. There are regular mock attacks to test the defences. Finally, visitors to the town will be surprised to find that the inner eastern ring road is, for several hundred yards, raised above a marsh. These swamps are quite extensive and originally formed a part of the Saxon defences of the town. After a period of wet weather one can see just how formidable they were. There can be few towns of any size in the whole of Europe that have what is virtually a primeval swamp within a hundred yards of their Civic Centre.

STANDON *5m. N of Eccleshall, which is 6m. NW of Stafford.*

The village straggles up the hill from Coates Heath and the ugly gantries of the electrified main line railway. There are a few cottages

Stafford, Highfields in early morning mist.

and a mill on the banks of Millmeece Brook, and near the foot of the hill is the church of All Saints. The 14th Century tower was built into part of an existing Norman church to which belong the present nave and N aisle. The N doorway of the old church is still in its original position. The whole building was restored and partly rebuilt by Gilbert White in 1846. Of the windows only those in the clerestory are original. There are memorials to Francis Ross, died 1500 (in the vestry) and to Nicholas Hyde, died 1526. Standon Hall lies in attractive country 0·75m. WNW of the church. It was built in 1910 and the architect was J. Francis Doyle of Liverpool. The 'L' shaped mansion is of red sandstone in Elizabethan style with mullioned and transomed windows. The Hall was used as a National Health hospital for some time, but is now a private establishment. In 1066 Siward held Standon. In 1086 it was owned by Robert of Stafford and held from him by Bryant. There was a village of some size with at least 18 households and a mill.

STANTON 3·5m. W of Ashbourne.
Stanton is a small, isolated village of stone farms and cottages on the Weaver Hills. It is known for the prehistoric circular burial mounds that lie to the W of the village : Skrip Low, 0·25m. N, and Over Low, 0·3m. W, both of which are about 90ft. in diameter. Slightly further W again are more burial mounds. Gilbert Sheldon, Archbishop of Canterbury, was born at Stanton in 1598. His father was Lord Shrewsbury's steward and the cottage *Dewpond near junction of A52 and A523.*

in which Gilbert Sheldon was born still stands in the middle of the village. Though his parents were poor he accumulated great wealth and became Chancellor of Oxford University. He paid for the theatre built in Oxford by Sir Christopher Wren, which was named the Sheldonian (1669) after him. He died in 1677 and was buried at Croydon. The church of St. Mary at Stanton is of 1846 by W. Evans of Manchester. It has lancet windows and a bellcote. It is an unassuming and pleasant little building of nave and chancel only, but beautifully positioned with wide views over the surrounding countryside.

STATFOLD 2·25m. NE of Tamworth.
Statfold Hall lies close to the Warwickshire border on the edge of its small Park, which is adjacent to the A453 Tamworth to Ashby de la Zouche road. The Hall and stables lie close to the medieval chapel, which was once the parish church, and to the north are the earthern platforms of medieval houses. In front of the Hall are pasture fields with the characteristic ridge and furrow marks of old, ploughed arable land. There was a village at Statfold but in the late Middle Ages it was deserted. The change from arable to pasture was a major cause of rural depopulation. An acre of pasture grazed by cows and sheep requires much less labour than an acre of corn or any other crop which entails ploughing, sowing, fertilizing, weeding, cropping and storing, all of which are labour intensive activities. The Hall has an Elizabethan core and is dated at about 1571 from a dovecote now demolished. The narrow polygonal tower at the back of the house is of 1671, the E and W bay windows were inserted in 1777, the N and S wings were added in 1817-19, and the N wing was demolished in 1937. The overall appearance of the house is Georgian. It was the home of the Pipe-Wolferstan family who first arrived at Statfold in 1465. The Chapel is at the back of the house. It has a plain Norman W doorway, a Decorated S doorway, 2 small 13th Century windows in the nave, a 14th

Century window in the chancel, a window of about 1600 in the E chancel and a window of 1906 in the nave. Amongst the memorials are effigies of 2 ladies holding their hearts in their hands, of the late 14th Century, and a large tablet to Francis and Frances Wolferstan of 1676. In the S window is a stained glass medieval bishop.

STEWPONEY *near Stourton, which is 2m. NW of Stourbridge.*

It has been suggested that the name Stewponey is derived from Estepona. It is said that a soldier returned from the Peninsula War with a Spanish bride, and that he named his inn after her home town. The reverend Sabine Baring Gould wrote a novel entitled Bladys of the Stewponey. The Foley Arms was named after the Foley family who were early ironmasters in this area. They lived at Prestwood, 1m. N of Stourton, in a 16th Century house, made Gothic in the early 19th Century, which was burned down in the 1920's. The gardens were landscaped by Humphrey Repton. Today the site of the old house is occupied by a hospital. The woods to the W fringe the Staffordshire and Worcestershire Canal and beyond is the

View over the Potteries from Hartshill.

River Stour. Stourton Castle stands on the site of a 14th Century brick house and former royal hunting lodge. It was rebuilt in the early 19th Century by Sir Robert Smirke in Gothic style with battlemented walls and gateway. It is now used as office accommodation. Laneswood House is an attractive Italianate building with a tower and stuccoed walls of about 1845. At Stewponey the short Stourbridge Canal (1776) joins the Staffordshire and Worcestershire Canal.

STOKE ON TRENT *An introductory note to the Potteries.*

Stoke on Trent is both the name of an individual town and the collective name for the 6 towns that comprises the Potteries — Tunstall, Burslem, Hanley, Fenton, Longton and, of course, Stoke on Trent (or Stoke upon Trent as the individual town is sometimes called). The collective name dates from 1910 when the County Borough was formed. Although the towns have grown outwards towards each other, and now form one more or less continuous built-up area, they all still have quite seperate identities. Their one common link is a tradition of pottery making. There have been finds of ancient pottery in the area dating back to Neolithic times (in the Manifold valley), and 1st Century Roman pottery has been discovered in Trent Vale, south of Stoke on Trent. In the Middle Ages names such as 'le Potter' (1280 at Audley) and 'le Throwere' (1327 at Biddulph) began to occur. By the middle of the 17th Century Burslem had developed as a centre of pottery making, and from then on the trade became established and spread southwards to the nearby villages now called The Potteries. The industry developed here for two reasons: the close proximity of ample supplies of coal, clay and water and the availability of the men to organise and develop the trade both technically and commercially — Wedgwood, Adams, Whieldon, Astbury, Elers, Bentley, Twyford, Davenport, Spode, Littler, Minton and others. The major development in the pottery industry — the event that took it out of its small craft roots — was the opening of

Stoke-on-Trent, Queensway and the Trent and Mersey canal.

299

the Wedgwood factory at Etruria in 1769. The Dutchman, Elers, had shown the way 70 years earlier in Newcastle-under-Lyme, but now there was a large factory dedicated to producing quality ware using refined techniques. The Pottery towns lie in a line from N to S — the line of the outcrop of long-flame coal. (The long-flame with which the local coal burned had the great merit of heating large surfaces evenly). They are linked by the main line railway, the Trent and Mersey Canal and most recently by the A500 dual carriageway. This new road leaves the M6 at junction 15, loops eastwards through the Potteries and rejoins the Motorway at junction 16. In this book the articles on the individual towns appear under their own names.

STOKE ON TRENT *1·75m. ESE of Newcastle-under-Lyme.*

In 1910 the pottery towns were federated and instead of being named after Hanley, which was easily the largest of the 6 towns, Stoke gained the honour. Strangers are always surprised to find that the town is apparently quite small. In fact, it is larger than it looks but is very spread about and broken up. First the canal, then the railway and more recently the A500 (Queensway) have effectively divided the town into two parts. East of the road are the Station and the Polytechnic, and W of the road is the old centre where most of the shops, the church, the Town Hall and the Spode factory are to be found. Up until about 1700 Stoke appears to have consisted of the church of St. Peter and Vincula and 3 houses, those of the Rector, his Curate and the Parish Clerk. The land about was flat and muddy. On the hill nearby was the medieval village of Penkhull (a Celtic name). Stoke, or Stoc, is old English for 'a place', but usually means a holy place, The church was old, a Saxon foundation, and when the present church was being constructed in 1829 to replace the previous Norman church, pieces of a Saxon preaching cross were uncovered. The font is also Saxon. In the churchyard are 2 arches, 2

The North Staffordshire Hotel, Stoke.

piers and some other pieces of stone. These are reconstructions, by Lynam in 1888, of medieval church remains discovered in the mill race of Boothen Mill when the mill was demolished in 1881. (Old churches were often quarried and the stone re-used for other buildings). The present church is a Commisioners' type designed by Trubshaw and Johnson with tower, nave and chancel,

Stoke-on-Trent, statue of Josiah Wedgwood.

300

Stoke, the church and the Town Hall.

Perpendicular windows, a 5 light E window, and battlements. Josiah Wedgwood's grave is by the reconstructed arches. The Hide Market was built in 1835 as a covered market, though it was subsequently used as a fire station and the cellar as a jail. The New Town Hall at Stoke is one of the grandest buildings in the Potteries. Work began on it in 1834 but the wings were not completed until about 1842 (north) and 1850 (south), It has a 19-bay ashlar front with a giant upper portico of Ionic columns in an overall classical design. The centre was originally designed as a market and this duly moved there in 1845. However, in 1888 it was moved out and the accommodation converted to house the mayor's parlour and offices. In 1911 the Kings Hall was added to the rear of the Town Hall. The Spode China works are in the main street of the town, opposite the old Town Hall. Josiah Spode came to this works after his training at Thomas Whieldon's factory in Fenton. He came as

Stoke-on-Trent, the Spode factory.

Cobbled alley behind the Spode factory.

master potter and Works Manager but by 1776 was the owner. Much of the old factory still remains amongst the present buildings. Josiah I died in 1794 and his son, Josiah II, took over. About 1800 he perfected his bone china. Calcined bone was mixed with clay and glassy material and the result was an excellent imitation of true porcelain. Josiah II made a fortune and expanded the factory by buying up adjoining property. Many of the houses he bought were incorporated into the works with very little alteration, a remarkable conglomoration covering 14 acres, some of which still stands. In 1842 there were 19 ovens, 272 working rooms, 19 slip kilns, 42 warehouses and 33 offices. The third Josiah had an accident in the factory and lost an arm. He spent most of his time at The Mount, a large brick house with 2 large domes, which stands in wooded gardens on the hill at Penkhull. The house was built in 1803 by Josiah II and has 7 bays, 2 storeys and

Stoke-on-Trent station.

an ashlar central bow with columns. It is now the Blind and Deaf School and recent extensions have been added to provide further accommodation. When Josiah III inherited the business he left management of it to William Copeland. After the death of Josiah III his widow and Josiah IV left the area *(see Armitage)* and William Copeland took control of the business. It has remained in the hands of that family to the present day. The other pottery firm based in Stoke was Minton's. Thomas Minton was the equal of Josiah Spode and Josiah Wedgwood. He had been apprenticed at the Caughley works in Shropshire, a factory renowned for the excellence of its wares which are highly sought after by modern collectors. The modern Minton premises are on the same site as the original factory. His reputation for quality was such that he attracted the very best craftsmen, many coming from the workshops of his competitors — from Spode and from works in Derby and Worcester. 'Nearly as good as a Minton' became a phrase of high praise. The Minton factory we see

today is of 1950-2. Opposite Minton's is the 7 bay Gothic School of Science and Art of 1858-60 by James Murray. Next door is the Library of 1878 by Charles Lynam, a building of some character with wide eaves, large round windows and mosaic and tile panels. Perhaps the most important event in the development of Stoke was the coming of the railway. The North Staffordshire Railway Company built the handsome station in 1848. A year later an equally handsome Hotel and Regional Offices were built with

Stoke-on-Trent, the Mount at Penkhull.

302

Stoke-on-Trent, the Polytechnic.

black diapers in a Jacobean style and mullioned and transomed windows. The area between the station and the hotel is called Winton Square and here is the statue of Josiah Wedgwood by Edward Davies, 1863. There are a few trees and the whole area is most pleasing. Stoke had become the railway centre of the Potteries and this, perhaps more than anything else, established her name nationally. In this respect, and of no little consequence, was the publicity the

Stoke-on-Trent, The Villas, London Road.

town achieved through its Football Club. Stoke City F.C. was formed in 1863 and is the second oldest club in the country. Their ground, the Victoria in Boothen Road, can be seen quite clearly from the A500. The club has produced more than 30 international players. Perhaps we can now explain why the federation of pottery towns was called Stoke. That was the name the nation knew because of a railway station and a football club. Some churches and their dates: St. John, Newcastle Road, Trent Vale, 1909 by A.R.

Piercy who incorporated the nave of the previous church as the S aisle; All Saints, London Road, Boothen, 1888 by Lynam and Rickman; Our Lady of the Angels (Roman Catholic), Hartshill Road, 1857 by Charles Hansom, a striking building of yellow and red brick, Gothic with presbytery and convent attached; St. Thomas, Penkhull, by Scott and Moffatt, Middle Pointed and paid for by the Rev. Thomas Webb Minton; Holy Trinity, Hartshill Road, 1842 by Gilbert Scott, in Middle Pointed and paid for by Herbert Minton who, no doubt, also supplied the plentiful tiles, and who also paid for the school, the parsonage and the Gothic brick houses near the church. To conclude, mention should be made of The Villas, a charming cul-de-sac off the London Road, with Italianate houses of about 1840 which have short towers, pantile roofs and stuccoed colour-washed walls; and Whieldon's Grove, the great Thomas Whieldon's 18th Century house of 2 storeys, 5 bays with a later wing, Ionic columns and a pediment, located E of Stoke, off City Road, and technically in Fenton.

STONE *7m. N of Stafford.*

Here Iron Age man built a fort, here an Anglo-Saxon king slew his children and through here passed one of the country's greatest coaching roads. Stone is a very old town and we have yet to unravel much of its early history. The Iron Age fort is on Bury Bank. It has a much eroded single bank and ditch with an interned NW entrance, and covers 3 acres on top of the heavily-wooded hill at the junction of the A34 and the A51 at Darlaston, 1·3m. NW of Stone. It will have been passed by millions of travellers because this was the point where the medieval road from London (now the A51) forked left to Nantwich, Chester and Ireland, and right to Newcastle-under-Lyme, Carlisle and Scotland. Chester was a port before it silted up in the 18th Century, the actual docks being on the site of the present racecourse. Darlaston itself never developed much

Stone Station.

beyond its present size — a handful of cottages, some new houses, a garage and a pub called 'Yesterdays' — but Stone, being the nearest town of any size to this important junction, thrived on the coaching trade, especially in the 18th Century when the roads were improved by turnpiking and the traffic greatly increased. Industries of some importance in Stone in the 18th and 19th Centuries, were leather tanning and shoe making. The tanneries were mostly alongside the Scotch Brook in Stafford

Street, but were pulled down when the stream was culverted and the area turned into a road and a car park. The shoe factories were numerous. Behind the shops in the High Street there are several small factories and larger works in Lichfield Road, behind the old cinema in High Street and around the modern Lotus factory. Today Stone is a flourishing small market town with a busy centre, a small market square and an essentially Georgian look. At the N end of the High Street is Granville Square. Here is the handsome Post Office and an attractive thatched pub called the Crown and Anchor. Half way down the hill is the Crown Hotel, which is a lot bigger then the facade would suggest. It was built by Henry Holland in 1778, presumably replacing an earlier inn. It has 2 brick bays and a central porch of Ionic columns. This was the most important coaching house in Stone. Back up the hill a bit is the very Georgian facade of Joules' Brewery Offices, with 2 ground floor bow windows and a porch with Tuscan columns. At the back was the old brewery which

Stone, Granville Square.

304

Stretton Mill.

and transepts were rebuilt in 1860. Adjacent to the church is Stretton Hall, a charming early 18th Century country house set in a pleasant park with a lake. It originally had only 2 storeys but a third was added about 1860. The house is built of brick and has even quoins, a central pediment and cupola, long sash windows with moulded surrounds, a Victorian porte-cochère, and inside a fine staircase. The Congreve family had acquired

Stretton, the Telford Aquaduct over the A5.

Stretton by marriage in the 14th Century and built a house here shortly afterwards. The present mansion was built by John Congreve. It was sold to the Conollys in the mid 18th Century and from them it passed to the Moncktons of Somerford who are the

Stretton, the lodge to the Hall.

present occupiers. The Staffordshire Moncktons are descended from the 5th son of the 1st Viscount Galway, who married the daughter and heiress of Lord Pigot of Patshull. Several members of the family have been Members of Parliament. One mile SW of Stretton the Shropshire Union Canal crosses the A5 by means of the black and white painted aquaduct constructed by Thomas Telford in 1832.

SWINDON *1·5m. SW of Wombourne, which is 4m. SW of Wolverhampton.*
It lies along the Staffordshire and Worcestershire Canal with locks to the N and S, old warehouses, a pub, a Post Office and a red brick church of 1854. There was an iron forge here from at least 1668 when the ironmaster, Thomas Foley (died 1677), took the lease on it. There was an iron furnace here even earlier, in the 1620's, which was said by Dud Dudley to be smelting iron ore by burning coal (rather than by burning the usual charcoal) more than 100 years before Abraham Darby 'rediscovered' the techniques at Coalbrookdale. The old craft of working tempered iron into edge-tools such as scythes, reaping hooks, axes, etc., was called 'whitesmithing'. There were

whitesmiths in several parts of the county during the mid 17th Century, and in Swindon there was a blade-mill that ground a sharp edge on the tools they produced. There was also a blade-mill at nearby Himley.

SWYNNERTON *9m. NNW of Stafford and 5m. NNE of Eccleshall.*
In 1086 it was part of the vast estates of Robert de Toni, standard bearer to King William during the Conquest. The lord of the manor was the Saxon, Wulfgeat, who had also held it before 1066 and was one of the few to keep his position under the new Norman aristocracy. Swynnerton is a handsome village that lies on a gentle hill amongst pleasant pastoral country. There is a pub, a rustic garage, a thatched cottage amongst several old red brick houses, and on the fringe of the village is a beautiful water tower. This has tall arches in yellow and red brick and was built in the 1890's. There once lived in the village an eccentric odd-job man who, until his death in 1987, lived in a tiny hut, without water and electricity, in the

grounds of the Fitzherbert Arms, the village inn. The parish church of St. Mary has 2 Norman doorways in the base of the tower; the upper part is of the 16th Century. The nave, chancel and nave arcades are 14th Century Early English, and there are Perpendicular traceried windows. The S chapel was the original church. In the SE chapel is a magnificent 7ft. high statue of Jesus dated between 1260 and 1280. He is seated and pointing to the wound in his side. This sculpture was certainly never meant for a humble country church and probably came from Lichfield Cathedral. It was found buried under the floor of the chapel and had probably been intered at the time of the Reformation. The stained glass of the E window was made by Powell to a design by J.D. Sedding. Under a canopy in the S wall of the chancel is the effigy of a cross-legged knight of the mid 13th Century, probably Sir John Swynnerton who died about 1254. In 1856 the tomb was opened and a body covered in lead an inch thick was found. When this was removed a young man of

Swynnerton Hall.

312

Swynnerton, the entrance to Army Camp.

Swynnerton, the yellow brick water tower. 609

ruddy complexion, with auburn hair and beard and with 2 front teeth missing was revealed. The body and the effigy agreed in measurement and other details, but on exposure to air the body quickly turned to dust. East of the church is the former Vicarage called Queenswood, a house of 5 bays and 2 storeys, of 1760 by Charles Cope Trubshaw. Swynnerton Hall stands within the village but turns its austere back towards the humbler abodes of the common folk. The park, which is now a conservation area, lies to the front of the south-facing Hall and is cut through by public roads. Amongst the green pastures is the ground of the village cricket club. The Hall itself was built by Francis Smith of Warwick for Thomas Fitzherbet in 1725-9. It is a classical ashlar house of 3 storeys, with a substantial cornice below the top storey. The 3-bay centre has giant Roman columns, the quoins are of equal length and the windows have moulded surrounds. In 1812 there were additions and alterations by James Trubshaw but some of these have recently been demolished. From the front of the house there are splendid views over Staffordshire to the S and Shropshire to the W. The estate passed by marriage from the Swynnerton family to William Fitzherbert in 1562. In the 18th Century the widow of Thomas Fitzherbert married George IV and played an important part in public life. The house is still home of the Fitzherberts and they still farm the estate of some 8,000 acres. The Roman Catholic church of Our Lady of the Assumption stands close to the hall and was built for the Roman Catholic Fitzherberts in 1869 by Gilbert Blount. It is a little austere without, but within it is richly decorated. The overall style is Gothic Middle Pointed. Due to the influence of the Fitzherberts a good half of the church-going population of Swynnerton is Roman Catholic. West of the church and tastefully hidden from sight is an estate of modern houses. Two miles S of the village, on the road to Eccleshall, is the entrance to the huge Swynnerton Camp, where specialist training is given on new weapons and equipment. A few years ago the area was coated with a radio-active dust during an exercise to simulate a nuclear attack. It is here that convoys carrying atomic warheads, en route from Scotland to the south for servicing, are parked overnight. Close by is the Weapons Testing Centre at Coldmeece. there are several marl pits in the Swynnerton

313

area. Marl is a clay rich soil which is mixed with poor, light soils to bind the particles together.

SWYTHAMLEY *3m. NE of Rushton Spencer, which is 5m. NW of Leek.*
Swythamley lies in the North Staffordshire Moorlands amongst some of the finest countryside in England. There is no village in the accepted sense, just a scatter of farms and cottages. The Hall is not large and the church (of 1903) has been abandoned; yet there is magic in the air, for this is the setting of the great medieval epic poem 'Sir Gawain and the Green Knight'. In the Middle Ages Swythamley belonged to the Earls of Chester and in 1180 the 5th Earl died at his hunting lodge here. (Swythamley lay between the forests of Leek and Macclesfield.) In 1214 the Cistercian Abbey of Dieulacres was established at what is now called Abbey Green, 1m. N of Leek. This

Swythamley, the Dane valley.

monastery had been founded at Poulton, on the River Dee near Chester, in 1146, and probably moved to Leek at the request of the Earl of Chester. The Earl endowed the Abbey with lands which included Swythamley. In 1540, at the time of the Dissolution of the Monasteries, Henry VIII granted Swythamley to the Trafford family. Their manor house was burned down in 1813. In the mid 19th Century the estate was purchased by Philip Lancaster Brockelhurst and he rebuilt the house. However, the centre block of the present Hall seems to be from the old, original manor. It is made of sandstone, whereas the wings to either side and the porch to the front are of brick. The house is irregular, of 2 storeys and has dormer windows. It is not altogether a friendly building, an opinion shared by the organisers of the Transcendental Meditation group who occupied it for several years before leaving in 1987. There are various outbuildings and two lodges with good iron gates. The abandoned rock-faced church lies near to the E lodge. Though the house is nothing special the setting is magnificent. To the front of the Hall is a delightful small Park in which sheep graze and to the rear are the jagged rocks of the Roaches. Close by are wild moors and deep wooded valleys, an archetypal romantic landscape. It is very likely that the author of 'Sir Gawain and the Green Knight' either lived at Swythamley Hall or very close by. Briefly, the tale tells of Sir Gawain's quest for the Green Knight, an elfin knight whom Sir Gawain had beheaded but not killed. Gawain journeyed from S Wales to the Wirral and from there he followed the old 'Earlsway' route used by the Earls of Chester to visit their lands in Staffordshire and Derbyshire. He reached the Meerbrook marshes and turned N into the valley between the Roaches and Gun Hill to Swythamley. Here he found a beautiful white castle with towers and turrets and here he sojourned as a guest of the owner, Sir Bertilak. Whilst Sir Bertilak was out hunting deer, boar and fox, Sir Gawain was seduced

Swythamley Hall deer park below the Roaches.

Sywthamley Hall.

Swythamley Hall deer park.

by his host's wife. To say more would spoil the story. The descriptions of the scenery in the poem are very fine indeed, and so many tally with natural features around Swythamley that there can be little doubt that the poem was set here. The cliffs called 'the rocheres' are the Roaches; 'the flosche', meaning a 'marshy place' is Flash; 'a knot', a rare word meaning 'a rocky formation', is Knotbury (a plateau just beyond Flash with semi-circular layout of tracks and houses around the common which is quite possibly an ancient settlement site); the place where the boar is trapped in a hole in a water course near a rock is probably Pincher's Hole in the valley of the River Dane, just S of Knar Farm, where there is a hollow between the river banks; 'valley to wild valley' is Blackbrook to Dane; the 'rughe, knokled knarres with korned stones' are the Castle Cliff Rocks near Lud's Church; and lastly, the mysterious 'Green Chapel', the forbidding cleft in the rock where the story reaches its conclusion, just has to be Lud's Church itself which lies in the woods of the Back Forest, 1m. NE of Swythamley Hall. This is most easily approached from Gradbach in the Dane valley. At Gradbach there is an old mill, now a Youth Hostel, and a footpath leads westwards through lovely country along the banks of the river. Lud's Church is not well signposted and the actual entrance could be easily be missed. The cleft in the rock is intially narrow but widens and deepens as one progresses. It is quite eerie.

The moss-covered rocks drip with water and trees and ferns overhang from above — hence the 'Green' Chapel. The sun never shines here. Altogether, Lud's church is about 100 yds. long, 30 to 40 ft. deep and 6 to 10 ft. wide. The cleft was caused by the Millstone Grit rocks slipping along a bedding plane which caused fractures, which were later eroded. It is a place that one should visit, though the climb is steep and rough in places. 'Sir Gawain and the Green Knight' was written by an anonymous author in about the year 1400. He used a dialect peculiar to the NW Midlands. The ballad is considered to be 'the finest alliterative poem of the age outside Chaucer's works', though comparison with Chaucer's work is impossible because of stylistic and language differences. The mystery of the poem is the location of the castle. There is no sign of a castle at Swythamley, or of any other building that even remotely fits the description. It is likely that this was simply a poetic invention, though who is say what excavation on the site of the Hall may reveal. There are 2 translations of 'Sir Gawain and the Green Knight' currently available. One is by Brian Stone, published by Penguin Books, and the other is by Tolkien, published by Unwin Paperbacks. A quarter of a mile NNW of the Hall, and within the park, is a prehistoric burial mound. When the Brocklehurst family sold the Swythamley eastate they burned most of the old papers relating to the house, much to the chagrin of *Swythamley, Gradbach Mill in the Dane valley.*

Swythamley, cottage in a wood
Swythamley, view from the road to Flash.

Swythamley, Lud's Church.

Swythamley, bridge near Gradbach.

the County Archivist. Note: Lud's Church is said to have been used for secret services by the Lollard religious sect, who were followers of John Wycliffe (1330-84). On one occasion their singing betrayed their presence to soldiers who were searching for them. In the struggle that ensued a beautiful 18 year-old girl called Alice was killed and was buried beneath an oak tree at the entrance to the cleft. She was the daughter of Walter de Lud-Auk after whom the 'church' is named. The Lollards were early Nonconformists who despised the wealth and arrogance of the established Roman Catholic church. Another local name for Lud's Church is Trafford's Leap, after one of the squires of Swythamley Hall, whose horse lept over the chasm whilst they were out hunting. The Swythamley Estate is famous for its wild wallabies. In 1938 the brother of Sir Philip Brocklehurst introduced imported wallabies in to his enclosed private zoo at

Roach House at the southern end of the Roaches. Some of these animals escaped and bred in the wild. Their descendants still live in the rocks and woods hereabouts and are seen every now and then though they are very shy and their numbers not very great. *(See Upper Hulme.)*

Swythamley, the R. Dane at Gradbach.

TALKE O' TH' HILL *1m. WSW of Kidsgrove.* Talke is a large mining village which lies along the A34. The name is from the Welsh meaning 'high place'. The little brick parish church of St. Martin is of 1794 with a Victorian bellcote, a stone-built N transept and a modern parish room adjoining the W end. On the main road are 2 early 19th Century lodges of the now demolished Clough Hall, which was the home of the Kynnersley family. Harecastle Farm lies on the A34 just N of its island junction with the A500 (Queensway). This is a Jacobean stone house with a recessed centre. The upper windows are regular but on the ground floor

Talke o' th' Hill, Harecastle Farm on the A54.

the door is left of centre and the middle window right of centre. This is because the Hall is not centrally placed. The Harecastle Canal tunnels run 0·75m. to the E. Reginald Mitchell, the designer of the Spitfire fighter aircraft, was born at 115, Congleton Road, Butt Lane, Talke.

TAMWORTH 24m. SE of Stafford.

The name is from the River Tame which is joined here by the River Anker. Tamworth Castle stands guard at their confluence. For over a thousand years it stood alone but now has the incongruous company of 6 blocks of council flats 15 storeys high. Below the castle are attractive public gardens leading down to the wooded banks of the river. Beyond the river, on the wide reaches of its flood plain, are the Castle Pleasure Grounds, and W of the now pedestrianised Lady Bridge is Lady Meadow. Tamworth itself lies on higher ground beyond the castle. It is a busy market town of some 50,000 people with a good range of shops and 2 modern shopping precincts. In 1965 it was designated an

Expanding Town to absorb the overspill population from Birmingham. This explains the acres of modern housing that now surround the ancient settlement. Tamworth has come down in the world not a little since it was the capital of the Kingdom of Mercia. Indeed, it was virtually the capital town of the country during the reign of King Offa, from 757 to 796, for he was overlord of England, the acknowledged King amongst Kings. He was a figure of international repute who dealt on equal terms with the great Charlemagne. Offa had his royal palace

Tamworth, the castle and the tower blocks.

at Tamworth, probably in the area now occupied by Market Street. The town continued to be the royal seat until it was burnt to the ground by the Danes in 874 and Mercia ceased to be an independent kingdom. In 913 Tamworth was fortified by Ethelfleda, daughter of King Alfred. Ethelfleda died in 918 and when her nephew, Athelstan, became King of England in 924 he again established a royal residence at Tamworth. His sister, Editha, married Sitgtryg, the Danish King of Northumbria. However, the marriage failed and Editha established a convent at Tamworth and gave the rest of her life to God and good works. In 943 the town was again attacked and burned by the marauding Danes. It was never to be the seat of a royal residence again. The Saxon fortifications were of earth and timber and except for the castle mound there is nothing above ground to be seen of these, though excavations in the town centre have recently produced some archaeological finds. After the Norman Conquest the castle and the manor became the property of Robert le

Tamworth Castle from the gardens.

Despencer and then of his nephew, Roger le Marmion. They then passed by marriage to the de Frevilles in 1291, the Ferrers in 1423, the Shirleys in 1688, the Comptons in 1715, and finally in 1751 to the Townshends. In 1879 Tamworth Corporation bought the castle. The castle they bought was the work of the Normans. The circular shell keep was built by the Marmions; the lower part of the herringbone walling is 11th Century and the main battlemented shell keep is 12th Century. Incorporated into the keep is a

Tamworth, the Peel statue and the Market Hall.

Tamworth Castle, herringbone masonry.

forge in association with a cotton factory in Lady Meadow owned by Robert Peel's third son. One of Mr. Peel's other sons was Sir Robert Peel, M.P. (1788-1850), who represented Tamworth and who became Home Secretary and later Prime Minister. His famous Tamworth Manifesto of 1834, which expounded his ideas on free trade, was delivered from the steps of the Town Hall, in front of which his statue now stands. In 1846 he repealed the Corn laws, an action which split the Conservative party and forced him to resign. The Town Hall in Market Street is one of Tamworth's few buildings of note. It was built in 1701 and paid for by Thomas Guy, of Guy's Hospital fame, who was an M.P. for Tamworth between 1695 and 1707. It is a building of some character with broad, open stone arches supporting a 2 bay-brick front with arched windows, a pediment and 5-bay sides with a cupola on top. Thomas Guy, who made a fortune out of the South Sea Bubble Scandal, also paid for the charming Almshouses in Gungate (a Danish name) which were completely rebuilt in 1913. In Market Street there are a few Georgian houses but also some untoward modern development. Buildings deserving mention include: the facade of G. Griffin & Sons, Jewellers, in George Street; the Job Centre in Church Street, a splendid 18th Century Georgian stuccoed house of 3 storeys and 5 bays with giant angle pilasters and a pedimented doorway; Rutherfords, solicitors' offices in Holloway, neo-Gothic of 1845, built to house Sir Robert Peel's Savings

tower. Within this ancient framework are buildings of a later date, principally the Hall which has survived in its Jacobean dress of the time the Ferrers held the castle. The exterior front was faced with ashlar and the Jacobean mullioned and transomed windows were Gothicized by the Marquess Townshend in 1786. The gabled Warder's House adjacent to the tower is original Jacobean. There is a beautiful wooden chimney-piece here, and 2 more in upper rooms S of the Hall. All the main rooms — the State Drawing Room, the Oak Room, the Haunted Room, the Long Gallery etc. — are well furnished and the castle houses the local authority Museum. The exhibits include displays of Saxon and Norman coins from the Tamworth Mint and information on the unique Saxon Water-mill. The castle has been lived in continuously from Norman times to the present day, though in 1790-2 the Banqueting Hall was used to house a

Tamworth, the street market.

was of some importance being part of the 'Parliamentary' mail-coach route from London to Holyhead. The village of Tettenhall is split into two parts. Halfway up the hill is Lower Green. Here is a sloping green with some attractive old houses and the church of St. Michael. This was an important medieval church, a Collegiate church under Royal control. Sadly, in 1950, it was almost totally destroyed by fire. Only the Perpendicular tower and the much later porch by A.E. Stuart of 1883 were salvaged. The rest was rebuilt by Bernard Miller. He made no concessions to the past and based his design on unusual cross-gables with circular and oval traceried lights. Some like it; some hate it. At the top of the hill is the large Upper Green, studded with mature trees and cut through by roads. Shops face the lawns on 2 sides and only parked cars mar a most picturesque area. On the other side of the main road there is a paddling pool, and beyond that a huge open area on part of which is the cricket ground — a ground of sufficient standing for it to accommodate

Minor County matches. A few old houses have survived. The Old Farmhouse of 1520 with stone mullions, on Stockwell Road, for

Tettenhall, Stockwell House.

example, and the black and white cottage opposite the Roman Catholic church. The longest established residential areas are along the rock edge, where handsome houses lie in large gardens, though it must be said that the gardens get smaller every time a house is sold. The temptation to make an extra £30,000 or so by splitting off a small building plot is irresistable to most vendors.

Tettenhall, the church of St. Michael.

326

Thorpe Constantine, the church of St. Constantine.

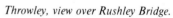
Throwley, view over Rushley Bridge.

Throwley, view from Throwley Cottage to the NW.

Very little is known about the Hall. It was the home of the Meverells in the late Middle Ages but when Robert Meverell died in 1626 his daughter and heiress married the 4th Lord Cromwell (who was distantly related to Oliver Cromwell). The ground about the house is much disturbed and there is a pond near the road. The site is almost certainly very ancient and is likely to have been occupied in prehistoric times. Next to the Hall is a farmhouse. The outbuildings of the farm include several very substantial stone-built barns with mullioned windows. One

Throwley Hall, the ruins over the pool.

has 2 floors of 7 bays and is called the Barracks. The hills around are littered with prehistoric tombs. Some are marked on the Ordnance Survey map and some are not. Even more have doubtless been destroyed by farmers and treasure seekers. A hoard of Saxon gold coins and broaches was found in Beeston Tor Cave (SK.108.541) in the Manifold Valley, 1m. N of Throwley Hall. The site is best approached from the road that runs just to the N of the caves or from the path that starts at Weag's Bridge. Throwley and the area around was intensively investigated in the middle of the 19th Century by S. Carrington of Wetton, a local schoolmaster. He showed that there had been a large population here during the Noelithic, Beaker and Food Vessel periods. Recent excavations have been made at the Cheshire Wood Cave (SK.116.536) and Falcon Low (SK.104.532) by Keele University Extra Mural Archaeology classes. In Falcon Low, on Old Park Hill, they found a sepulchral cave probably of Neolithic age. Six people had been buried there — 2 adults

Tipton, the Factory Canal Junction.

and 4 children. There were also the remains of dog, hare, wild cat, marten, pig, sheep and water vole. The cave had been blocked with boulders and covered with earth. At the top of the hill to the SW is Throwley Cottage. Note the tall trees. They were planted primarily as a windbreak but also function as a landmark. When the hills are covered in snow and visibility is bad, even people born and bred on the moors can become disorientated and in need of help to find their way home. There is also a small disused quarry. Much of the material for the dry-stone walls came from such local quarries; it was not all just picked off the land when clearing fields. It is strange to think that these bleak, green, hills were once forested. Prehistoric man cut down much of the woodland. Once the land was grassed over grazing animals ate the seedlings of any new natural tree growth that attempted to establish itself. Experiments in Scotland have shown that if hillsides are protected from sheep, woodland can regenerate without any assistance from man. Of course,

if existing woodland is not close by, the process can be very slow because it takes time for sufficient seeds to be brought in by natural processes such as by the wind and droppings from birds, etc.

TIPTON *5m. SSE of Wolverhampton.*
The Norman scribes who compiled Domesday Book often made mistakes in writing down the names of the towns, villages and manors they visited. They were, after all, French speakers writing down colloquial Anglo-Saxon. Whether or not their notation of a place we now call Tipton is correct we will never know. They called it Tibbintone, a delightful name if ever there was one and certainly an improvement on Tipton. The original name was in fact probably Tipstone. A 'tip' was a stave or spear and Tipstone might well have referred to a spear shaped stone — a megalith of prehistoric origin — that once stood here. Tipton is the archetypal Black Country town, a place of some character and some unusual claims to fame. For example, before some of

331

the canals were filled in it is reputed to have had more miles of waterway than Venice, and is indeed often called the 'Venice of the Midlands'. At one time, almost unbelievably, the town had 7 passenger railway stations and 6 goods depots belonging to different 19th Century companies. Yet another surprising fact is that the Parish Registers here date from December, 1513, the earliest in the whole country. Until about 1700 Tipton was a small village surrounded by fields. The only event of note to have occurrred in the area was the Battle of Tipton Green in 1644. This was an indecisive engagement between the troops of Lord Denbigh, who were intent on taking Dudley Castle, and the Royalists. By the early 18th Century the small medieval coal, iron and limestone workings were rapidly expanding. Mining continued through the 18th and 19th Centuries and coal was being extracted until about 1920 when excessive flooding, amongst other reasons, forced the pits to close. The extent of the old workings was illustrated by a report on the area in 1984 which said that 25 acres would have to be abandoned because the ground was too unsafe for new building, or even for use as recreational parkland. There is a honeycomb of old limestone caverns beneath the surface, and 37 uncapped mine shafts have been discovered. The iron trade flourished in Tipton, and Barrows and Hall at Bloomfield (presumably the site of an early 'bloomery' iron works) were the largest producers of iron in the Black Country until the firm closed in 1906. Another famous works was the Horsley Iron Company who in 1821 made the world's first iron steamship, the Aaron Manby. The old Horsley works still exist as a part of a larger company. The centre of the town is Owen Street, which was once a lively, thronging place between the canal at Factory Road and the level crossing. However, in the 1980's it was redeveloped. The S side was demolished and replaced by a shopping centre and town houses. On the corner of Factory Road is the Fountain Inn,

Tipton, canal and works at Factory Junction.

for long associated with the Tipton Slasher, a pugilist of great repute. His real name was William Perry and from 1850 to 1857 he was the champion prize fighter of England. The 'Slasher' was a canal boatman who became a publican in West Bromwich on winning the title, and is buried in the churchyard of St. John's, Kate's Hill, Dudley. He was born in 1819 and died in 1880. The railway station of **Dudley Port** is actually in Tipton. It got its name in the days before the Dudley Canal Tunnel was cut under the limestone ridge that bisects the Black Country. Here goods for Dudley or for the canal system on the other side of the ridge were unloaded and carried by pack horse up the hill. So, although actually in Tipton, this was the port for Dudley. Later, when the railway came through, it became the station that served Dudley and a branch line to the town — the Dudley Dodger — was built. The Tipton Harriers are a well-known athletics club.

332

Tutbury Castle, John O'Gaunt's Tower.

Tutbury, the bridge over the R. Dove.

Tutbury and included within its boundaries the present counties of Stafford, Derby, Warwick, Nottingham and Lancaster. The Duke encouraged minstrels to attend his court and granted them a charter. Authority over the minstrels was in the hands of the King of the Minstrels, who was elected annually, and disputes amongst them were settled at the Minstrels' Court. The Court

Tutbury, view from the ridge northwards.

Ferrers in the 1080's and attended by monks from Pierre-sur-Dives in Normandy. The monastery is gone and the church is not complete. It originally had an apse, a large choir, transepts and a crossing tower. A new chancel and apse were added by Street in 1866. The outstanding feature of the church is the great, and much photographed, W front doorway which has 7 orders of receding decoration most elaborately carved. The outside order is alabaster, this being the first use of that material in England. The nave has large Norman columns and the present clerestory was the original Norman triforium into which Perpendicular windows have been inserted. The S aisle door is Norman and on the lintel is depicted a boar hunt. The N aisle is of 1822 by Joseph Bennett. In medieval times Tutbury was famous for its Minstrels' Court. John O' Gaunt spent quite a lot of time at Tutbury which was the administrative centre of the Honour of

ensured, amongst other things, that the minstrels served a 7 year apprenticeship before playing for gain. The court was held on the Feast of the Assumption of the Virgin Mary and every musician in the Honour had to attend. This organization and assemblage was unique in England. After the election of a new King of the Minstrels there was a banquet, and after the banquet all the musicians assembled for the bull-running. A bull was shorn of his horns, had his ears cut off, his tail cut to a stump, his body smeared with soap and, finally, his nostrils blown full of pepper. The populace of the town was commanded to 'attend to their safety' and not to come anywhere near the enraged bull. The animal was released and the musicians had to try and take a piece of the bull's hair or hide. He who did so won the bull, which was then brought to the High Street, baited with dogs and killed. This bull-running was practised from about 1377 to 1778 when the custom was abolished because one of the participants was killed. Tutbury is also famous for its Treasure. In 1320 Thomas, the 2nd Earl of Lancaster, along with other English Lords, allied himself to Robert the Bruce, King of Scotland, and received a large quantity of silver coin to finance his fight with Edward II, King of England. At the battle of Burton Bridge Lancaster was defeated and fled to his castle at Tutbury where he ordered his treasurer, Leicester, to convey his treasure chest of English, Flemish and Scottish coin to Pontefract with all possible speed. However, as the train was crossing the River Dove, at the foot of the castle, the chest fell into the raging flood waters. The King was only half an hour behind him so Leicester had no time to recover the treasure, being more intent on saving his life. The treasure then appears to have been forgotten. At least it was not recovered by Leicester or anyone else in his retinue. Then, on the first of June 1831 the workmen of a Mr. Webb were removing a quantity of gravel from the bed of the River Dove, on the S side of the bridge, in order to accelerate the flow of water to the mill. 'While thus employed the workmen found small

Tutbury, the Dog and Partridge Inn

Tutbury, the Priory church of St. Mary.

pieces of metal, which on examination they perceived to be silver coins. Upon this discovery a general scramble commenced and large numbers of people soon flocked to the place. Almost numberless coins in close rows came forth together with many beautiful encrustations of horse shoes, sword handles, with other war-like remains.' The Chancellor of the Duchy ordered the place to be cleared and soldiers patrolled the river banks. A search was made by Duchy officials and 1,500 more coins were found. The workings were then back-filled with gravel. In 1838 further official diggings were made and a large number of coins were again recovered. It has been estimated that the total number of coins found exceeded 100,000. This has to be a guess, of course, because so many were taken in the first, unauthorised, scramble. Some of these coins are on display in the museum at Hanley. It should be noted that the old bridge over the

Dove was further upstream from the present bridge. The town of Tutbury is a pleasant enough place. The wide High Street lies on the slope of a hill and has some handsome and varied buildings. The Dog and Partridge is a timber-framed public house of great character, and opposite is a house with a charming little doorway in Venetian style. The Croft House is Georgian with 3 bays and a pedimented doorway. There are several other good Georgian houses both here and in Castle Street. There are, unexpectedly, 2 craft manufacturers of ornamental glass and crystal ware in the town. Both are situated near the centre and both have factory shops. Tutbury alabaster is world famous but in fact the mines were all nearer to Hanbury, 2·5m. WSW of Tutbury. The last of these, which is still producing gypsum, is the huge mine at Fauld, 1·5m. W of Tutbury. (Alabaster is a special kind of gypsum suitable for carving. It is now in very short supply and is only used for small craft ware. *(See Hanbury.)*

UPPER HULME *2·25m. NNE of Leek.*

The access road to Upper Hulme leaves the A53 Leek to Buxton road and drops into the little valley, where the tiny village lies crammed between the hills, a waterfall and a factory. A factory is not exactly what one expects but this is just the kind of place in which the early mills were sited. Manufacturing began in the country and only later became centralised in towns. In fact the mill at Upper Hulme was once world

Upper Hulme, the waterfall in the village.

345

renowned as Tatton's, the yarn dyers, who were especially famous for their black dyes. It is still a dyeing works though part of the premises are now occupied by an engineering company and a furniture manufacturer. The original stone mill-house still stands and is some 300 years old. It was a rope works before the dyeing trade came. The dyers found the water from the stream especially good. The road continues on around Hen Cloud, the outlying hill of the Roaches, and passes above Windy Gates (SK.004.618). This house is dated at 1634 and is superbly positioned with long views over Tittesworth reservoir. It has 2 gables, transomed windows, and the porch has a stepped lintel. On the other side of the road from Windy Gates, in the rocks of the southern tip of the Roaches, is Rock Hall (SK.006.622), which has no water and no electricity, and which was made a Listed Building in 1987. This remarkable and extremely picturesque cottage includes a room which is actually a cave. The present occupiers, 'Doug' and his

The Roaches, 'Doug' who lives at Rock Hall.

The Roaches, Hen Cloud from the south.

346

The Roaches, view NW over Meerbrook valley.

The Roaches, the delightful Rock Hall.
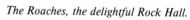

The Roaches, an abandoned farm.

hard, coarse sandstone used for grinding wheels before synthetic carborundum was developed. To the left are magnificent views over the green meadows of Gun Hill, and to the right are jagged rocks with ruined stone cottages standing forlorn in rough hill pasture. At Roach End there are farm gates to be opened and closed before proceeding. The road circles around the Roaches and there are more incredible views over the great bowl of Goldsitch Moss. Ultimately, one returns to the Leek — Buxton road. A journey not to be missed. This is not a place that only looks right in the summer sun. It looks good in any season but in different ways at different times.

wife, have lived there for 10 years. It was built by the squire of Swythamley Hall for his game-keeper. Queen Mary visited the house as a child. It is said that there were caves here which were destroyed, taken for the stone to build cottages. It is also said that the flat stone to the right of the cottage was used as a place of sacrifice by pre-historic man. The road runs parallel with the Roaches and continues past the disused quarries and the Five Clouds to Roach End. Roach means 'rock' and these rocks are millstone grit, a

Note: The Roaches used to belong to the estate of Swythamley Hall. In 1938 the squire of Swythamley was Sir Philip Brocklehurst. His brother lived at Roache House (SK.011.605), which is at the southern end of Hen Cloud, at the southern end of the Roaches, where he had a private zoo. In 1938 wallabies were introduced here, but shortly

The Roaches, view NNW from near Roach End.

348

The Roaches, view over Goldsitch Moss.

after Sir Philip's brother left to fight in the First World War. Whilst he was away the fences became broken and the animals escaped. All of them were recaptured except some of the wallabies. Sir Philip's brother

The Roaches, a wallaby at Hanley Museum.

was killed in Burma but the wallabies have managed to survive and now live and breed on the Roaches. They are shy and their numbers not large but they are still there. They have some favourite haunts, but we will not say where these are in the interests of their safety.

UTTOXETER *13m. NE of Stafford.*

The name Uttoxeter (or Uttchiter as the locals pronounce it) means 'Wittuc's homestead in the heather'. The 'xeter is not a corruption of 'cester – meaning a Roman fort. However, in the fields to the S of the town there is a large quadrangular earthwork which is almost certainly the remains of a Roman defensive position. The N entrenchment is the best preserved and lies in a field called Sandfort. The S and W sides are also discernable. Pottery has been found on the site and nearby an amphora was located. Many finds were made in Bradley Street which was probably the site of a Romano-British pottery. Finds include a quantity of grey clay, an unfinished pot, a bronze disc, the handle of a bronze key, a quern, a coin, pieces of iron, pottery, boars' tusks and part of a glass fibula enamelled in red, etc. Small potsherds and coins have been found all over the town. Near the church was an old well surrounded by a pavement, a foot below ground level, that was believed to be Roman. It was lined with sandstone for its full length and pottery was found in a bank nearby. Very little Roman Samian ware has been found and much of the pottery found is Romano-British. Little is known about the area in the Dark Ages, but in 1066 Uttoxeter was held by the great Earl Algar. After the Norman Conquest King William took the manor for himself and at the time of Domesday Book there were at least 37 families living here, a considerable settlement for the time. The Norman scribes called Uttoxeter Wotoche-shede. The village officially became a town about 1140 when the Earl of Derby sponsored a borough and the right to hold a market was obtained. To induce new tenants to take residence the burgesses were offered right of grazing and other rights in Needwood Forest. The new town was a great success and both the landlord and tenants prospered. By the 15th Century Uttoxeter and the lower Dove valley in which it is situated was an area renowned for its dairy products. Leland, who passed through in 1540 said, 'there be wonderful pastures upon the Dove'. The potters of Burslem were kept busy making butter pots for the traders and farmers at Uttoxeter market. Indeed, they had to be constrained from making pots too shallow – done no doubt at the request of the farmers – because customers were getting short measure. In 1596 and again in 1672 there were major fires which destroyed almost all the old timber-framed medieval houses. Despite its prominence as a market Uttoxeter was the last North Staffordshire town to be linked (in 1763) to the new, improved, turnpike-road system. The Uttoxeter canal that ran to Rocester some 4m. to the N has long been abandoned and the warehouses have been converted to other uses – as a corset factory in Uttoxeter and a railway warehouse in Rocester. There was a large malthouse in the centre of Uttoxeter until 1968 when it was demolished. Market towns are often venues for horse racing and Uttoxeter is no exception. Regular meetings have been held here since the late 18th Century. The Racecourse is situated alongside the railway line to the SE of the town, on the back road to

Uttoxeter. Market Square and the domed Weighing House.

350

Uttoxeter Racecourse.

Marchington. On the slopes of the wooded hills overlooking the course are some attractive old houses. The town centre consists of 2 adjoining irregular squares collectively called the Market Square. In the larger square is the small, domed and pedimented classical structure that was built in 1854 as the Weighing House. It is now used as a newsagent's kiosk. It was in Market Place (about 1780) that Dr. Johnson, as an old man, stood bald-headed in the rain and did penance for having disobeyed his father 60 years earlier. Johnson's father was a seller of second-hand books and had a stall at Uttoxeter market. (Dr. Johnson himself suffered from Tourette's Syndrome which manifests itself as facial and bodily tics, convulsive movements, whistles and noises, gesticulations and compulsive actions like touching posts and measuring one's footsteps). There are attractive and interesting buildings around the Market Street corner of the square. The Talbot Inn is part black and white, the shop of T.G. Sargeant is timber-framed of about 1600, restored in

1980, and opposite is an ironmongers' shop in Gothic stone with a gable, an arched window with carvings and a turret. The building, of which this front is a part, housed the old Bamford (JCB) offices. The firm is now at Rocester but its original factory was in Uttoxeter on the road to Stafford. The premises still stand. The main shopping street in Uttoxeter is High Street, a busy place at most times, but thronging on market days despite the great lorries that still vibrate their way along the narrow road. Here is the Classical Town Hall of 1854 by Thomas Fradgley, now standing forlorn with shuttered windows and flaking paint. A passage leads to the Cattle Market that stands behind the Town Hall. Also in the High Street is the 3-storeyed Uttoxeter House, still handsome despite the later work of unsympathetic hands. Here, too, is the Old Bank House of 1798 with 5-bays and an engaged Tuscan columned porch. There is a small shopping precinct off the High Street, a rather misrable affair done on the cheap and completely out of character with the rest of

351

the town. The brick Methodist church is of 1812, in Classical style with arched windows and a pediment. Buildings worthy of mention include the following: starting in Church Street there are the County Court Offices, with a Gothic pointed arch doorway; the Manor House of 5 bays and 2 and a half storeys with a 3 bay pediment, 3 tall urns and a handsome Tuscan columned doorway — possibly the best house in Uttoxeter; the Jervis House with 2 canted bay windows; and the Headmaster's House of Alleyne's Grammar School (about 1858). In Carter Street is the white-painted White Hart which has Tudor panelling in the dining room taken from Beaudesert Hall when it was demolished. Opposite the White Hart is a group of 3 timber-framed cottages. In Balance Street are some good Georgian brick houses and the Roman Catholic church of St. Mary, built in 1839 by Pugin but much altered since. The parish church of St. Mary faces straight on to the pavement at a busy corner. The tower is early 14th Century and has a recessed spire. Most of the rest was

rebuilt by Trubshaw and Johnson in 1828 with alterations to the chancel in 1877. It is a light, airy church with galleries and contains the 16th Century tomb of Thomas Kinnersley of **Loxley.** Loxley Hall lies on the hill above the hamlet of Lower Loxley, 2m. WSW of Uttoxeter, along the A518 to Stafford. Legend has it that this is the Loxley mentioned in the old Robin Hood Ballads. The Hall is a large 11 bay house with ashlar facade of about 1795 and a 4 columned porch. Much of the house was rebuilt in 1817. Parts of the previous house remain, notably the old panelled hall which has been brought into the house by the extension of the front. The panels are of about 1650 and the small inset pictures are Catholic. In the frieze over the large mantel-piece are heraldic shields dated at 1607. The Hall is located on a good site and it is likely that there has been a house here since Saxon times, although in 1066 the land was said to be 'waste' and in 1086 was still in that condition. Between the road and the Hall is a large brick Dovecote still occupied by birds. The Hall is occupied by

Loxley Hall.

Loxley Hall, a door in the hall.

children for it is now a County Council Special School, with the usual mundane and unsightly modern extensions that such institutions attract. The Dove Bridge lies 1m. NE of Uttoxeter town centre. It crosses the River Dove close to its confluence with the River Tean. It has two 14th Century pointed arches and two later round arches, probably of the late 17th Century, all with substantial cut-waters. Alan Gardner, an 18th Century sailor and native of Uttoxeter, was promoted to the peerage and chose the name of the town for his title. In 1648 the 1st Duke of Hamilton came to Uttoxeter with the remains of his army, after their defeat by Oliver Cromwell at Preston, and surrendered to Lambert. Hamilton was executed three months later.

WALL *2.25m. SSW of Lichfield.*
Wall lies along Watling Street. The A5 makes a slight detour S of the Roman road here. The village is presumed to have taken its name from the upstanding remains of the old Roman fort and settlement of Letocetum. Most of the modern village lies on the hill above the Roman site. It is a dignified settlement of mostly large red brick houses and farms. Near the church is a substantial Classical mansion with stuccoed walls. The small church is of 1843 by Scott and Moffatt. It has a nave, short chancel, a small steeple and is pleasant enough. The site must surely be old and indeed there is good reason to believe that here, or hereabouts, was a pagan temple — a Celtic church of the Cornovii. A number of carved stones with human horned heads have been found built into the walls of the Roman settlement just below the church. It is believed that the name Cornovii means 'worshippers of the horned one'. (The Cornovii were the Celtic tribe that occupied most of Staffordshire, Shropshire, Cheshire and Herefordshire at the time of the Roman invasion.) It is thought that the Romans destroyed the shrine but re-used the stones, which they turned upside down, as a small gesture to the Celtic gods should they in fact exist. The bones of Celtic oxen with down-turned horns have also been found in the area, and they may be the remains of animals ritually slaughtered and then eaten. The name Letocetum is a Latinised version of the Celtic word meaning 'the grey wood'. The Romans first had a large but simple marching camp here. Later, they built a succession of

Wall, the church of St. John.

Wall, the Roman ruins of Letocetum.

1st Century wood and earthern forts. The last of these forts was abandoned about 80 A.D. because the area had been pacified. In the 3rd Century new defences were constructed to make a strong point on the road. Parts of this were built in stone and stand astride Watling Street. The Civil Settlement has been partly excavated and can be viewed by the public. Here are the sandstone foundations of a mansio (an inn) and of a bath-house with the usual sequence of rooms of different temperatures. There was also a stable where a change of horses could be obtained. Two houses in the vicinity worthy of mention are Pipe Place, 0·75m. NW as the crow flies (but approached off the A461 N of Muckley Corner), which has 5 bays, 2 storeys, cross-shaped windows and a hipped roof, dated at about 1700; and Aldershawe House, 0·5m. N of Wall, which has half-timbered gables above, and brick below, to a design by Samuel Luxton of the 1890's.

WALSALL *6m. E of Wolverhampton.*
The town planners in Walsall may have tried but they have failed. The centre of the town is cut through by nightmarishly busy roads and junctions, made worse by a one-way system that so infuriates drivers that many become homicidal maniacs intent on mowing down anyone who dares even to think of crossing the road. Walsall is not mentioned in Domesday Book, but the manor passed to the Ruffuss family about 1159. The town has 2 charters: one granted by William Ruffuss in, it is thought, the early 15th Century and another of 1309. In 1390 *Walsall, the Town Hall and the white County Court.*

Weeford, 'Thick Groome', on road to Shenstone.

Walsall, statue of Sister Dora.
Walsall, tower blocks from Darlaston road.

the manor passed to the Earls of Warwick and remained with them until 1488. (This explains the appearance of the Warwickshire bear and ragged staff symbol in the Walsall coat of arms). The old town lay on the slope between the church at the top of the hill and the bottom of the valley below. The church of St. Matthew (formerly the church of All Saints) almost certainly replaced an Anglo-Saxon church. St. Matthew's was built in the 13th Century but all that remains from this time are the tower and the crypt, which is something of a feature of this church. It was altered in the 15th Century and in 1819-22 the nave walls were encased in ashlar stone and the windows re-made and given iron tracery by Francis Goodwin. Ewan Christian remodelled the chancel in 1877-80 and the spire was largely rebuilt in 1951. Inside there are three galleries and a good Georgian Gothic ceiling. There is a battered effigy of Sir Roger Hilary, died 1399, in the S aisle. Other churches are: St. Mary, Roman Catholic, 1825-7 by Joseph Ireland; Vicarage Walk Baptist Church, 1879, Italianate; St.

Paul by J.L. Pearson, 1891-3; St. Peter, 1841 by Isaac Highway, brick with polygonal buttresses; and St. Michael at Caldmore, 1871, by J.R. Veall, Early English style in red sandstone. Coal, iron-ore and limestone have been quarried and mined in and around Walsall since the 14th Century. Iron was worked here from at least 1554 and in 1570 men from Walsall were felling trees at Bentley Hay (which was part of Cannock Chase), to make charcoal. Iron was also exported to several other areas, including the Paget furnaces on Cannock Chase and Middleton in Warwickshire (1592). The limestone workings are very extensive and there is a honeycomb of uncharted tunnels and caverns below the town which could one day cause a disaster. In 1824 the Mayor of Walsall was drowned in a flooded derelict quarry along the Lichfield Road, and another man died trying to rescue him. In 1874 the Arboretum and Lake Company was formed to convert this quarry (which belonged to Lord Hatherton) into a pleasure garden. The company failed and the council took over

Walsall, bass relief on the Sister Dora statue base.

356

long for comfort. Here is the Old Library of 1907 by Stephen Holliday, built in brick and stone with fluted columns and pediments, and paid for by Andrew Carnegie. Next door is the Town Hall of 1875 by Alexander Henman in brick to a Gothic style. The only other building of note in High Street is Christ Church of 1821 by Francis Goodwin. It is in Perpendicular style with iron window tracery and 3 galleries. On the roundabout at the S end of the High Street is an arched stone gateway which came from the now demolished Sandwell Hall, a reminder that West Bromwich is the centre of the new Metropolitan Borough of Sandwell. Sandwell Park covers a large area to the west of the town. There are nature trails, a farm, woodland and pools, totally surrounded by suburbia and sliced through by the M5. Here was the site of a Medieval Benedictine Priory. Recent excavations have revealed the foundations of both the Priory and its church, also the drinking fountain fed by a natural spring, the 'sanctus fons' or holy well which became San(d)well. Sandwell Hall

was rebuilt in the early 18th Century on the site of the ruined Priory by the Legge family who were to become the Earls of Dartmouth. They exploited the natural resources of the area, principally coal. When the industrial region encroached upon their private domain they abandoned Sandwell Hall and went to Patshull near Wolverhampton. Sandwell Hall was demolished in 1928. Although the first known blast furnace in the Black Country was at West Bromwich (1590) the area did not develop much until the early 19th Century. Coal and ironstone were discovered in the open heath to the S of the old village centre and the area became a 'boom town'. This explains why today the modern centre is so far away from the parish church and the Old Manor House. Between 1801 and 1901 the population increased from 5,700 to 65,000. Many things were made here but especially irons, stoves, bedsteads, grates and coffee mills. The church of All Saints lies 1·5m to the NE of the town centre. It has a tower of the 14th and 15th Centuries but the rest was rebuilt in 1872 by Somers Clarke.

West Bromwich, the Manor House.

Inside, there are alabaster effigies believed to be of Anne Whorwood, died 1599, and Field Whorwood, died 1658, both members of the family who lived at the old Sandwell Hall, before it was rebuilt by the Earls of Dartmouth. There is also a wooden chest, all of one piece, carved out of a solid block. Local personalities include William Salter, a late 18th Century businessman, who made several things but especially springs. His firm continued and by 1960 was making over 500,000 different kinds of springs! Jess Pennington played for West Bromwich F.C and England (25 times) in the early 20th Century and is still remembered as a great player. Madeleine Carroll, the film actress, was born in West Bromwich in 1906. She starred in several classic films, including The Thirty Nine Steps of 1935 and The Prisoner of Zenda in 1937. In 1837 James Fellows started the most famous of the canal transport companies, namely Fellows Marton and Clayton, which at one time had 200 narrow boats. They were known as Joshers after Joshua Fellows. The firm closed in 1948. Some 2m. NE of the West Bromwich High Street is Bishop Asbury's Cottage. Asbury, or Ashbury, spent his childhood here, became a Methodist preacher and went to America to spread the gospel according to John Wesley. He travelled extensively in the new continent and fought for many social improvements. He became the first Methodist Bishop, much to the despair of his old teacher, Wesley, who

West Bromwich, Bishop Asbury's cottage.

decried such pomp. Nevertheless, Asbury is highly regarded in America and is considered to be one of the 'founders of the

West Bromwich, Metal Closures Ltd.

nation'. In the mid 19th Century a man called Hudson invented dry soap powder. For many years he had a small works at West Bromwich before opening a large factory in Liverpool which was taken over by Lever brothers of Port Sunlight in 1908. To the north and the south of West Bromwich are

West Bromwich, the M5 from the A4041

366

long, straight stretches of canals with deep embankments which can be quite dramatic. The best known is the New Main Line (1829) to the S of the town on the border with Smethwick. At one point (SK.002.898) the M5 crosses the main line railway and the canal, which here are within yards of each other.

WESTON ON TRENT *5m. NE of Stafford.*

Weston lies in the valley of the River Trent, which here is paralleled by the Trent and Mersey Canal (1777). The village stands at the crossing of the A518 Stafford to Uttoxeter road and the famous coaching road now called the A51 from Rugeley to Stone. It is an attractive place with an enormous village green and retains a deal of character despite the new houses. Facing the green is the Woolpack and almost opposite the pub is an old factory with a chimney. This has been various things including a dairy and an alabaster works. Alabaster was formerly mined at Norman's Wood near Stowe by Chartley and brought down to Weston to be

Weston-on-Trent, the village green

processed. Behind the factory is the Laing Construction equipment depot. The firm came here in 1963-4 when the M6 was being constructed and has been here ever since. The yard occupies the site of the old Salt Works, established alongside the canal by Earl Talbot in 1820. Parts of the impressive brick building designed by James Trubshaw survived until 1963. There were 8 large pans in which the brine was heated and the water removed by evaporation. *(See Shirleywich.)* By the short canal spur that served the works

Weston-on-Trent, the Old Hall.

367

Weston, canal spur to the old salt works.

dredging, as a flood control measure. In the village is the parish church of St. Andrew, famous for its sturdy and handsome 13th Century Early English tower with lancet windows. Above the tower arch, the arcades and the chancel arch are also 13th Century. However, much of the church was rebuilt by Gilbert Scott in 1860 (N aisle) and Butterfield in 1872 (S aisle and clerestory). The chancel windows are of about 1400 but are not in their original positions. The E window glass is by Gibbs. The church has 2 bells of about 1400, some of the oldest in Staffordshire. Opposite the church, screened by trees, is a handsome Jacobean-style house called Abbeylands, built in 1858 by Gilbert Scott. Here lives Sir Harmer Nicholls, father of Sue Nicholls, the actress, who has appeared in several contemporary television 'soap operas'. Also opposite the church is a most attractive stuccoed dwelling, and to the right-hand side of the church, almost totally

Weston-on-Trent, Abbeylands

is a cluster of cottages which probably had a connection with the industry. The most impressive building in Weston is Weston Hall. Indeed it is one of the most impressive houses in the county. The Hall stands 0·5m. to the W of the village on the lower slopes of Weston Bank on the A518. Gaunt and strong-looking it is a stone Jacobean house with 4 gables, 3 storeys plus attic, and mostly transomed windows. The porch was added in Victorian times. At the turn of the century it was sold to pay gambling debts and has since been converted to flats. It is a pity that the owner of the greatly extended cottage adjacent to the Hall has seen fit to plant the tall, straight line of coniferous trees that now partly obscure this handsome house. The small brick shed in the valley below is the old pump house which supplied water to the Ingestre Estate. Close to it is an area of landslip where springs issue forth. The River Trent has been lowered hereabouts by

hidden by trees, is a splendid and substantial thatched cottage.

WESTON UNDER LIZARD. *7m. W of Telford (Oakengates).*

Two miles to the SW of the village, over the border in Shropshire, is the wooded Lizard Hill under which the settlement lies. Lizard itself is said to be either a corruption of the name of a local Norman lord of the manor or of Lazar, meaning a leper, of which there is reputed to have been a colony hereabouts. Weston is very much an estate village and had it lain on a more peaceful road than the busy A5, it would be considered most attractive. The cottages are of several styles, all handsome, though it is sad to see the proud vicarage in its wooded gardens being sold for 'development'. The Hall and the church are hidden from the road by a high wall and a screen of trees. Weston Hall is very much open to the public and the main entrance is to the west of the village at a minor, and very dangerous, crossroads. Opposite the entrance gates is the estate plant nursery and saw mill. In the Middle Ages the Weston estate passed from the Weston family to the Myttons and then by marriage to the Wilbrahams, and again by marriage to the Newports (Earls of Bradford). Finally, in 1762, it passed to the Bridgemans (Earls of Bradford of the second creation). The 6th Earl of Bradford is the

Weston-u-Lizard, the Old Rectory.

Weston Park, estate cottages.

current owner of Weston Hall. The present classical house was built in 1671 to a design by Lady Wilbraham, wife of Sir Thomas Wilbraham. The S front has a central stone bay, and to the left and right segmental gables. Above the E front is a pediment and a Victorian porch (1865). There is a balustrade

Weston Park, the Butterfly House.

around the whole of the top of the house and some good chimneys. The low E wing was added in Victorian times and joins on to the 11-bay 17th Century Stable Block which has a central pediment, weather vane and cartouch of arms. Beyond the stables are the handsome 18th Century Farm buildings. Alongside these there is now a small menagerie — ducks, donkeys and exotic birds etc. — and also a pottery and a shop. In the Orangery of 1865 is a cafe. The church of St. Andrew (1701) has an entrance to the N. to the main road, but is attached to the Hall. Like the Hall it was designed by Lady Wilbraham. Part of the previous church was

Weston Park, the deer park.

Weston Park, the Hall.

incorporated, namely the tower, in which there are some Norman stones, and the E wall which has a 14th Century window. In 1877 Ewan Christian added a family chapel in Norman style. In the E window are re-set parts of the original 14th Century glass in a work by Hardman of 1876. There are monuments to various members of the Bradford families including, of course, Lady Wilbraham, died 1705. The Park was landscaped by Capability Brown. The woods contain many specimen trees, such as the magnificent plane tree by the house, and in the meadows there are deer and rare breeds

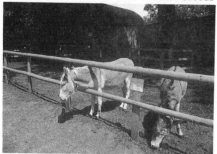

Weston Park, donkeys in the Pets Corner.

of sheep. In the grounds are several ornaments. The Temple of Diana is a substantial domed orangery standing above the deer wall. This and the Roman Bridge with its 'sentry boxes' are by Thomas Paine of about 1760. Beyond the bridge is the Swiss Cottage with its wooden trellis verandah. There is also an Obelisk, a Mausoleum of 1870, Boathouses and various urns and vases. To the S on Tong Knoll is the Tower, a

Weston Park, the Stew Pools.

Weston Park, lilies on the top lake.

Victorian folly with a polygonal turret. There are various attractions in the park these days: an Adventure Playground in Temple Wood and beyond that a Miniature Railway; an Aquarium in the old boiler room beneath the Orangery; a Butterfly Farm beside the Church Pool; and the Museum of Country Bygones. There are Walks in the woods, the charming Temple Pool and the freshwater tanks in which fish from the lake were kept for some weeks to improve their taste before being killed and eaten. (These are by the Toddlers' Playground.) Inside the Hall nothing is left of the 17th Century. The

Weston Park, the Temple of Diana.

finest rooms are the Tapestry Room with Gobelin tapestries (1766) and the Dining room made in the mid 19th Century. There is a marble staircase and an important collection of paintings including works by Holbein, Reynolds, Gainsborough, Hoppner and many others. In the former dining room, now the Library, there is a collection of rare books, some of which were stolen recently. The present Earl is young and full of enthusiasm for his House and Estate. From April to November a wide range of events is held at Weston — Steam Engine Rallys, Dog Shows, a stage of the famous R.A.C. Rally, meetings of Microlyte Flyers, and Horse Trials etc. One mile N of Weston Park is Blymhill which is very much a Bradford estate village.

WETLEY ROCKS *6m. S of Leek.*

It lies on the A520 Leek to Stone road, 1·25m NNE of its junction with the A52 at Cellarhead. The Rocks are an outcrop of Millstone Grit which have been quarried since the early 19th Century. The red and white stone was originally used only for kerbstones and steps, but in 1833 St. John's at Wetley Rocks was rebuilt of local stone, and by 1850 Wetley stone was in great demand as a building material for churches and chapels. The stone was being worked until at least 1890. St. John's has a nave, tower and aisles of 1833, paid for by the Sneyd family of Ashcombe park, and a chancel of 1901 by J. Beardmore. Wetley

Wetley Rocks.

Abbey lies 0·75m. SW of the village, down a track off the main road (A520). It was probably an old house enlarged greatly in 1836. It has a cruciform shape and Gothic features with a pediment and an ornamental motif of the cross and mitre — a somewhat strange house. The Victorian painter, George Mason Mills lived here. It is now a Nursing Home.

WETTON *8·5m. NW of Ashbourne and 1·25m. W of Alstonefield.*

This is the heartland of the Staffordshire Moorlands — hills and dales with pastures divided by dry-stone walls. Even in summer the village looks cold. In this high place prehistoric man lived and died. His burial mounds are still numerous here, though many have been ploughed out. In the 19th Century most of the larger tumulii were opened and their contents removed by Samuel Carrington of Wetton and Thomas Bateman of Hartingon. The pottery, bones, coins and other grave goods that they found are now mostly in Sheffield museum. There

Wetton. the village.

are caves too. The best known of course is Thor's Cave which lies 0·5m. SW of Wetton, approached by a track. The cave overlooks the Manifold Valley and the views are dramatic. It is, however, quite dangerous. The rocks at the entrance to the cave are very worn and shiny, making them quite slippery. Anyone falling from here would be unlikely to survive. The approach track is safe enough though and the views from the bluff are

The Manifold Valley, from Thor's Cave.

excellent. Many prehistoric and Romano-British finds were made in the floor of the cave when it was excavated. Between 1848 and 1852 the fields known as the 'Borough Hole' near Wetton were archaeologically examined and the remains of many dwellings found. These were probably the homes of workmen in the Roman lead mines. There were numerous finds of pottery, iron utensils, coins (from A.D. 253 – 337), glass, a bronze ring, skeletons and enamelled jewellery. The site has long been

Wetton, Thor's Cave

used by local people as a source of building stone. At Long Low Cairns (SK.122.539), 1·25m. SE of Wetton, at the end of a track that leads directly to them, are 2 round mounds linked by a stone bank. This is unique. The larger mound is 8 ft. high and 75 ft. in diameter, and inside was a closed stone grave chamber containing 13 bodies and 3 leaf-shaped flint arrowheads. These were probably Late Neolithic people who lived about 2,000 B.C. The village of Wetton is

Wetton, Weag's Bridge

373

small, nucleated and built of stone. There is a pub and a church. St. Margaret's has a strongly built medieval tower, but most of the rest was rebuilt in 1820 to a Gothic style with pointed windows. The large corner stones are a feature of the structure. Samuel Carrington lies buried here.

WHEATON ASTON *8·5m. SW of Stafford.*

The village lies 1·5m. N of the A5. In the centre are some attractive old houses. One large black and white house is especially good but has been spoilt by having lost its garden to development. All around modern estates proliferate. This is no longer a country village. The church of St. Mary is of 1857 with a chancel of 1893 and stained glass by Kempe in the E window. There is also a Primitive Methodist Chapel of 1856 in Georgian style with a round-headed window. The NW edge of the village is touched by the Shropshire Union Canal, and where landway and waterway meet is the Hartley Arms. The country around is flat and was presumably an area where wheat was grown. Aston, of

Wheaton Aston Old Hall on the A5.

course, means East Town. Pennocruciam lay 3m. SE of the village around Stretton Mill on the River Penk. Wheaton Aston Old Hall lies alongside the A5. The New Hall stands close by but is set back from the road .

WHISTON *3m. NE of Cheadle.*

A substantial stone-built village on the A52 in the hills 1m. E of Froghall. The church of St. Mildred is of 1910 by J.M. Becket and is pleasant enough. Whiston Hall (or Manor Farm as some call it) dominates the village. It lies on the top of the hill, large and built of ashlar stone and very blackened. It is now the club-house of the local golf course. Behind the Hall is the Whiston Incline. The Incline is made of earth and supported a plateway which carried trucks of limestone that came from Cauldon Lowe quarries and went on down to the Caldon Canal at Froghall. Between Cauldon Lowe and Froghall is a distance of 4m. and the vertical drop is 649 ft. Copper from the great Ecton mine, 10m. to the NE, was smelted at Whiston from 1770 to 1890. Almost the only

Whiston Eaves, cottage built against a rock.

Whiston, the Incline.

sign of this industry today is slag, some of which has been used as a building material. In the 1680's stone for use as hearths in iron furnaces was quarried on Whiston Moor. Coal outcrops in the area about Whiston. **Whiston Eaves** lies 0·5m. SE of Whiston along the road to Oakamoor. There is little but a few cottages and the ashlar gatehouse-stable block of Whiston Eaves Hall. The Hall was pulled down and the stone taken away and re-used to build houses for the senior management of British Industrial Sand, a

local farmer told us. One of these houses is at Hollington. B.I.S. have huge quarries here from which they extract sand. This is processed in what is said to be the most advanced purification plant in Europe. Flint glass sand is supplied for the manufacture of a variety of commodities — glazes, pottery paint, asbestos sheets, abrasive cleaners and even milk bottles. The quarries are connected to the main line railway by the old North Staffordshire Railway line that follows the Churnet Valley northwards through

Whiston Eaves, the B.I.S. Moneyash Quarry.

375

Whiston Eaves, the B.I.S. Moneyash Quarry.

Consall Forge and Cheddleton. Most of the sand is taken to the Pilkington works in St. Helens, Lancashire. Near Whiston Eaves, on the road to Oakamoor, is a quaint little smallholding. The house is built against a rock outcrop, a place of great character.

WHITGREAVE *3·5m. NNW of Stafford.*
It lies between the A34 and the M6, a little

Whitgreave, the village over the M6.

rural village spoiled by the roar of the motorway. The church is of the early 19th Century in brick with a bellcote and pointed windows.

WHITMORE *4m. SW of Newcastle under Lyme.*
Whitmore lies on the A53 Market Drayton to Newcastle-under-Lyme road. It is an unpretentious but most attractive village. The first lord of the manor we know by name is John de Whitmore (died 1208) but what we see today is very much the making of the Mainwearings, who can trace their line and tenure of the estate as far back as 1546 when Alice de Boghay married Edward Mainwearing. In all that time the manor has never been sold and has only passed on by inheritance. The present squire maintains a keen interest in the village. There are trim little estate cottages, the Mainwearing Arms, a craft shop in the premises of the original pub, a bridge across the stream and the charming church of St. Mary and All Saints. This has a timber-framed bell-turret and a timber-framed gable. Parts of the N and S walls are Norman and inside is an alabaster effigy of Edward Mainwearing, died 1586. The Hall faces the church down an avenue of mature lime trees — a most splendid sight.

Whitmore Hall, the avenue of lime trees.

The old 4-storey timber-framed manor house is encased in brick. The handsome S front that faces the church is of 1676. It has 9 bays and 2 storeys with a top balustrade. The porch is of 1847 and the entrance hall with its Corinthian columns is mid-Georgian. The Stable block is as good as the house. It dates from about 1625 and the horse boxes are in beautiful, original condition. A road leads northwards to Keele, past the Stable Block, and on up the hill from where one can look down on the lake embowered in trees. The lane continues up and a track forks left to the

Whitmore, the village over the bridge.

Moathouse and Woodhouse, both names implying late forest clearance. Whitmore Heath lies 0·75m. SW of the village. Here are some good modern houses on the hillside which overlooks the Whitmore Gap, a low point in the Trent-Mersey watershed which is utilised by the main line railway. At the top

Whitmore, the squire outside the old pub.

of the hill, NW of the village, the A53 is joined by the A5182 to Trentham. This was a new road made in 1845. Samuel Stone, the author of the famous hymn 'The Church's One Foundation', was born at Whitmore.

WHITTINGTON *3m. E of Lichfield.*

To the N and E the village is bounded by the Coventry Canal, and to the S are the 'danger areas' of army rifle ranges. On Whittington Heath, 0·5m. S, are the grim bastions of Whittington Barracks, home to nine regiments. Adjacent to the main road (A51) is an army museum. In the village church of St. Giles is the rather grand 17th Century pulpit, which had been removed from Lichfield Cathedral by Gilbert Scott during his restoration of the building in the second half of the 19th Century. The tower of St. Giles is medieval, the brick nave and the ashlar bays are of 1761, the chancel is of 1881 by Ewan Christian, and there is some restored 15th Century stained glass. Preserved in the church is the flute of William Bass who accompanied the singing here from 1800 to 1867. All manner of both solo instruments and 'rustic ensembles' of violins, trumpets, oboes and the like were common in country churches in the days before organs became common place. Whittington Hall is mostly of 1891 when the 17th Century brick house was much enlarged

Whittington, Packington Hall.

for Samuel Lipscomb. On the garden side is the handsome stone porch from the original house. The gate posts are also original and dated at 1673. On the road to Fisherwick, just past the Hall, are 2 splendid half-timbered houses, Old Timbers and Long Meadow. The infilling is of brick and they stand about a cobbled court facing the road. Both have been extremely well renovated and restored. **Fisherwick** Park lies 0·75m. NE of Whittington on the wide, flat plain of the River Mease. Here the Marquis of Donegal had a large country house surrounded by

Whittington, Long Meadow on the Fisherwick road.

landscaped gardens, all built and designed by 'Capability' Brown in 1774. (Lancelot Brown was also an architect.) Sad to say, in 1810 the estate was bought by the Howard family of Elford who demolished the house and ploughed up the park. All that remains are the large gate piers and a lodge house. There is a local tradition that the bricks used to construct the wall of the Park were originally intended for the unbuilt centre part of the house Charles Pye partly erected at Clifton Campville. Just to the E of Whittington Barracks and clearly visible from the A51 is the handsome, cream washed 18th Century **Packington** Hall. It is fronted by a line of trees and stands amidst huge arable fields. It is now used as offices by Gills Cables Ltd. The sound of gunfire echoes all around from the army rifle ranges which encircle it to the rear.

WIGGINGTON *1·25m. N of Tamworth.*
Wiggington is a small village 0·5m. N of the suburbs of Tamworth. It is an Anglo-Saxon settlement and after the Norman Conquest was kept by the king. It lay within the Royal Forest of Cannock and in 1266 it was noted that the tenants of the manor had rights of 'husbote and heybote' in a wood owned by the manor. By 1340 there was a fulling mill here. The attractive brick church of St. Leonard is of 1777 by Joyce of Burton with a later Gothic chancel of 1862. It has a gallery, round-headed windows and 2 columns which support the small square turret-tower.

WIGHTWICK *2·25m. W of Wolverhampton town centre.*
Wightwick used to belong to the manor of Tettenhall. Today they both belong to Wolverhampton and both are up-market residential areas — the leafiest of leafy suburbs. There are many good houses here, ranging from the large, red brick Wightwick Hall (now a council special school) to little, old cottages. Wightwick lies on the bluff that overlooks the Staffordshire and Worcestershire Canal to Castlecroft and is best approached along the A454

Wolverhampton to Bridgnorth road. The star attraction here is Wightwick Manor. Superficially it looks old, but is in fact of the late 19th Century. It was built by Edward Ould of Liverpool for Theodore Mander, who paid for it from the profits of his paint and varnish business. (His main factory was right in the heart of Wolverhampton where the Mander Centre now stands.) The Manor is not only a beautiful and interesting house, it is also on a scale that is suitable for living in. The left-hand half of the house (as seen from the garden) was built in 1887 and is part timber-framed and part bright Ruabon brick and hung tiles. On this side is the short tower that contains the entrance. The right-hand side is of 1893 and is almost all timber-framed and highly decorated above the low sandstone foundation plinth. The chimneys on this side are tall and have candy twists. The entrance leads to a long corridor. In the left and older part of the house are the Drawing Room and the Library. In the right-hand part are the Great Parlour of 2 storeys, the Dining Room and the Billiard Room. All the rooms are decorated with an impressive collection of the works of the Pre-Raphaelites and the William Morris school of design. There are stained glass windows by Kempe, rugs, textiles, wallpapers and tapestries by Morris, and tiles by de Morgan. The furniture, though, is a motley crew and

Whitwick, the Pear and Partridge at Perton.

includes a settle by Bodley, a folding chair by Swinburne, a cupboard painted by Treffry Dunn, an Italian Renaissance chimney piece

Whitwick Manor, the garden at evening.

and some neo-Jacobean plaster ceilings by L.A. Shuffrey. The gardens surround the house with both formal and natural areas and were designed by Alfred Parsons, with a later terrace by T.H. Mawson. The Lodge and the Barn are all that is left of the previous late 16th Century Manor House and they have been grossly over-restored by Ould. In 1937 Sir Geoffrey and Lady Mander made over the house and gardens to the National Trust. North-east of Whitwick Manor is the Mount Hotel in Mount Road. This was the home of Charles Benjamin Mander, cousin of Theodore. It was built about 1870 and extended in 1891 and 1908. In Church Road is Christ Church, constructed of rusticated stone in 1866 by Bateman and Corser with some stained glass by Kempe. Abounding Whitwick to the N was the old wartime Perton aerodrome on which, in the 1980's, have been built several large, modern housing estates.

WILLENHALL *3m. E of Wolverhampton.*
At the time of Domesday Book 'Winehale'

belonged to the king and was a Royal Manor. By the 19th Century the following rhyme was current: 'A tumbledown church, A tottering steeple, A drunken parson, And a wicked people.' There is many a true word spoken in jest. The church did in fact become unsafe and was rebuilt 3 times; the Reverend Moreton was a 19th Century vicar who drank, gambled and interrupted sermons to attend cock fights; and Willenhall was known nationally as a cruel place where young and old worked longs hours for little pay and where the children were 'beaten shamefully with horsewhip, strap, stick, hammer, handle, file or whatever tool is nearest to hand'. The tool nearest to hand would probably have been one used in the manufacture of locks. Ninety per cent of the locks made in England today are made in Willenhall. It was for long a craft industry because most of the parts of the lock mechanism had to be filed by hand. This was not only skilled work, it was hard work and the men of Willenhall were known for their stoops and humpbacks — 'Upshire' they called the area in other parts of the Black Country. Not until 1856 was the drop forge used to press parts into shape. Two of the largest firms today are Josiah Parkes, who were originally iron-merchants and turned to lock making in 1896, and Yale, founded by the American Linus Yale, who invented the pin tumbler lock and also set up in Willenhall in 1929. There are 2 lock museums in the town. One is at the public library in Walsall Street, and the other is the privately owned National Lock Mueum in New Road which is housed in an old locksmith's shop that has been in continuous use since the 1840's. In the Market Square there is a large stone sculpture of a lock with inscriptions around the base. The parish church of St. Giles is dedicated to the patron saint of cripples, reputedly because in Spring Lane there was a well whose waters cured the sick, especially those who suffered complaints of the eyes and skin. The present church has a tall tower with pinnacles, and was built by W.D. Griffin of Wolverhampton in 1867. St. Stephen's in Wolverhampton

Willenhall, Gipsy Lane.

Street is also by W.D. Griffin, of 1854. St. Anne's in Ann (sic) Street is by H. Jeavons, of 1856. In 1849 there was an outbreak of cholera in the town and not enough room in the churchyard to bury the victims. Dr. Richard Wilkes gave a piece of ground to take the overspill and 211 (out of 292) corpses were interred there. The burial ground is known as Doctor's Piece and is now a Memorial Garden. Between the centre of Willenhall and the M6 is Bentley where once stood Bentley Hall. This was the 17th Century home of Colonel John Lane and his

Willenhall, Market Place.

sister, Jane, who gave comfort and succour to Charles II in September 1651 after his defeat at the Battle of Worcester. The church at Bentley is All Saints. It stands on a good site overlooking the Motorway and was built by Lavender, Twentyman and Percy in 1951. It is dedicated to Alfred Ernest Owen of Rubery Owen and Co., Darlaston, and replaces a church of 1872 by Street which was destroyed by a landmine in the Second World War. By the Bentley Canal in Willenhall is Mumper's Dingle where Isobel Berners camped and where fought the Flaming Tinman in George Borrow's 'Lavengro' (1851).

WILLOUGHBRIDGE 6m. NE of Market Drayton.

Willoughbridge is most easily approached off the A51 — the old coaching road between Nantwich and Stone. Turn off on the road signed to Winnington and Mucklestone. There is no village in the accepted sense. There probably was one once but it has long gone. The centre of interest here is

Willoughbridge Lodge. It sits dramatically outlined against the sky on a hill like a medieval castle. It is in fact quite old and was built by the Gerard family about 1600 as a Hunting Lodge. (The Gerards lived some 4m. to the SE at Gerard's Bromley.) The Lodge is built of sandstone, presumably taken from the quarry which is now surrounded by pine trees at the end of the drive. The NW facing front is most handsome with battlements, a turret and an ogee cap which consists of tiles decorated with a scale-like design. Around the central block are short wings to the left and right, and to the rear all the windows are mullioned. The Lodge is now a farm and has been somewhat spoiled by red brick extensions to the right side and the rear. There are several estate cottages close by, some of which are derelict. Near the foot of the slope, to the left of the access drive as one approaches the house, is a small wood in which are several pools fed by natural springs. A quarter of a mile NE of the Lodge is an impressive moated site — a sizeable,

Willoughbridge Wells, the well house.

Willoughbridge, the Dorothy Clive Gardens.
Willoughbridge Lodge at sunrise.

Wightwick, the Hall.

Willoughbridge, springs near the Lodge.

square, mounded, enclosure surrounded by a now dry ditch. The mound is covered with tall grasses and bullrushes. A small brook passes by the moat and a short distance upstream is an ancient pond-bay. Whether this was constructed as a fishing pool or for a water-mill is not known. This is altogether an interesting area and one worthy of detailed investigation. Along the lane in the direction of the A51 is Willoughbridge Farm, a curious collection of large brick buildings and a farmhouse with stone mullioned windows. Opposite this farm is a lane that leads to a small quarry and also to the back entrance of Willoughbridge Wells. Here is a charming house, set amongst trees with lawns that run down to a small, islanded lake. In the late 17th Century Lady Gerard attempted to establish a health spa here based on the warm springs that feed the lake. She built a small, square, stone bath house (dated at about 1682), which is still there, though now

roofless. Much of Willoughbridge Park has been quarried for sand and gravel and is still being worked. Indeed, the front entrance drive to Willoughbridge Wells House is at the end of the access road to the A.R.C. quarry which leads off the A51. Also on the A51 are the delightful Dorothy Clive Gardens. These were created in this century in memory of the owner's wife. They are both interesting and beautiful and well worth a visit.

WILNECOTE *2m. SE of Tamworth.*
It lies on Watling Street, close to the Warwickshire border, and was at one time in that county. In 1935 Doulton's built a factory here to make acid-proof stoneware and porcelain for the chemical industry. Reliant cars are also made in the village, for village it is though now joined to Tamworth by suburbia. Wilnecote Hall lies S of the main road. It has 3 bays of brick with stone dressings separated by giant pilasters and a steep pediment, all of the 18th Century. The turreted Gothic church of Holy Trinity lies 0·25m. NW of the Hall, on the other side of Watling Street. To passers-by it presents a stoney face; to the back it is brick.

WOLSTANTON *See Newcastle-under-Lyme.*

WOLVERHAMPTON *16m. S of Stafford.*
Wolverhampton is an ancient hill town and the raised mound on which the parish church is built is quite possibly of prehistoric origin. By the mid 9th Century it was an Anglo-Saxon religious centre and the 14 ft. high pillar that stands by the entrance of St. Peter's church dates from this time. It is covered in badly worn carvings, one of which appears to be of a dragon and was almost certainly a Preaching Cross. The first church was probably of timber construction. In 985 Lady Wulfruna, the sister of King Edgar, was granted land in Heantun by King Ethelred, and in 994 she endowed this land to the church of St. Mary. Shortly after, Heantun (meaning 'High Town'), became Wulfruna's

384

Heantun, later corrupted to Wolverhampton. The Minster Church of St. Mary served a wide area. The parish system was not yet established and the Christian religion was administered by priests who travelled out from Minster Churches. They preached under trees, often yew trees, at specially erected preaching crosses and even in old pagan temples. In the reign of Henry III (1216-1272) the church of St. Mary was re-dedicated to St. Peter. It was now a collegiate church, a Royal Free Chapel, answerable to the King, not to the church. Collegiate churches were powerful, influential and richly endowed with land. St. Peter's is a large church and reflects both its own prosperity and that of the town. Wolverhampton grew rich on the wool trade in the 14th and 15th Centuries. There was a large market place to the SW of the church and the memory of this is preserved in names

Wolverhampton, St. Peter's church.

Wolverhampton, restored cottage in Victoria Street.

such as Blossom's Fold, Mitre Fold, Wadham's Fold, Exchange Street and Cheapside. The word Cheapside is derived from the Old English for 'market'. There are also more Folds in other parts of the town: Pountney Fold in Dudley Street, Bennet's Fold in Salop Street, and Farm Fold in John Street. The market place has been in-filled with buildings since Victorian times and the process was completed in 1978 when the new red brick Civic Offices (designed by Clifford Culpin) were erected in the last open space between the Old Town Hall and the church. Wolverhampton in the 15th Century was a handsome place full of richly adorned merchants' houses, inns and hostelries. As late as 1868 Elihu Burrit was able to write of Wolverhampton: 'Look at this town ...... Few in England wear seemingly more antiquity in general aspect. Here are houses built in Elizabeth's day .....' One of the houses that Burrit saw was the Old Hall, the moated mansion of the Leveson wool merchants and future Dukes of Sutherland, whose house survived to be used as a late 19th Century japanning works, and which stood on the site now occupied by the Central Library. The road at the back of the Library is still called Old Hall Street. Another old house was the Deanery, reputedly the most beautiful Elizabethan house in the town. It stood on the site of the new Polytechnic and was demolished in 1921. The only building to survive from this period is the small 16th Century timber-framed house on the corner of Victoria Street and St. John's Street, which was zealously over-restored in 1979-81. After the decline of the wool trade Wolverhampton continued to prosper through the 16th and 17th Centuries as a market town, and in the 18th Century a variety of industries took root. Architecturally the early 18th Century is represented by 2 buildings. The unexciting and currently boarded-up Molyneaux Hotel is of about 1740-50, the old home of the Molyneaux family. It has 2 fronts. The earlier faces the Ring Road and has 5 bays and 3 storeys. The new front is at the back and has 2 richly decorated Venetian windows. The turret is Victorian and there have been several extensions. A little earlier in date, at 1728, is Giffard House, the town house of the Giffard family of Chillington which stands near the Civic Hall. The Roman Catholic church of St. Peter and St. Paul was built on to the back of the house in 1828. The stuccoed church was designed by Joseph Ireland and has shallow domes and high moon-shaped windows. Both buildings are now in the process of being renovated. Also of the Georgian period is the 18th Century George Street with elegant houses leading to the E end of St. John's Church. The church was built in 1758-76, by either William Baker or Roger Eykyn. It is ashlar, is not altogether in proportion and inside has 3 galleries. The organ is of about 1682 by Renatus Harris and was formerly in the Temple Church, London. It is an instrument of some renown. One of the most attractive streets in Wolverhampton is King Street where a row of small Georgian houses form a delightful ensemble. They have recently been renovated and the street pedestrianised. The continuing prosperity of the town can be judged by the fact that by 1763 no less than 7 turnpiked roads met here. Not only was there a Corn Exchange, a weekly market and a horsefair, but the metal trades were becoming established, the canals were arriving and Wolverhampton was entering an age of prosperity matched, perhaps, but not exceeded, by any other town in England. That this is not reflected in its public buildings has been noted by more than one

Wolverhampton, Lichfield Street and the Art Gallery.

Wolverhampton, Galisbury House, Tettenhall Road.

observer. The explanation seems to be quite simply that 'they took their money home and spent it their'. Certainly, the workers saw little of the profits. However, drive down Tettenhall Road to Tettenhall, Penn Road to Penn or Compton Road to Compton and you will see the houses the wealthier Victorians and Edwardians built. Around the town centre were the courts and passages of the artisans, the slums and squalor that led to outbreaks of cholera in 1832, 1849 and 1872. In 1849 an asylum was established for children made orphans by the plague. This became the now highly respected Royal Wolverhampton School in Penn Road. The impressive buildings date from 1853 and were designed by Joseph Manning, with wings added in 1863. The Headmaster's House is of 1885 and the chapel, which has stained glass by William Kempe, is of 1895. The town became a Jack of All Trades and because of this diversity was never hit by the recessions that inevitably affected some undividual industries. Of particular importance were iron-working (Bayliss),

japanning (Mander), lock making (Chubb), railway rolling stock (G.W.R.), bicycles (Rudge), motor-cars (Sunbeam), motor-cycles (A.J.S.), lorries (Guys) and brewing. Little wonder that between 1801 and 1901 the population of the town rose from 12,500 to 95,000. In 1848 Wolverhampton became a borough and its first mayor was George Benjamin Thorneycroft, an ironmaster. Two

Post war pre-fab in Hendon Road.

years later the Oxford and Worcestershire Railway arrived, followed by the Shrewsbury to Birmingham and Great Western in 1845.

387

During the 19th Century the town was virtually rebuilt. As was so often the case the wealth created by industry financed wholesale and largely indiscriminate redevelopment. It was 'farewell and adieu to Old England' and 'all hail the Age of Steam'. The greater part of Wolverhampton is today Victorian (1837-1901) and Edwardian (1901-1910) but there has also been some rebuilding in recent years, especially in the Chapel Ash area, at the end of Darlington Street, where amorphous concrete giants clad with red brick stand gazingly coldly at the traffic rushing around the new Ring Road. Having done their worst at the west end of town the planners are now exercising their talents on the east end, which at the time of writing has been bulldozed flat. More sensibly, the council recently organised the mass modernisation of Victorian terraces in areas like Whitmore Reans. From the humble to the high, a further word on the parish church. The red sandstone church of St. Peter is an ancient foundation but the fabric that we see today owes much to the vigorous restoration carried out by Ewan Christian in 1852-65. What is old are the crossing arches which support the crossing tower, the excellent 5 light E window and the piscina (wash basin) in the S wall, all of which are of the 13th Century. The N transept, the embattled and pinnacled tower itself and the windows in the S transept and the nave clerestory are all Perpendicular. The nave is of about 1460. The chancel and apse were rebuilt by Christian and the porch is largely Victorian. The pulpit was donated by the Swynnerton family. There are monuments to the Levesons in the S (Leveson) chapel, including a bronze of Admiral Sir Richard Leveson, died about 1634, by le Seour; and in the N (Lane) chapel are monuments to the Lane family, including the tomb of Thomas and Katharine Lane (1582) and the wall monument to Colonel John Lane, died 1667, who aided King Charles II in his escape after the Battle of Worcester. There are stained glass windows by Kempe and Powell, and some 16th and 17th Century Dutch and German stained glass medallions in the chancel. The stalls are 15th Century and came from Lilleshall Abbey. They were given to the church by the Leveson family in 1546 (at the Dissolution of the Monasteries). In 1479 Edward IV united the Deanery of St. Peter's with that of Windsor and this Royal

Wolverhampton Polytechnic extension

Peculiar lasted until 1846. The markets, both open and covered, have long been banished to the edge of the town centre (Salop Street — School Street) and are housed in a building by A.G.E. Chapman, who must have been given a very small budget. Opposite the new red brick Civic Offices are the old Town Hall of 1869 by Ernest Bates and the unprepossessing Civic Hall of 1938 with its giant Classical portico. The village green of the original settlement was called High Green and occupied the site now called Queen's Square. The Queen, of course, was Victoria. In Queen's Square is a statue of Prince Albert on horseback (1866) by Thomas Thorneycroft. This was unveiled by Queen Victoria herself and was her first engagement after the death of her Consort. It was whilst travelling here for this engagement that she is reputed to have ordered the blinds to be drawn over her railway carriage window so that she would not have to witness the horrors of the Black Country. On arrival at the station in Wolverhampton she walked beneath a triumphal arch of coal, especially erected as a

watered by a stream about 0·7m. NE of Wombourne, just off the A47 to Sedgeley. It is a Jacobean house that was well restored by G.F. Bodley in the 1870's, and given additional external ornament by C.R. Ashbee and his Guild of Handicraft in the years 1896-8. The following was their work: the gables, the parapet, the sundial in the porch and the wrought iron weather-vanes. The stables are Georgian brick and have a cupola and a central pediment. The Bratch is a hamlet 0·75m. NW of Wombourne. Here is a well-known and much photgraphed canal lock and lock-keeper's office complex on the Staffordshire and Worcestershire Canal where it is crossed by a bridge that carries the road to Trysull. On the opposite side of the road is a car park, and adjacent to this is the red brick Waterworks of 1895 dressed up with little corner turrets to give the impression of a Gothic castle.

WOODLANE 8·5m. N of Lichfield.

Woodlane is a hamlet in Needwood Forest, 1·25m. N of Yoxall, on the A515. There is a

handful of cottages, a telephone box and the Roman Catholic church of St. Francis de Sales. The church is of 1795 and was commissioned by the 15th Earl of Shrewsbury, whose father had lived at nearby Hoar Cross Hall. It is of brick, in a Gothic style and was enlarged in 1834. Attached to the church is the Presbytery.

WOOTTON LODGE 6m. WSW of Ashbourne and 1·5m. ENE of Alton Towers.

Wootton Lodge must be the most handsome house in Staffordshire and the equal of any in England. In addition, it is set in the most beautiful Park — a valley of woods, meadows and lakes stocked with deer of several kinds. It is such a terrible misfortune that the strident music from the enormous fun fair at Alton Towers drifts across this perfect idyll. The Lodge was built for Sir Richard Fleetwood, 1st Baronet, about 1600. The architect was probably Robert Smythson, died 1614. Sir Richard was a recuscant Catholic and a Royalist, and in 1643, during the Civil War, the Lodge was attacked and

Wootton Lodge Park.

Wootton Lodge, the finest house in Staffordshire.

Wootton Lodge, the deer park.

badly damaged. The 3rd Baronet sold the house in the Late 17th Century and it was bought by an ironmaster from Stourbridge, John Wheeler. He repaired the exterior and completely re-made the interior in about 1700. The balustrade, the steps and the detached side pavillions date from 1700. The Wheeler family and their relatives, the Unwins, occupied the Lodge until the Second World War. Since then it has changed hands once or twice and is now owned and occupied by a member of the Bamford family of the J.C.B. company, who manufacture earth-moving equipment in their new factory at Rocester. The founder of the company started with virtually nothing after he was demobilised at the end of the war, and yet has built in his own lifetime a large, profitable amd internationally-known company of high repute. Mr. Bamford has used his own equipment to good effect at Wootton where the lakes have been greatly extended and new terraces constructed. The house is tall and symmetrical. It is 3 storeys high, plus basement, and is 5 bays wide. On either side of the central projecting porch bay are canted bays, all rising the full height of the building. Around the top is a balustrade. The chimneys are small and neatly aligned. The sides have semi-circular bow windows. The fan-shaped entrance steps lead to the entrance porch which is decorated with pairs of fluted Ionic columns on which are obelisks. The windows are mullioned and transomed. The detached pavilions to either

The Kevin Quarry, near Wootton.

side of the house at the front are quite acceptable but modern attached extensions at the back are not good at all. There are several other buildings on the estate — farms, workshops, lodges and the like — and all are fitting and well cared for. Wootton Lodge and its park really are most excellent. The old rhyme 'Wooton under Wever, where God came never' may have applied to the village 1m. NE, but to the Lodge he most surely came. The entrance to the estate is not signposted. It lies at the end of a lane off the road from Upper Ellastone to Wooton. Note: Wever is the old name of the Weaver Hills, and is still used by many local people.

WORDSLEY *2·5m. N of Stourbridge.*

Wordsley hardly has a separate identity merging, as it does, into Brierley Hill to the E and Amblecote to the S. The village lies

Wordsley, Stuart Crystal museum.

along the A491 Stourbridge to Kingswinford road and it is here that the Redhouse Glass Works of Stuart and Sons Ltd, stand (SO.894.864). The glass industry came here early because all the necessary raw materials — coal, fireclay, sand and potash — were available locally, and was given an impetus when the Stourbridge Canal (1779) was driven through. *(See Brierley Hill).* There are still many companies making glass here but Stuart and Sons kept their glass-cone, which is now the only surviving building of its kind in the Midlands. (There are only 4 in the whole country — 2 more in the N of England and one in Scotland.) The cone is 87 ft. high

Wordsley, the Stuart Crystal Kilnhouse.

396

and tapers from 57 ft. at the base to 10 ft. at the top. The building is now used for storage but it originally had a 12-pot furnace which was in use until 1939. Around the furnace were; the 'dog hole' for pot storage ; the pot arch which pre-heated the pots (the pots were made of fireclay); an annealing kiln; a metal room where the glass mix ready for melting into glass was stored; a 'glory hole' where glass was reheated whilst being worked; a second glory hole and another kiln; and the coal entrance to the kilns which connected to the canal. Almost all these ancillary buildings have been demolished. The works probably date from about 1788 when Richard Bradley, a glassmaker, bought the site. The company is still very much a going concern and there is now a museum, a coffee shop, a workshop which repairs minor damage to glass products, and a factory shop. The complex is open on Sundays, as are several other glass factory shops in the area.

Wordsley, repairman at Stuart Crystal.

For the rest, Wordsley is a place typical of the Black Country — factories, large and small terraced houses, corner shops and the occasional grand Georgian house. The parish church is Holy Trinity in High Street. It is a substantial and impressive building raised by Lewis Vulliamy in 1829-30 with an E chancel window of 1857. The traceried side windows with 2 lights are of about 1300 and inside there are high arcades, galleries and flat ceilings. The School is also by Vulliamy with stepped end gables and a mid gable. Wordsley Hospital was the former workhouse. The central block with gables and tower is of about 1900.

WYCHNOR *7m. NE of Lichfield.*
Wychnor Bridges Farmhouse is on the horrendously busy and dangerous A38. It is a 7-bay, 2·5-storey house with a canted 3-bay centre supported by Tuscan columns. Opposite this substantial house is the lane to Wychnor. A bridge carries the lane over the Trent and Mersey Canal which here runs alongside the main road. Half a mile down this lane is a turning to the left. This leads to the church of St. Leonard which stands on the edge of a low terrace overlooking the flood plain of the River Trent. It is mostly of about 1300 (Decorated) but the E arch of the tower is of about 1200 and the brick top of about 1600. Next to the church is the Old School House. In the field to the front of the church and the school house is an area of disturbed ground. This is probably part of the site which was excavated in 1973 when

Wychnor, the bridge over the canal.

remains of an early Anglo-Saxon settlement of some size were found. The Angles came into the Midlands along the valley of the River Trent. The group that settled at Wychnor were the Hwicce, after which the settlement was named. The medieval village was deserted either because of flooding or, more likely, because of a change from arable to pastoral agriculture. Just SW of the church, on the island, is the site of a moated farmhouse or manor. Today, all that is left of the village is the church, the old school house and across the fields 2 farms. Wychnor Hall lies 0·75m. W of the church. It stands in a small park with a few cottages and a plant nursery. The old moated Hall has been replaced by an 18th Century mansion which has a main range of 7 bays, 3 storeys high, with a recessed centre and a Tuscan columned porch. To the right of the main block is a 2 storey range of the same height. It is not a handsome house and the grounds are uncared for. What is worse, the present owner tells with glee how he disposed of the ancient custom of the Wychnor Flytch. In

1347 the manor was granted to Sir Philip de Somerville by John O' Gaunt on the condition that a flitch of bacon should always be kept in the Hall to be claimed by any man of the manor who could prove absolute fidelity and happiness in his marriage for a year and a day. The custom fell into disuse but a token flytch made of painted wood was kept in the Hall right up until about 1980 when it was sold to a private person for a pittance and left the Hall forever. That was a great pity. The A38 is, of course, Ryknild Street, the old Roman road that was kept in repair throughout the Middle Ages, and was a major highway in the 12th Century. The bridges over the River Trent at Wychnor were therefore of some importance. (Note: The Hwicce were the 'salt people'. 'Wich' is derived from the name and usually denotes an area where salt is, or was found — Nantwich, Shirleywich near Stafford, etc. It does not necessarily mean that the Hwicce tribe were the settlers in all those places. It is also now believed that Hwicce may be a Celtic name, adopted by the Angles).

Wychnor Hall.

YARNFIELD *2·5m. WSW of Stone.*

Yarnfield is most easily approached off the A34. The road climbs the hill of Bury Bank and passes the Iron Age fort in the woods to the right. A little further along, and also on the right about 0·33m. from the road, is the conical hill of Saxon's Lowe (SJ.875.366), a large 38 ft. high burial mound. It is most easily seen in the winter when the trees close to it have no leaves. The road crosses over the M6 and on the outskirts of Yarnfield are the derelict prefabricated buildings of Duncan Hall, the old G.P.O. training centre. These have just been sold (1987) and will soon be replaced by modern houses, not that Yarnfield needs any more. They already envelop the old village to the extent that it is no longer a country place but more like the suburb of a town. Nevertheless, the long village centre still retains some kind of character. There is a half-timbered barn at Ivy Cottage, a pub called the Labour in Vain and St. Barnabas, the tiniest of tiny churches, which is simply a red brick box with a slate roof, but quite endearing. The village green is very large with an unexpected wild area near the stream. There are several older brick cottages, the attractive Gorsty Hill Farm and a rendered Village Hall of 1932. Close to the centre of the village is the new college, almost a small town in its own right. The large, multi-storeyed, many-windowed teaching blocks of about 1970 are not at all pleasant. However, the student accomodation is quite reasonable and the new buildings constructed in 1987 are superb. They have low, varied roof lines with pantiles, and red brick walls with smooth brick dressings. The green window hoods and dark glass add just the right amount of colour and they are positioned so that they can be seen to their best advantage. Today the centre is known as the British Telecom Training College. There are some 1,000 students and about 500 staff to instruct and administer them.

YOXALL *7·5m. NNE of Lichfield.*

The village lies in flattish country on the A515 NE of King's Bromley. It is a substantial settlement and although not picturesque is a pleasant enough place. The River Swarbourne flows parallel with the E side of the main road and is crossed by 4 bridges. The name Yoxall is thought to mean 'a secluded piece of land small enough to be ploughed by one team of oxen'. In 1778 nearly 40 urns of coarse brown pottery were found in the village and it is probable that they marked the site of a Romano-British burial ground. This suggests that Yoxall is a Celtic settlement in origin. (One of the urns is in Lichfield Museum.) In the late 18th and early 19th Centuries there was a woven cloth tape-making industry in the area. At Morrey, 0·5m. W of Yoxall, there was a large tape-mill. It was built in the 1790's and operated in conjunction with a bleaching works until the mid 19th Century. In Woodhouses, 0·75m. E of Yoxall, a small tape factory was established in 1817 in the mansion of Highwall Hall, but after 1818 nothing more is known about it. The church of St. Peter was rebuilt by Woodyer in 1865-8 but still retains a S doorway of about 1200, Decorated arcades, and a W tower which looks Perpendicular but is believed to be of the 17th Century. There is stained glass by Wailes and there are monuments to Humphrey Welles, died 1565, and Admiral Meynell, died 1865. Noteworthy buildings include: The Rookery, 0·25m. S, an 18th Century house of 3 storeys and 5 bays with a pedimented doorcase; and Yoxall Grange, a timber-framed house infilled with brick and with 2 gables. Yoxall Lodge (now demolished) stood NE of the village and was the home of the Rev. Thomas Gisborne, a friend of William Wilberforce who often visited here and spent many weeks discussing his reforms with the Reverend. At Bond End, on the eastern fringe of Yoxall, are the remains of a Malthouse. Well into the 19th Century it was not uncommon for innkeepers and the owners of large estates to brew their own beer in their own breweries. Some also had a malthouse, but a large floor area was required on which to spread the barley, so most bought their malt from specialist malthouses. One such was the malthouse at Bond End. It is especially interesting because the accounts have been preserved. Of the buildings, the brick and tile malthouse and part of the kiln still survive. The main range runs alongside the road and is 83 ft. long by 21 ft. wide and 3 storeys high. The top 2 floors are laid with gypsum plaster, a surface prized by maltsters from at least 1680 to 1870. The kiln formed a cross wing at the W end and was built in 1776. The premises are now used as a builder's store. Finally, near Mill Stream, is a rectangular moated site 300 ft. by 110 ft.

THE END

Glossary of Architectural Terms

Apse A semi-circular or polygonal end to the chancel and or a chapel of a church. It is usually vaulted.

Arcade A range of arches supported by either columns or piers and usually of structural importance. *(See Blind Arcade.)*

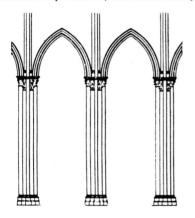

Ashlar Blocks of squared stone, smooth faced, even in size and usually laid in courses like bricks. The blocks can either be structural or merely a facing to a brick built building.

Bailey An enclosed and protected open space within the walls of a castle.

Bargeboards Boards which hide the join of the roof and the wall on a gable and which are often ornamented.

Battlement The alternately raised (merlons) and lowered (embrasures) configuration of a parapet, usually associated with the tops of the walls and towers of a castle but also used as a decoration on civilian buildings. An alternative word for battlemented is crenellated.

Bay A bay is a vertical division of a building either by internal or external features. The most common feature used to define the number of bays is the arrangement of the windows as seen from the outside. *(See the illustration of 'Queen Anne Style' house. It has 7 Bays.)* The building in the drawing has 5 bays.

Beaker People Late Neolithic (New Stone Age) people who came to Britain from Europe. They introduced weapons and tools made from metal and buried their dead in round barrows.

Belfrey It can be either a specially built bell tower or the upper floor of the main church tower where the bells are hung. In the Middle Ages a belfry was a moveable seige tower and later came to mean a a watch tower from which the alarm was raised by ringing a bell.

Bellcote A simple framework from which bells are hung. It is often an extension of a gable end but can mean anything that literally 'houses a bell'.

Broach Spire When an octagonal tapering spire meets the square tower on which it stands, sloping half-pyramids of wood, brick or stone are positioned at the base of the four oblique faces of the spire to 'square the octagon'. *(See diagram on next page).*

401

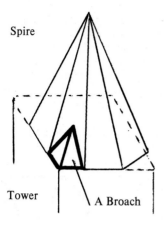

Spire

Tower — A Broach

Cable Moulding A decorative band usually carved in stone or wood imitating a twisted rope or cable and much used by the Normans.

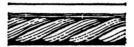

Capital The top part of a column or pilaster usually highly decorated. It tapers outwards from the column beneath to provide a platform from which an arch may spring or upon which an entablature may rest.

Blind Arcade A series of arches supported by columns or pilasters arranged against a wall almost always as a decorative, not structural, feature. The Normans were very fond of it.

Broken Pediment A pediment in which the horizontal base line has a gap at the centre.

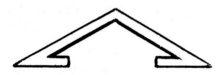

Bronze Age Bronze is a mixture of tin and copper. It was the first metal that man was able to work with effectively. In Britain the Bronze Age lasted from about 2000 B.C. (the end of the Stone Age) to about 600 B.C. (the beginning of the Iron Age).

Canted Bay Window A protruding window the front of which is straight and parallel to the main building, and which is joined to the main building by side walls set at an angle of more than 90 degrees.

Cartouche An ornament in the form of a tablet or shield with an ornate frame, often in the form of scrolls made to look like paper, and which usually bears either an inscription or a coat of arms.

Castellated Identical in meaning to 'battlemented'.

Chancel The part of the church, usually the east end, where is placed the altar. In a cruciform church it is the whole of the area east of the crossing. The sanctuary is the area immediately around the altar.

Chantry Chapel A chapel either inside or attached to a church or other religious foundation in which prayers were said, and the mass was chanted, for the founder or other particular person (often a relative of the founder). The founder usually built the chapel himself and endowed (i.e. left money or land) to the church to pay for the clergy to officiate after his death.

Chevet A French word meaning the east end of the church.

402

Classical   A building or style based on Roman or Greek architecture.

Clerestory   Derived from clear-storey. The upper part of the main walls of a church, above the aisle roofs, which are pierced by windows. *(See Triforium diagram.)*

Cob   Walls constructed of mud or clay mixed with straw and, or, cow dung. The exterior surface of the cob was white-washed to protect it from rain and properly maintained is a durable material. The houses of the poor in Britain were commonly made of cob, and some still exist in the south-west. However, if neglected and exposed to water they almost literally melt away. Whole villages, once abandoned, could disappear in a matter of years.

Corinthian   See Order.

Cornice   A projecting ornamental moulding around the top of a building, arch or wall. *(See illustration to 'Queen Anne Style' house.)*

Crenellation   Means battlemented.

Crossing   The area where nave, chancel and transepts meet.

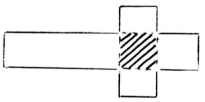

In a cruciform church the tower is usually built above the crossing.

Cruck   A curved beam that supports both the walls and the roof of a timber-framed building.

It was usually obtained from a tree that had a major branch leaving the trunk at an angle of about 45 degrees. The tree was then cut down and the main branch and the trunk trimmed of side branches. This curved timber was then spilt in two. The two parts were then erected opposite each other to form an arch. Several such arches were constructed and these formed the basic structure of a 'cruck house'. The area between the arches were called bays.

A two-bay cruck house.

Cruciform   In the shape of a cross, usually meaning a Christian cross.

Crypt   A room below floor level and usually at least partly below ground level, most commonly positioned at the east end of a church underneath the chancel. The crypt normally contained graves and religious relics.

Cupola   A small dome, usually circular but sometimes polygonal, that either crowns the roof of a building or a tower or caps a turret.

Decorated   (Sometimes called 'Middle Pointed'.) A style of English Gothic current in the period 1300-1350 or thereabouts. As the name suggests ornamentation was rich in this period. *(See Gothic.)*

Doric   See Order.

Dormer   A window placed vertically in the sloping plane of a roof. If it lay in the plane of the roof it would be a skylight. *(See illustration of 'Queen Anne Style' house.)*

Early English   Sometimes abbreviated to 'E.E.' and sometimes called 'Lancet' or 'First Pointed'. Early English is the earliest style of English Gothic and was current between 1200 and 1300. It is characterised by a simplicity of line; by tall, pointed, untraceried, lancet windows; and by slender spires and tall piers. *(See Gothic.)*

Easter Sepulchre A recess in a wall (usually the N wall) of the chancel in which is a tomb chest. An effigy of Christ is placed here during the Easter ceremonies.

Embattled It means there are battlements. *(See Battlement.)*

Fan Vault A vault is an arched interior roof of stone or brick. A fan vault is a late medieval vault where all the ribs from the same springer are of the same length, the same distance from each other and the same curvature.

Fluting Vertical grooves or channels in the shaft of a column.

Foliated As of foliage; the materials are ornamented with carvings of plant foliage, especially leaves.

Gable The triangular upper part of a wall that rises to the slopes of a pitched roof. The gable at the side of a building is called the End Gable. Gables facing to the front or back of a building are simply called gables.

Gallery In a church a gallery is an upper floor over an aisle which is open to the nave. There is also sometimes a gallery at the west end to house the organ.

Gazebo A small pavilion or summerhouse in a garden or park. When placed on the roof of a building it is called a Belvedere.

Georgian Buildings constructed in England during the reigns of of the four King Georges, 1714-1830, in a style influenced by Greek and Roman (Classical) ideas are said to be Georgian. Neatness, formality and symmetry are to the fore. Famous architects associated with the Georgian styles include Robert Adam, John Nash, James 'Athenian' Stuart and James Wyatt. Many of the great English country houses were either built or were given new facades in the 18th Century.

Gothic Gothic is a style that can only be defined by listing its characteristic features: the ribbed vault, the pointed arch, the flying buttress, the traceried window, the lofty steeple, the panelled stonework, the triforium, spacious clerestory windows etc. When all or many of these elements are present in a building it can be described as Gothic. The word 'Gothic' was not used during the period called Gothic, that is between the later 12th Century and the mid-16th Century. It was first used in the late 16th Century to describe the architecture of the previous centuries. It was a term of abuse. To say the style was Gothic meant that it was barbaric and uncivilised, as were the ancient German tribes called Goths. Gothic architecture had absolutely no connection with the Gothic tribes themselves. The style, though always recognizable as one style, underwent changes over the years. The main historical sub-divisions in England were:

Early English	1200-1300
Decorated	1300-1350
Perpendicular	1350-1550

These dates, of course, overlap and are only a rough guide. It should be remembered that individual elements of the Gothic style can be present in buildings that are not Gothic. It is the coming together of several elements that defines the style. Gothic evolved out of the Norman style and so some later Norman churches might best be described as Transitional.

Hammerbeam Horizontal timbers 'projecting' out from opposite sides of the walls supported by brackets. From these, vertical timbers called hammer-posts rise to support the purlins.

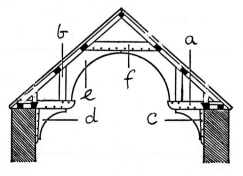

a — hammer beam
b — hammer post
c — bracket
d — brace
e — arched brace
f — collar beam

Herringbone A design created by laying bricks, stones or tiles so as to make a zig-zag pattern.

Hipped Roof A roof which has sloping ends, not vertical ends with gables as is usual. *(See illustration of 'Queen Anne Style' house.)*

Ionic See Order.

Iron Age The Iron Age began when iron working was introduced into Britain by invading Celtic tribes who arrived on these shores in about 600 B.C. The Iron Age lasted until the coming of the Romans which was effectively A.D.43. However, in some remote areas the Iron Age continued until the coming of the Anglo Saxons in the 6th Century A.D.

Linenfold Tudor panelling, usually of wood to an interior wall, decorated with a stylized representation of a piece of linen laid in vertical folds. The pattern is contained within one panel and repeated in every other panel.

Lower Palaeolithic See Palaeolithic.

Lancet A tall, slender, one-light window with a sharply pointed arch, much used in early Gothic 13th Century architecture. They can be either single or arranged in groups, usually of 3, 5, or 7.

Mansard A pitched roof with two slopes, the lower being longer and steeper than the other. Named after Francois Mansart (sic).

Mesolithic Means Middle Stone Age, the period of man as hunter and fisher from about 8,000 B.C. to 3,500 B.C.

Megalith A large stone or block of stone, often irregular and either rough hewn or left as found. Such stones were erected by prehistoric man as monuments between about 4,000 B.C. and 1,000 B.C.

Middle Pointed Another name for the period of English Gothic more commonly called Decorated. *(See Decorated and also Gothic.)*

Misericord Sometimes called a Miserere. A bracket attached to the underside of a hinged choir stall seat, which, when the seat is turned upright, provide support for a person in the standing position. They are frequently carved and because they are not seen by the congregation the subjects are sometimes non-religious and on occasion even verge on the profane.

Motte Means a mound, usually of earth, on which the main fort of a motte and bailey castle was built.

Mullion A vertical post that divides a window into seperate lights. The term is usually reserved for substantial uprights of brick or stone. *(See Transom).*

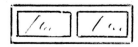

Nave The western part of a church, often with aisles to the sides which are occupied by the congregation.

Neolithic Means New Stone Age, the period of pre-history in Britain from about 3,500 B.C., when settled farming communities were established, to the emergence of the Bronze Age about 1,800 B.C.

Norman What in England is called Norman is really Romanesque. The Norman architects and builders did not have a style particular to themselves. They built in the manner current on the Continent at that time. Indeed, there are in England examples of 'Norman' work — such as Westminster Abbey — that were constructed before the Conquest. *(See Romanesque.)*

Obelisk A pillar of square section that tapers to the top and ends with a pyramid. It can be of any size but is usually of stone, large and erected as a monument.

Ogee An arch introduced into Britain about 1300 and very popular during the 14th Century. It has a characteristic double curve, one concave and the other convex, and is best described by a drawing:

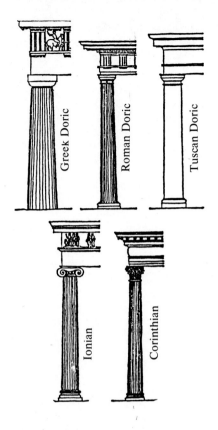

Order In Classical architecture an Order is a complete system which comprises a column and its associated base shaft, capital and entablature (a horizontal table or lintel supported by the columns). The number of inventions and permutations is endless but a mere handful achieved popular acceptance in Rome and Greece and are still used. They are Greek Doric, Roman Doric, Tuscan Doric, Ionian and Corinthian.

Palaeolithic Means Old Stone Age and lasted from about 26,000 B.C. to the start of the Middle Stone Age (the Mesolithic) about 8,000 B.C. As it is such a long period it is sometimes divided into Lower (the early part) and Upper (the later part).

Palimpest When a metal plate, usually of brass, is re-used by engraving on the back the plate is said to be a palimpest; likewise a parchment re-used after removing the original writing; and a wall painting where one painting overlaps and obscures an earlier work.

Pantile A tile with an 'S' configuration. When laid such tiles give a roof a corrugated surface.

Pediment A low-pitched gable much used in Classical architecture and essentially of an ornamental nature. Pediments can be found not only at roof level but above windows, doors and porticos. *(See illustration of 'Queen Anne Style' house.)*

Perpendicular A style of Early English Gothic current in the period 1350-1550. It is characterised by the vertical lines in the window tracery and the vertical articulation of the panelling in the stonework — hence Perpendicular. *(See Gothic.)*

Pier A pillar-like support but square (or composite) in section, usually of masonry. The brickwork or stonework between windows and doorways in a building can be described as piers.

Pilasters A shallow pier or rectangular column projecting only slightly from a wall.

Piscina A stone basin, complete with drain, in which the Communion or the Mass vessels are washed. It is usually set in or against the wall south of the altar.

Porte Corchere A coach porch.

Portico A porch with columns and a pediment decorating the main entrance to a building. If it projects forward, as is commonly the case, it is said to be 'prostyle'. If it recedes into the building (with the columns arranged in line with the front wall) it is said to be 'in antis'.

Presbytery Has two meanings. It is part of the church east of the choir where the high altar is placed. It is also the name given to the house of a Roman Catholic priest.

Priory A monastery whose head is a Prior or Prioress, as distinct from the Abbot or Abbess of an Abbey.

'Queen Anne Style' A style developed in England by Eden Nesfield (1835-88) and Richard Norman Shaw (1831-1912) and very much influenced by 17th Century Dutch brick architecture and the William and Mary style (1689-1702). *(See the illustration)* Queen Ann reigned from 1702-1714.

Queen Anne house

1. Pediment
2. Quoins
3. Cornice
4. String course

Quoins Stones, usually dressed, at the corners of a building. Sometimes they are of equal size; more commonly they alternate long and short. *(See illustration of 'Queen Ann Style' house. It has long and short quoins.)*

Recusant A person who refuses to submit or comply. Most commonly means a practising Catholic in the period when that religion was suppressed, that is, between the Reformation and Catholic Emancipation in the early 19th Century.

Reredos A wall or screen, usually well decorated, that lies behind the altar in a church.

Rib-vault A vault with diagonal ribs projecting along the groins. 'A framework of diagonal arched ribs carrying the cells which cover the spaces between them.'

Rock-Faced Masonry cut to regular blocks but deliberately roughened on the exposed surface to look rough-hewn. The aim is to

407

look natural, but usually the result is most unnatural.

Roll Moulding A decorative moulding of semi-circular and more than semi-circular (but less than circular) cross section.

Romanesque A Continental term for what in England is called Norman, and which covers architecture of the 11th and 12th Centuries. The style is characterised by the round arch, thick walling, small windows, bays clearly marked internally by vertical shafts from floor to ceiling, arcading, tunnel vaults and apses. Ornamentation was vigorous and depicted foliage, birds, animals and monsters, and utilised various bold geometric designs such as zig-zags and chevrons.

Rood A cross or crucifix (Saxon).

Rood Screen A screen which separates the chancel from the nave. Above, or fixed to, it is often a rood (a crucifix or cross).

Saddle-Back Roof This is a normal pitched roof, as on an ordinary house, but placed above a tower.

Saltire Cross A cross with four equal limbs laid diagonally i.e. an X shaped cross.

Sarcophagus A coffin, usually of stone and ornamented with carvings.

Screen A porclose screen separates a chapel from the rest of the church.

Screens Passage The passage between the kitchen and other work places, and the screen that protected the privacy of the occupants of the great hall of a medieval house.

Sedilia Masonry seats for use by priests on the south side of the chancel of a church. There are usually three in number.

Segmental Arch An arch with a profile that is part of a circle in which the centre of the circle is below the springing line; that means that it will always be less than a semi-circle.

Solar An upstairs living room in a medieval house.

Spandrel The triangular space between the side of an arch and the horizontal line drawn through its apex and the vertical line drawn from the side of the opening below the arch.

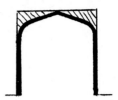

Spire A tall cone, pyramid or polygon that is placed on top of a tower. it has no structural purpose and its function is primarily to act as a landmark.

Steeple A term that means the tower and spire of a church taken together.

Strapwork Decoration consisting of interlaced bands similar to leather straps. It can be open (like fretwork), as in a vertical partition or screen, or closed as in plasterwork on ceilings. It was especially popular during the Renaissance.

String Course A horizontal band projecting from an exterior wall.

Stucco Plaster or cement rendering to walls or ceilings. The term is most commonly used to describe external wall rendering which is usually given a smooth finish.

Three-Decker Pulpit A tall pulpit with three seats, one above the other: a reading desk, the clerk's stall, and the preacher's stand.

Tomb Chest A stone coffin shaped like a chest, often with an effigy of the deceased placed on top. Some times the side walls are elaborately carved. It was commonly used in medieval times.

Tracery In the Middle Ages it was called form-pieces or forms. It is the intersecting ornamental work in the upper part of a window, a screen, a panel, a blank arch or a vault.

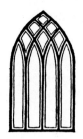 

Transept The transverse arm of a cruciform church which usually projects out from the junction of the nave and the chancel.

Transom A horizontal bar across a window opening which divides the window into separate lights. The term is usually only applied to a substantial bar, one commonly made of stone.

Triforium A galleried arcade facing on to the nave between the wall arcade (below) and the clerestory (above).

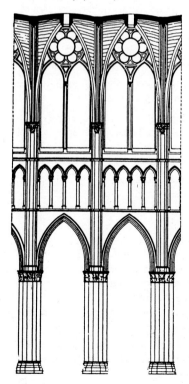

Turret a small tower, round or polygonal in shape.

Tuscan See Order.

Undercroft A vaulted room under a church or other building, sometimes below ground level.

Upper Palaeolithic See Palaeolithic.

Venetian Window A tripartite window. The central part is arched and wider than the square-topped parts to either side. It was developed from the Italian Serliana.

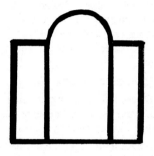

Victorian Architecture and general style associated with the period during which Queen Victoria reigned in Britain, 1837-1901.

Weather-Boarding Horizontal exterior overlapping boards, usually of a timber-framed building but sometimes used decoratively on a stone or brick structure.

Index of Place Names

(p) indicates a photograph separated from the text to which it relates.

British Industrial Sand Moneyash quarry at Whiston Eaves.

413

417

418

Typographical errors. Much to the author's consternation the following list of typographical errors was mislaid at the proofing stage, and not until almost the whole book had been printed was it discovered that the corrections had not been made. Fortunately, all but a handful of the errors are of a minor nature and do not affect the meaning of the text. Those to which attention should be drawn are:

5.2.23; **67** caption; **99** caption; **107**.1.2; **229**.1.19; **247** photograph and **256** photograph.

The location of each error (with the exception of captions and photographs) is given by three numbers: the first, printed in bold type, is the page number, the second the column and the third the line. Caption lines are not counted but article headings are. Mis-spelled words and incorrect punctuation are given duly corrected but without repetition of the original text for comparison; repetition is only made when confusion might otherwise occur.

Credit Page: rear cover illustration should be 'Manor Thatch' not 'Old Thatch'; the postal code of the publisher's address is ST18 9LY. **4**.1.34 Bagot's **5**.2.23 insert 'hill' at the end of the line **14**.2.14 delete 'on' between 'passed' and 'to' **17**.2.24 incongruous **17**.2.14 and **19**.) **22**.2.23 fools' **22**.2.31 purpose-built **23** Caption top right photograph 'moon rise' should be 'moonrise' **24**.1.16 'the' should be 'a' **26**.1.30 'were' should be 'where' **27** Caption to photograph Hall o' th' Wood **38** Caption bottom right photograph *Sunset* should be *sunset* **39**.1.2 'on' should be 'in' **40**.1.26 lace, **46**.1.20 window **48**.1.10 delete 'Century' **48**.2.20 Old **49**.1.2 'a' should be 'the' **49**.1.15 eye-catching **52**.2.11 The **54**.2.16 turned **60**.1.12 It **62**.2.5 Hanley **63**.2.14 Wyrley **67**.1.34 persons' **67** Caption bottom left photograph 'Arnold's' should be 'Bennett's' **67**.2.28 (fort-settlement) **69**.1.1 Monasteries **71**.1.23 Leicestershire **71**.1.33 delete comma after 'Saxon' **71**.1.34 delete comma after 'Wulfric' **73**.1.10 altar **73** Caption top right *cast-iron* **76**.1.16 'on' should be 'in' on both occasions **76**.2.20.) **76**.2.29 camp- **78**.2.12.) **80**.2.15 fort-settlement **82**.2.20 iron-working **83**.1.21 & 22 robber-knights **85**.2.22 wool- **85**.2.23.) **93**.2.2 Staffordshire, **93**.1.2 SK **95**.1.4 'Shallowford' should be bold **99** Caption top right photograph should read: *Church Eaton, the Old Rectory.* **101**.2.37 'Maunton' should be bold **103**.1.7 Italianate **104**.1.36 'the' should be 'its' **107**.1.2 the date 1834 should be 1847 **108**.1.15 delete comma **109** Caption top left photograph *'limstone'* should be *'lime'* **118**.1.15.) **123**.1.14 'front' should be 'font' **127**.1.9 This **128**.2.7 high-banked **128**.2.14 stone-built **132** Caption bottom left photograph *Newcomen* **138**.2.25 Street **140**.1.28 prison **140**.2.11 valley **141**.1.14 'The' before Ecton should be 'the' **143**.1.45 1822; **150**.2.9 Italianate **151**.2.21 delete 'the' at the beginning of the line and insert it before 'arched.' **154**.2.6.) **158**.2.24 'were' should be 'are' **161** Caption top left insert *the* between *in* and *church* **167**.2.16 Wars **168** Caption top left photograph *Tyreley* should be *Tyrley* **168**.2.17 occurred **168**.2.33 master's **171**.2.6 monastery **173**.2.16 'in' should be 'to' **174**.2.30 Many **176**.2.9 insert 'a' between 'at' and 'later' **182**.2.36 'eyes' should be 'eye' **184**.2.45 Remembrance **184**.2.45 'wih' should be 'with' **184**.2.29 high-walled **184**.2.29 'nodel' should be 'model' **186**.2.3 delete 'the' before 'gold' **190**.1.12 incongruous **192**.2.29 gables, **196**.2.40 'country' should be 'county' **198**.2.32 'Old Thatch' should be 'Manor Thatch' **199**. Caption bottom photograph *'Old Thatch'* should be *'Manor Thatch'* **200**.1.10 originally **200**.1.18 stone-built **210**.2.14 Pensnett **205**.1.12 grounds **211**.2.40 altar **213**.2.11 visitor **216**.2.18 Anglesey **218**.2.15 Bennett **219**.1.29 'far' should be 'for' **220**. Caption bottom left photograph *Manor House* should be *Old Hall* **227**.1.31 insert 'in' between 'is' and 'an' **228**.2.7 mid-19th **229**.1.19 'easterly' should be 'westerly' **229**.2.14 mid-18th **231**.2.20 fine, **237**.2.10 off **239**.2.13 England. **239**.2.14.) **243**.2.38 received **245**.1.18 chandler's **245**. Caption top right photograph *Wyreley* should be *Wyrley* **246**.1.1 Wyrley **246**.2.45.) **247**. Photograph bottom left captioned *High Offley* was printed the wrong way round. **250**.2.29 'the girth' should be 'a girth' **253**.2.23 Wyrley **256**. Photograph captioned *Penkridge, Cuttlestone Bridge* has been printed the wrong way round. **256**.2.5 Victoria **262**. Captions to both photographs *Hampstall* should be *Hamstall* **263**. Caption left photograph *Hampstall* should be *Hamstall* **264**.2.14 yds. **268**.1.11 delete commas after 'thane' and 'Algar' **270**.2.24 medicine **275**.2.13 road, **277**.2.22 Anglo **284**.2.19 2-bay **286**.1.1 inheritance **297**.2.22 earthen **298**.2.3 Reverend **300**.2.7.) **300**.2.8 Commissioners' **301**.1.10 (south). **301**.1.1 5-light **306**.1.20 bursts **306**.1.25 practise **306**.2.3 3-bay **307**.2.34 Archaeological **307**.2.10 Stone. **308**.2.27 well-known **310**.1.23 fire-charred **311**.2.5 mid-18th **312**.2.16 interred **312**.2.21 mid-13th **313**. Caption top left photograph insert *the* before *Army* **316**.1.34 initially **318**.1.22 into **321**.2.19 2-bay brick **322**.2.46 Birmingham **323**.2.7 Mr. Griffiths **324**.1.3 small, **325**.2.8 Wolverhampton **328**.1.38 Derby **328**.2.32 4-centre **334**.2.30 single- **336**.1.10 delete 'the' before 'Earl Talbot' **3361**.10.) **336**.2.27 Britain **341**.1.3 Blue' **341**.1.12 Piccadilly **342**.2.7 O' should be o' **342**.2.10 insert 'to' after 'Lancaster' **345**.2.23 ware.) **345**.2.23 *ware, see Hanbury.)* **351**.2.21 5 bays **351**.2.24 miserable **352**.1.8 3-bay **352**.2.10 11-bay **352**.2.11 4-columned **354**.1.6 'this' should be 'these' **356**.1.5.) **358**.2.22 'Church' at the beginning should be 'Hall' **362**.1.14 lectern **366**.2.4 mid-19th **371**.2.17 mid-19th **378**.1.22 commonplace **379**.1.14 cream-washed **387**.1.3 there **388**.1.29 5-light **390**.1.6 insert 'style' between 'Gothic' and 'by' **390**.1.17 well-known **390**.1.31 questionnaires **390**.2.6 thieves, **393**.1.2 Sedgley **393**.1.13 photographed **398**.1.21 2-storey **398**.2.2 O' should be o' **398**.2.25.) **399**.1.34 accommodation **399**.2.22 mid-19th **401**.2.30.) **405**.2.19 provides **405**.2.29 separate **408**.2.8 It